MEN AND BOOKS

OR

STUDIES IN HOMILETICS

LECTURES INTRODUCTORY TO

THE THEORY OF PREACHING

BY

AUSTIN PHELPS, D.D.

LATE BARTLET PROFESSOR OF SACRED RHETORIC IN ANDOVER
THEOLOGICAL SEMINARY

NEW YORK
CHARLES SCRIBNER'S SONS
1882

𝔉𝔯𝔞𝔫𝔨𝔩𝔦𝔫 𝔓𝔯𝔢𝔰𝔰:

STEREOTYPED AND PRINTED BY RAND, AVERY, AND CO.

BOSTON.

PREFACE.

A THOROUGHLY trained preacher is first a man, at home among men : he is then a scholar, at home in libraries. No other profession equals that of the pulpit in its power to absorb and appropriate to its own uses the world of real life in the present and the world of the past as it lives in books. A very essential part of a preacher's culture, therefore, concerns his use of these two resources of professional power. The large majority of the topics commonly treated by professors of homiletics as *miscellanies* will be found to arrange themselves naturally in these two lines of discussion. By so arranging them, I have sought to gain the concentration of unity and the cumulation of order.

Like the Lectures on "The Theory of Preaching," in a former volume, these discussions retain the form and style of the lecture-room in which they were delivered, in response to the practical inquiries of students on the eve of entrance upon their life's work. Almost no other changes have been made than those which were necessary in the mechanical revision for the press.

It should be observed, respecting that portion of this work which discusses the study of books, that its design is limited. I have by no means attempted to give an analysis of English literature, nor to plan the studies of men of literary leisure, nor to advise respecting the reading of miscellaneous classes, as President Porter has so usefully done in his work on "Books and Reading." My aim is to answer the inquiries of young pastors whose collegiate training has created literary aspirations which ought to be perpetuated in the lifelong labors of their profession.

It will be objected, to some of the counsel given in these pages, that to many young preachers it is impracticable. This objection is treated at length near the close of the volume. But at present this should be said of it : that any plan of effort or of study auxiliary to the work of the pulpit, to be largely useful, must, from the nature of the case, be largely *ideal* in its character. One of its chief virtues must be its power to sustain the aspirations of a preacher, rather than to measure his achievements. Diversities of gifts, diversities of culture, diversities of health, and diversities of leisure, must create such diversities of condition among pastors that no two of them can find precisely the same plan practicable to them both.

All that professional criticism can do, therefore, is to present to all, as to one, the true ideal of the labor auxiliary to homiletic culture, and trust to the good sense of each to decide for himself how far, and with what eclectic skill, it is practicable to him. It is worth much to have a good ideal of any thing that is worth doing. The grandest lives are but approaches to grand ideals. The very sight of a good library, though just now unused, is a stimulus and a cheer to a missionary in the backwoods. So an ideal of a life's work is valuable as a suggestion of effort, perhaps for ever impracticable in the full, yet for ever susceptible of approximation.   Such an ideal does much for a youthful pastor, if it marks out the line of ascent on which he will gain the loftiest altitude and the broadest vision, with the least waste of mental and moral forces.

TABLE OF CONTENTS.

LECTURE XI.

LECTURE XII.

LECTURE XIII.

LECTURE XIV.

LECTURE XV.

LECTURE XVI.

LECTURE XXII.

MEN AND BOOKS;

OR,

STUDIES IN HOMILETICS.

LECTURE I.

INTRODUCTION. — STUDY OF MEN; OF A PREACHER'S
OWN MIND; OF OTHER MEN.

THE first orator in the order of time had nothing to
make him an orator but his head and his heart and his
study of men. He had no treatises, no models, no objective eloquence in any form, to guide him. He had
only human nature to work with as well as to work
upon. The instinct of speech he improved into eloquence by experiments upon men as hearers of speech.

Then, when the reflective process began in his mind,
and he reasoned out the first crude science of his art,
he must have reasoned upon the simple facts of his
experience. His primary question was not, What is eloquence in its philosophical germ? or, Has it any such
germ? It was, How is it that men are actually moved
by speech? What, in fact, persuades men? What has
done this as a matter of experiment? Upon that history of eloquence as an experience of living minds,

1

possibly of but one living mind, must have been laid the first stone of the arch of oratorical science.

But while the first orators, and, following them, the writers, — for speech must have preceded writing, — had only men to study, their productions became to their successors an additional source of oratorical culture. Observe: not an independent, but a supplementary source. It is a source, which, from the necessity of the case, could be valuable only so far as it embodied the results of a knowledge of human nature. Demosthenes, by incorporating into his orations the principles of eloquence derived from the study of men, rendered those orations a source of culture to all subsequent generations. We therefore have a second source of oratorical culture in models of effective writing and speaking.

Observe, that, when we speak of models of effective writing and speaking, we include all successful and permanent literature. The grand test of power in speech is the Napoleonic test of character, — success. The final test of success, from which there is no appeal, is permanence. All literature, be it oral or written, which bears these tests, may be a source of professional discipline to a public speaker. Not merely orations, speeches, sermons, but all written thought which bears the stamp of success, must embody some of the principles of power in the expression of thought by language. In defining the range of it, we do not inquire what authors and speakers have written and spoken according to one standard or another, by the rules of one authority or another, to the taste of one age or another, but simply who have succeeded. We do not ask who have succeeded in the right cause or the wrong, with good motive or bad motive, by honest purpose or by knavery, but who have succeeded in any cause, with any motive, by any means of *speech*.

Proceeding to apply the view here given to the studies of a preacher, I propose, in this and the succeeding Lectures, to speak of a preacher's STUDY OF MEN and of his STUDY OF BOOKS as sources of oratorical discipline.

I. Upon a preacher's independent study of men the following suggestions deserve remembrance : —

1. Every preacher may obtain much of oratorical culture from attention to the processes of his own mind. The study of men every man may pursue for himself. We have at least the same facilities in this respect that the first orator had. In the study of men a preacher should rank first his own mind. You have in your own selves an original and independent source of rhetorical knowledge. No other can be more so.

(1) In development of this view, let it be observed that every man's experience contains biographical *incidents* suggestive of oratorical principles. Every educated mind which is therefore accustomed to self-inspection has in itself a history of oratorical appliances. You have listened to public speakers ; you have heard sermons ; you have read successful literature ; you know, therefore, what truths have moved your own mind, and in what forms, and in what combinations with other truths. You have learned to distinguish between speakers who instruct your intellect only and those who move your sensibilities. Your memory is full of incidents of success or failure in experiments of speech which other men have made upon yourselves. Have you not unconsciously laid the foundations of your

self-knowledge, in part, in this knowledge of your own susceptibility to persuasive speech?

Here, then, is a general criterion by which to judge of your own appliances to other minds, — a general criterion, I say, because individualities differ in details. Very much spurious composition would collapse if the writer would honestly apply to it the test, "Would this move me? Would these thoughts, thus expressed, satisfy the cravings of my nature? Would this strain of argument convince my intellect, this style of reproof reach my conscience, this method of appeal sway my heart?"

Many a preacher knows that the best of his own sermons can not stand this homely test. The salient incidents in his own mental history, which are always most fresh in his memory, suggest something very unlike his own productions. His experience as a listener, and his practice as a preacher, are founded on different ideals of success. If he were to choose, on the spur of the moment, the preacher to whom he owes, more than to any other, his noblest conception of the power of the pulpit, he would choose the man above all others most unlike himself, and whose sermons, not only in degree of excellence, but in kind and in aim, are most diverse from his own.

(2) Not only do incidents salient in every man's life suggest principles of eloquent speech, but the more profound history of every man's *character* is full of similar suggestions. Every character has a history of changes. They lie deeper than transitory movements of intellect, and awakening of sensibilities. As preachers we have to deal mainly with fundamental changes of character. Our great aim is to produce changes,

some of which are revolutionary. The plow of the pulpit runs deep, if it runs at all to the purpose of the pulpit.

A preacher needs, therefore, to study the history of his own character. He needs wisdom to read it aright. Your own life antecedent to your religious awakening; the causes and the process of that awakening; the unwritten experiences which gather in your memory around the crisis of your conversion, if that crisis disclosed itself to you; and the visible stages in the process of your religious growth thus far, — are most vital resources of that kind of culture which you need as a guiding mind to others through similar experiences. Other changes auxiliary to these are scarcely less important. Changes of opinion, of taste, of mental habit; changes in the proportion of the spiritual to the physical in your nature; changes inevitable to progress from the infancy to the maturity of godly principle within you; any and every change which your self-consciousness marks as fundamental to growth of character, — are resources of knowledge to you respecting means and methods of working, combinations of truth most helpful to success, and the entire furniture of your mind for the work of training characters which are in need of or are undergoing similar changes under your ministrations.

Yet does not the history of the pulpit give evidence of inattention to this kind of personal history, which must lie back of it in the memory of the preacher? We preach too little of and from the work of God within us; too much, perhaps, about our external history, but too little about the principles involved in the deeper processes of spiritual life, which do not disclose themselves in events, nor provide the material for an anecdote, but are subterranean, and tributary to all growth. Much of the fanaticism of the pulpit would be forestalled, if preachers were more studious of God's method in the training of themselves. As a rule, fanatical preachers were not converted by fanaticism. They are never themselves improved by fanaticism. They know this, if they interpret honestly their own history. A regenerate man preaching from his own regenerate experience could not be a fanatic: he could not so disturb the divine balance of truth. Some short-sighted modes of doing good, some unnatural appeals to the consciences and the feelings of men, much claptrap, egotism, humdrum, animal magnetism, in the pulpit, would be displaced by more profound resources, and more intensely vitalized expedients, if preachers read human nature more adroitly in their own.

Preachers often attempt to influence audiences, not only by isolated arguments, illustrations, appeals, but by prolonged plans of ministerial effort, which they know, when they fairly awaken to the realities of the case, have no root in the underground of their own characters. Revivals of religion are sometimes labored for by expedients which are untrue to the preacher's own history. They are expedients which he knows would, if he had encountered them at a critical period of his life, have caused his own soul to revolt from the truth, to despise the truth, or to stagnate under the truth. He is the very last man, it may be, to have responded favorably to a prophecy of his own sermons.

Have you not yourselves observed the fact in the history of preaching, that ministers who fall into unphilosophical modes of preaching are themselves the most uninterested listeners to such preaching? Preachers are proverbially hard hearers. One reason is, that there is so much in preaching which is unreal to any-body's experience. They who preach claptrap are not edified by claptrap any more than their hearers. Those who preach humdrum are not interested in humdrum when they hear it. They sleep under it more pro-foundly, if possible, than other men. Seat them as listeners to such preaching, and, if their eyes are open, they are as the fool's eyes, like those of other hearers. A great and live soul, which can furnish its own fire, is required to get aglow under such preaching. The authors of it never do : they never feel even the crackling of thorns under such a pot. Ignatius Loyola might have been converted under such preaching, but never the Rev. Dr. Dunderhead.

The same is true of inordinately intellectual preach-ers. By this I mean those preachers in whom intel-lectual enthusiasm exceeds and overpowers religious fervor. Such preachers are not morally moved by the preaching of their peers. They are not religiously edified by extreme profundity, or by imaginative pyro-technics, or by mystical reveries, in other preachers. The men who move them are probably the plain men who talk right on. The text may move them ; the prayer may melt them ; the hymn may make them weep : but the immensely intellectual sermon, which is that, and nothing more — they know too well the stuff it is made of.

The phenomenon will sometimes discover itself to you in the experience of the pulpit, that a preacher's professional life and his personal life are at antipodes to each other. He preaches almost any thing, in any way, except the thing, in the way, which the Holy Ghost

has made a living thing and a living way to his own
soul. You perceive, then, the fundamental character of
the principle, that a preacher should study his hearers
in himself. Other things being equal, no other preaching is so effective as the preaching which is rooted in a
man's own experience of truth. Such truth he knows.
Comparatively speaking, he knows nothing else.

2. Every preacher has also a source of rhetorical
culture in the study of other men. Real life everywhere is full of power in speech. Character can scarcely express itself in language other than the dialect of
eloquence. Whether it be so denominated in books or
not, it is such in fact. Books should be conformed to
life, not life to books.

(1) *Individual* character in its rudest forms is power
in speech. The market-place, the streets, the fields, the
workshops, the counting-rooms, the court-rooms, the
schoolhouses, the platforms, the firesides, the steam-
boats, the rail-cars, the exchange, every place, every
thing, in which men are off their guard, and speak
right out what they think and as they feel, with no
consciousness of trying either to think or to feel, are
teeming with natural eloquence. Books bear no comparison with this eloquence of life. The world could
not contain the books which would have been requisite
to express this unwritten development of power in
oratorical forms of utterance.

You can not observe two men making a bargain without witnessing an example of something which enters
into the highest art of persuasion. You can not listen
to the words, constructions, intonations, of an angry
man, without meeting some of the elements of all
earnest oratory. A man chasing his hat in a gale acts

in pantomime a principle which Demosthenes could not safely ignore in striving for the crown. The slang of the street, the dialect of the forecastle, the lingo of collegians, illustrate principles of style which underlie forms of power in thought and utterance which have lived a thousand years. A woman over the couch of a sick child speaks in words which have roots running down into the original ideal of pathos in all literature. Animated conversation illustrates principles, and takes on forms, which no eloquence of the senate or the pulpit can do without. How often does our wearied criticism of a public speaker express itself in some such inward exclamation as this, " Oh that he would step down from his stilts, and talk as we heard him talk at the tea-table on a certain evening ! "

These most common and therefore neglected forms of individual character in daily life are full of the re-sources of homiletic culture to any one who will take the trouble to observe them for that purpose. At this point is seen one of the vital dependences of the pulpit on pastoral duty. No preacher can afford to be a preacher only, and live in his study alone, were it only for his need of homiletic suggestion coming directly from the homes and the business of his people. To know thoroughly one able man in your parish is the counterpart of a homiletic treatise in teaching you how to preach to all the peers of that man.

(2) The conduct of *secular assemblies* often discloses the working of power in speech. Much wisdom which preachers have occasion for may be learned from the answer to the question, " How do lawyers who gain their cases deal with juries? How do they work differ-ently in addressing a bench of judges?" If it were

possible, I would have every minister of the gospel
practice law. Some of our ablest preachers have been
subjected to that preliminary discipline, and never
without acknowledging their obligations to it through
a lifetime.

How are town-meetings governed by a few words
from a few plain men? How is it that an educated
man sometimes fails in such an assembly, outgeneraled
by a farmer or a blacksmith? How is a city mob
quelled by a dozen men with no weapons more deadly
than a billy? Why are a dozen policemen a match for
a hundred desperadoes? The elements of power which
explain that phenomenon have their parallels in oratorical forces. The principle which explains, in part, the
fact that an army of sixty thousand men keeps in subjection sixty millions of aliens in British India is the
same which explains, in part, the coming conversion of
the world by a handful of preachers with no auxiliaries to speech but prayer.

Edward Everett could hold in silence an audience of
three thousand scholarly minds by an oration which
passed at once into the standards of literature ; and
Charles Sumner could command the most intelligent
and independent Senate in the world, not one of
whom liked him personally, by a speech which became a
thesaurus of learning and a landmark of history. Yet
neither of these princely orators could get a hearing of
ten minutes from a crowd in the street, if the Hon.
Stephen A. Douglas were known to be there to oppose
them. What caused these diversities? Anybody who
will explain such facts as these truthfully must discover in the process some practical rhetorical wisdom,
and that the very last which a preacher can afford to lose.

Are some of these things done by other means than speech, and by foul means in part? Very true. But all successes in real life have their counterparts in speech. Foul means, to be successful, must appeal to elements of human nature which are normal to it. A right appeal to those elements a preacher may make with hope of equal success. The susceptibility of the human mind to such appeals is the basis of all eloquence. The business of real life, therefore, is full of it. The study of men succeeding and failing in that business must be prolific of wisdom to a public speaker. The late Lord Lytton gives advice to a young London author, saying, "Never write a page till you have walked from your room to Temple Bar, mingling with men, and reading the human face." He adds the fact that great poets have, for the most part, passed their lives in cities.

(3) We find also a specially valuable resource of homiletic culture in the study of masses of men *under religious excitement*. Sympathetic religious awakenings are phenomena of life as old as nations: to them is due by far the major proportion of Christian progress. More than half of the history of Christianity in this world would be blotted out if we should erase the record of the great sympathetic waves of religious sensibility which have rolled over communities and nations and races. The modern excitement which we term a revival illustrates only one phase of an experience of which, in kindred forms, history is full.

Revivals are often spoken of as an American product. It is true that American revivals have had peculiarities growing out of the national temperament and history; but in the sense of being in spirit limited to one country or another, or one nation or age rather than another, they are not American. Revivals are a normal working of human nature moved by supernatural forces. They have never been provincial. All the past is dotted over with them : all the future must be the same. Our hope of the world's conversion is a dream, if religious progress is to be measured by that of the intervals between these great awakenings of the popular heart.

Such awakenings, therefore, are a very vital object of a preacher's study. Generally, sympathetic religious excitements are the result of preaching. Consecutive plans of preaching should contemplate them, and be adjusted to them. Under a wise ministry, blessed of God, they are sure to occur. A pulpit not adjusted to them is like a system of husbandry not planned for a harvest. One of the saddest sights in the history of the pulpit is that of a ministry which regards revivals as abnormal, and which therefore adjusts itself in scholarly ease and refinement to the slow and well-nigh hopeless growth of periods which lie between revivals.

Such a ministry, you will observe, are very apt to find their chief interests and excitements outside of their profession. They give themselves to literature, to science, to art, to reforms, to social life, to the improvement of their private fortunes. Some of our standards in literature have been the work of clergymen who did the work, and could do it, because their professional plans did not contemplate nor aim at overpowering awakenings of the people. Few men in the pulpit can adjust themselves to the divine plans in this respect, as history has thus far given us the means of interpreting them, and yet find time and mental force to create literary standards which shall live to future times. The exhortations to scholarly aims which we give and receive are always to be accepted with this qualification, that, in a successful ministry, religious awakenings may overwhelm a preacher with professional labors to such degree as to render literary pursuits for the time impracticable. Such awakenings must command the profound and prayerful study of men who mean to be a power in the instrumental control of them.

The practical question is, How are they brought about? What procedure of the pulpit is conducive to them? A country village, remote from the excitement of metropolitan crowds, is agitated by a strange quickening of religious inquiry. Skeptics look upon it as an epidemic. What has Christian philosophy to say of it? What instruments have apparently wrought the change? What methods of preaching, what subjects in the pulpit, what auxiliary agencies outside of the pulpit, have seemed to be the working forces? Hard-featured and cross-grained men are subdued by a female Bible-reader; so that a quaint observer applies to them the old couplet in the primer, —

> "Whales in the sea
> God's voice obey."

What is the secret of her power? A roving evangelist whom three-fifths of the community despise reaches the other two-fifths with such power of moral suasion, that the majority are compelled to smother their contempt, or to express it in tones which echo a secret fear that he is right, and they are wrong. How does he do it? Prayer-meetings are crowded in the "Black Sea" in Boston. A motley assembly of five thousand, whom no other than a religious teacher could keep silent for ten

minutes, are thus held for an hour by the plainest of
plain religious talk in Burton's Theatre in New York.
Twenty thousand men and women in the Crystal Palace
at Sydenham are held in such stillness that they all
hear one voice intelligibly. How are these things done?
What is the philosophy of the success of such men as
Whitefield, Summerfield, Spurgeon, Finney, Moody?

Right or wrong, normal or abnormal, these are facts
in popular history. They are known and read of all
men. They assume the importance of crises in the
history of nations. In our own day they are growing
to the magnitude of the old Roman gladiatorial shows.
The simple power of speech seems now to be achiev-
ing results in popular excitement, which in Pagan life
could be created only by brutal and sanguinary spec-
tacles. What philosophy of speech can explain them?
Wise is the man who can give the reason why speech
should thus supplant the dagger and the lasso and the
trident.

As specimens of the questions on this subject which
a preacher needs to ask and answer, let the following
be specified: [1] Are revivals of religion a normal method
of divine working for the world's conversion? What
is their relation to divine sovereignty? Are any laws
of the working of the Holy Spirit in them discoverable?
In what condition of the popular mind are revivals to
be looked for? What agency of the pulpit is prepara-
tive to a revival? What agencies auxiliary to the pulpit
are most essential? Are evangelistic labors desirable
under a settled ministry? What types of theology are
dominant in the most valuable revivals? What place

---

[1] The majority of these inquiries have been published in the appendix
to the " Theory of Preaching."

should be assigned in them to doctrinal preaching? Has the service of song any special value in them? Are children proper subjects of conversion in revivals? What are the pathological perils incident to such awakenings? How are those perils avoidable? How can they be counteracted when not avoidable? Are minds of high culture naturally subject to these popular awakenings? Does the subsidence of a revival imply religious decline? Does popular re-action from a revival neutralize its value? What policy of the pulpit should characterize the period immediately following a revival? What are the differences, if any, between the type of piety of those who meet the religious crisis of their lives in revivals and those who meet it in more tranquil times? What is that change in professing Christians which often occurs in revivals, and is called "reconversion"? Is President Edwards's work on the "Religious Affections" adapted to the present religious inquirers?

If, by a philosophic study of these and kindred questions, we can come at those principles of human nature which underlie the divine economy in the sympathetic awakenings of society to the realities of eternity, we gain thereby the very pith and marrow of homiletic culture. I repeat, therefore, Study the great awakenings of the past. Investigate the spiritual life of the Reformation. Read Tracy's history of the "Great Awakening" in President Edwards's day. Observe critically the similar movements of our own day. Read the "Year of Grace in Ireland," the "History of the Hawaiian Islands," the "History of Missions in Madagascar." Study the lives of pre-eminent revival preachers. Read the memoirs of Whitefield, Wesley, Nettleton, Finney, Lyman Beecher, Dr. Kirk. Observe narrowly the facts

of current history bearing on the subject. Be familiar
with the ministries of such men as Mr. Spurgeon. Learn
something from them all. Study opposite characters
in the history of revivals.

Above all, preserve a docile state of mind in such
studies. Take an expectant attitude. Look for progressive evolution of wisdom in the administration of
the pulpit. Never allow your mind to settle down in a
quiescent state, under the conviction that the policy of
the pulpit is fixed by the past for all time.

A most fatal position to the clergy of a nation is that
assumed by a portion of the clergy of this country and
of England, which holds them aloof from the experience
of modern revivals, and which some of them avow as
antagonistic to such awakenings. Fatal, I say, is such
an attitude to the spiritual power of the ministry. A
pulpit thus sundered from these quickenings of the
popular heart can never be the pulpit of the future.
The work of this world's redemption will sweep grandly
over it, and bury it in oblivion. Or, if it lives, it can
represent only a fragmentary and sickly development
of religious life. It can only build up a Christian
infirmary in which shall be gathered the invalid classes
of Christian minds. All the signs of our age indicate
increase rather than diminution of these popular excitements. The ministry must understand them, must
be in sympathy with them, must be masters in the
control of them, or must perish under the billows of
them which are sure to roll in upon the church of all
coming time.

LECTURE II.

3. RESUMING the subject of the study of men where
we left it at the close of the last Lecture, let us now
observe the fact that this study is often undervalued,
because of a factitious reverence for books.

This must be recognized as one of the perils of studious minds engaged in a practical profession. True,
the opposite peril also exists; but it besets only indolent
minds. Mental indolence finds a very cheap pabulum
in underrating scholastic learning. But studious men
are tempted on the side of their scholastic tastes. We
need to see the relations of the two in some approach
to equilibrium. We will not say with Patrick Henry,
"Sir, it is *not* books, it is men, that we must study;"
but we say, "Books *and* men we must study."

A young man once inquired of me, "Can you direct
me to a book which shall teach me to write a sermon?"
I receive letters of inquiry founded on the same ideal
of homiletic discipline. "No," must the answer be:
"there is no such book. From the nature of the subject there can be none." Preaching is one of the arts
of life, — as much so as the use of the telegraph. It
never can be learned as an abstract science only. From
books may be learned principles, nothing more. Lec-

17

tures can portray the theory of preaching, nothing else. Criticism is that theory in fragments.

The peril here named is often aggravated by an excess of the conservative temperament. This entices men of books and schools often to live as if the acquisition and classification of printed knowledge were the chief object of life, rather than the growth and the use of character. The clergy, therefore, are often charged, and sometimes justly, with reverence for the past at the expense of the present and in distrust of the future. One of the most seductive positions which can be offered to a scholar is a fellowship in a large and ancient university. But scarcely could a more perilous position be accepted by a man, who, like a clergyman, looks forward to a practical profession as the work of his life.

Whatever has been once crystallized and labeled in our cabinet of thought, we are tempted to prize at the cost of those creations which are still in the fluid state, and in the seething process before our eyes. Clerical tastes, therefore, often need a counterbalance to the conservative temperament. We must remember that a vast scene in the drama of human history is now acting. We and our cotemporaries are the *dramatis personæ*. A link in the chain of historic causes and effects is now forging.

Specially should this be borne in mind, that divine communications to the world have always been made through the medium of real life. Living men live a great truth, and so truth comes to the birth. The Bible is almost wholly history and biography. Abstract knowledge is given in it only as interwoven with the wants and the experiences of once living generations. God took out of the circle of universal history a single segment, and the result is a revelation. Men lived under special divine superintendence and illumination, and the product is — a Bible.

So all the great truths which have moved the world have been lived. They have been struck out by collision of thought with the living necessities of the world. Monotheism exists only as an experience vital to living men : it has come into being as a revolt from living idolatries. Liberty is a possession sprung from the pressure of living despotisms. True theory in all departments of civilized culture is a life. It has grown out of the brooding of thought over an experience of living barbarism. Scholarship, therefore, is always the pupil of Providence when it is the leader of men. It must be studious always of Providence in the experience of living generations, if it would hold its leadership. That mind lags behind Providence which studies only the past. It is always a little too late in its opinions, its tastes, its culture, and therefore in its power of adaptation to uses.

Why should we not feel for the nineteenth century somewhat of the respect which men of the twenty-ninth will feel for it? Why not place the ages abreast with each other in their chances for rank in our literary regard? Studying in this manner the phases of a living civilization, we shall surely learn something which no records of a defunct civilization can teach us. No generation of men, in God's plan, lives for nothing. Every generation is a positive quantity in the world's problem. It adds something to the knowledge or the power of the world which its predecessors never knew. The world's life is thus a growth, always a growth, without retrogression and without pause. We should not allow ourselves, then, to undervalue for oratorical discipline the study of living men, through a morbid reverence for books as the sacred repositories of the past. "Books and men, men and books," should be our motto.

This view is enforced by the fact that accumulation is not the chief object of a scholarly life: if it were, we should never have been fated to spend one-third of our lives in sleep. The great object of life, and therefore of culture, is character, — the growth, the exercise, the use, of character. We gain, surely, as vigorous a character, and as much of it in amount, from the study of men as from that of books. No culture can be symmetrical which is restricted to either. Each needs the other as its complement.

It should be further remarked, that symmetry of culture in this respect is essential to a hopeful courage in the ministry. A minister who studies only the past is almost sure to be distrustful of the future, and despondent of the present. He sees the future in a false perspective: therefore to him the former times were always better than these, and the future is doomed to be worse than either. He is an incorrigible pessimist. Two clergymen, once companions in this seminary, met, after twenty years of labor in the ministry, in which both had had a fair measure of success. Said one in a brisk, cheery tone, "I have a hard life of it, but I enjoy a hard life. It pays to have a hard life. I have such a glorious trust in the future!" Said the other, unconsciously sinking his tone to the habit of his mind, "I have a hard life too. I try to endure it patiently, but I shall be glad when it is over. The future looks dark, very dark, to me. My chief satisfaction is in the past." This man was the more learned of the two, but he had worn out his courage by excessive conservatism. He was weary and footsore from walking backward. A few years later he was gathered to the fathers with whom his mental life had been buried for twenty years. His friend, I think, still lives ; and, if so, I venture to affirm that he still has a hard life, and enjoys it as hopefully as ever. Such men never grow old. Which of the two men illustrates the better ideal of a clerical scholar ? Which has been worth the most to the world ? Which has the most brilliant record of self-culture to carry into eternity ?

4. Enthusiasm in the study of men should be stimulated by that which is well known to be, in this respect, the popular idea of a clergyman.

The popular conception of a clergyman is that he is, *ex officio*, in respect to the knowledge of mankind, an ignoramus. Be it true or false, this is the popular notion of the clerical character. It produces not a little of that feeling towards the clergy which vibrates between amusement and contempt. In the popular faith we belong to a race of innocents. If not all Vicars of Wakefield, we are cousins-german to that reverend greenhorn. Men of the world feel it to be refreshing when an able preacher breaks loose from the hereditary conventionalisms of the clerical guild, and thinks and talks and dresses and acts as *they* do.

This popular notion is, of course, a caricature ; yet to some extent the habits of the clergy foster it. For instance, no other body of men are in so much danger of excessive seclusion from the world as are the clergy. Relics of the theory on which clerical celibacy was founded yet linger among the ideas which clergymen have of the clerical office. We do not avow it, yet many feel a special reverence for a celibate minister. So long as the Romish clergy keep alive that fiction in the persons of godly and faithful men, some Protestant ministers will make unconscious concessions to it.

The idea of a priesthood, also, yet remains in the Protestant conception of a clergy. So long as the Church of England keeps alive that notion, and makes it respectable by the culture and the industry and the piety of her clergy, the ministry of other churches will insensibly be drawn towards it. Seclusion from men for the sake of communion with God is the conception which lies at the bottom, not only of many of the popular ideas about the ministry, but of some of the notions which the ministry entertain of themselves.

One consequence of this drift of things is, that the ministry often stand aloof from the real world. Men often do not act themselves out in our presence. They do not express all their opinions in our hearing. Principles and practices grow up in a community, and pass unnoticed by the ministry for years, in some cases, because the ministry know nothing of their existence.

For illustration, take the change which has been going on for the last twenty years in the Christian theory of amusements. That change is a very significant one. It is one to which the ministry, whenever they recognize it, will find that they must yield something of the clerical theory of fifty years ago. Yet one may well be surprised at the apathy and apparent ignorance of some of our ministry on the subject. A certain Methodist conference once adopted a minute against the playing of croquet, and were supported in it by so clear-headed a man as President Finney; apparently ignoring the fact that Christian opinion in a multitude of our churches only laughs at such relics of a monastic age. The rising generation are in some danger of being swept into an extreme of license in popular amusements, for the want of an intelligent handling of the subject by their ministry.

The use of tobacco is not a sign of a heavenly mind. But that was a woful diagnosis of the condition of earthly minds which led an American publishing society to bear its written testimony against tobacco at the very time when men were boiling over at the refusal of that society to utter its testimony against American slavery. "What is this Christianity," men asked, "which shuts its eyes to the public sale of a woman on the auction-block, and opens them so very wide at a pipe in the laboring-man's mouth?" Such misuses of Christian truth involve a cost to the cause of Christ which would bankrupt it if it were any other than the cause of Christ. In ways which I have not time to detail, changes may come upon the opinions and temper of a people, which a secluded clergy may not detect till those changes develop themselves in some overt revolution at which we stand aghast.

In milder form the same error shows itself in the fact that the theory of religious life taught in some pulpits is not recognized by the people as a reality. That is one of the saddest illustrations of waste in clerical power, in which the people quietly shove aside the teaching of the pulpit as nothing but perfunctory deliverances. The preacher is imagined to preach them because it is his business to do it, he is paid for doing it: not that he believes it, not that he expects the people to believe it, as a matter of heart and life; but it is the proper outflow of professional routine. Is it not sometimes obvious that the theory of the pulpit has no even approximate representative in a living church? Do not instances occur in which preachers themselves, who are vicegerents of God in the pulpit, do not meet the people out of it as if they expected their viceroyal authority to be heeded, nor as if they were at all aware of the fact that it is not heeded in real life? Souls are lost, for which somebody must give account, by means of the contrast which the people sometimes feel between the intense fidelity of the preacher in the pulpit and the apparent obliviousness of it all by the man out of the pulpit.

5. This defect lies at the foundation of that notion of clerical character which is most common in the literature of popular fiction. The clergyman of literary fiction is the secular parson. He is a priest, or something equivalent, whose business is to perform certain official functions, and nothing more. He plods in routine; his preaching is routine; his prayers are routine; his parochial service is routine; his whole life is routine. The vital, rather the fatal, point is, that his life is chiefly outside of the life of his parishioners. They feel no sense of reality in any thing that comes from him to themselves. Substantially they live and die without him, except that he baptizes their children, and buries their dead. He may be a fox-hunter, and it shall make no difference that reaches them. If he is of upright character, he is an innocuous saint, who is but half a man. He knows nothing of this world, and he has no business here when men have any earnest work on hand. In whatever the people feel to be a reality such a clergyman is always in the way.

An engraving was exhibited for sale in London not long ago, in which a nobleman was pictured in the last gasp of life, having been fatally injured in the hunting-field. By his bedside stands a white-haired but ruddy-faced and smirking clergyman in gown and bands, with closed prayer-book under his arm. His professional duty to the dying man is over. His eager face shows that the departing soul is forgotten in his interest in the story of the hunt, which is going on in the chamber of death. A caricature, this, doubtless; but could it ever have found spectators to enjoy it, or a purchaser to pay for it, if it had no original in real life? Carica-tures which men laugh at and pay their money for are caricatures of *something*.

So is it with the parson of literary fiction. He is not nearly so vital a character in the affairs of life as an old Roman augur was. The augur did something to the purpose of real life. He told the people when to fight a battle, when to raise a siege, when to launch a fleet. The clergyman of fiction has no such dignity. Doubt-less the clergyman of fiction is an exaggeration. Upon large numbers of both the Romish and Protestant clergy it is a libel. Still, that it exists is evidence that more or less foundation for it exists. We give occasion to such a caricature by every word and act and silent usage by which we suffer the pulpit to become a subli-mated institution, aloof by its elevation or its refine-ment from the life men are actually living, the thoughts they are thinking, the habits of feeling they are indul-ging, and the pursuits in which they are expending the force of their being.

An opinion was reported to me a few years ago as coming from the superintendent of the police of one of our Atlantic cities, to this effect; that, so far as his observation went, there was no other class of men who knew so little of real life as the clergy. This judgment was not uttered in bitterness of feeling. I did not understand that the author of it belonged to that class of men, who are not few in any large community, who are best known as haters of ministers. He spoke from his experience of the phase of society with which he was most familiar. Whatever might be true of the clergy elsewhere, down there where he saw men and women in need of those influences which the clergy are supposed to represent he thought they were the least effective workers. They were easily imposed upon. They started impracticable methods of working. They could not get access to the vicious and degraded. I, of course, do not indorse this criticism. I give it as one of the waifs indicating what the world says and believes about us. We need to face the facts of the popular theory as they are.

Further: it should be observed, in illustration of the same point, that portraits of character given in the pulpit sometimes do not seem to the people to be true to real life. Preachers often paint character in the general. Depravity is affirmed and proved as depravity is in the abstract, not as it is softened and adorned by Christian civilization. Piety is illustrated as sainthood, not as it is deformed by infirmity and sin. Hearers sometimes, therefore, seem to themselves to be described as demons, when they know that they are not such, and other hearers to be described as saints, when they know that they are no more such. Have you not listened to sermons which no living man who knows what the world is would be likely to accept as true to life? Such work in the pulpit appears to hearers as a work of art. It is a fancy sketch. It may be praised or censured, as one would criticise the Dying Gladiator, by the very men of whom it ought to have been a breathing likeness.

It has been said of the old New-England ministers, that they knew being in general more thoroughly than they knew man in particular. So the modern world often believes of the modern preacher, that he knows man in the abstract more thoroughly than he knows men individually. A consequence of this popular idea of the ministry is a widening of the distance between the pulpit and the pew. Sometimes you will find the laity settled comfortably in the conviction that the pulpit does not mean to reach them. They may live as they list, and may repose in their immunity from rebuke; and yet their clergy shall be firing the shot of a sound theology, or intoning the periods of a venerable liturgy, over their heads all the while.

6. This sense of security from the aims of the pulpit is often at the foundation of the antipathy of hearers to that which they call "political preaching." Generally that antipathy is morbid. They are so unused to feeling the ministries of the clergy as a reality touching the vital affairs of life, that when, on the eve of a national crisis, they listen to a sermon on the duty of Christian citizens, they are disturbed by it as an innovation. It breaks up the repose they have been accustomed to enjoy in the sanctuary. To many good men it appears sacrilegious to discuss such mundane affairs so near to the sacramental table. They call it desecration of the pulpit. What does this mean, but a confession that they have been so long used to regarding the pulpit as standing on the confines of another world, that it is a

novelty to them when it presumes to concern itself with the affairs of this world by any such methods as to make itself felt?

This is one of the most astonishing distortions of Christian opinion which our age has witnessed. The extreme of it came to my notice, a few years before the civil war, in the case of a very worthy man, and an advocate of reticence in the church on the question of American slavery. To test his principle in the matter, I inquired of him whether he thought it the duty of Northern Christians to send preachers to Utah. "Certainly," was the reply. "What should a preacher do in Utah?" — "Visit the people, hold meetings, preach, as he would elsewhere." — "But what about polygamy?" — "He should let that alone." — "Do you mean to say that a preacher should go among a people who are living in a state of legalized adultery, and be silent upon that sin?" — "Yes." — "Then, what would you have him preach about?" — "*The gospel.*"

The courage of the man was refreshing. But what of the opinion? An instance not dissimilar came to my knowledge in Western New York on the day of the national fast following the assassination of President Lincoln. On the morning of that day the pastor of one of the churches in the village had ventured to utter in his sermon a few very moderate and saintly words, somewhat in the style of a bishop's benediction, on the guilt of rebellion to the powers that be. The language was not positive enough to disturb any but a morbid mind; but it ruffled the placidity of some of the audience very perceptibly. It was the theme of considerable comment after the service. Said one who had heard it, "That was a bold sermon, a very bold sermon." I ventured to suggest that it might have been bolder without disturbing Enoch. The reply of my companion was, "It was a great deal for *us* to hear. We are not used to hearing any thing from our pulpit that *means anybody*." Contrast this theory of the pulpit with the observation of Coleridge: "If I were a preacher at St. Paul's in London, I would not preach against smuggling; but, if I were a preacher in a village of wreckers on the coast, see if I would preach against any thing else!"

Why should not the usage of the pulpit be such, that, as a matter of course, hearers shall understand that we mean somebody? Why should not preaching be always so truthful in its biblical rebuke, so intelligent in its knowledge of men, so stereoscopic in its power to individualize character, so resonant in its reponses to the human conscience, that hearers shall be unable *not* to understand that we mean somebody? The pulpit should be a battery, well armed and well worked. Every shot from it should reach a vulnerable spot somewhere. And to be such it must be, in every sense of the word, well manned. The gunner who works it must know what and where the vulnerable spots are. He must be neither an angel nor a brute. He must be a scholar and a gentleman, but not these only. He must be a *man*, who knows men, and who will never suffer the great tides of human opinion and feeling to ebb and flow around him uncontrolled because unobserved.

7. Not only in the way of rebuke does the pulpit often fail in its mission, through the want of a masterly acquaintance with mankind. Often the failure is more marked in respect to its mission of comfort. If there

is one thing more obvious than another in the general
strain of apostolic preaching, it is the preponderance of
words of encouragement over those of reproof and
commination. In no other thing did inspired preachers disclose their inspired knowledge of human conditions more clearly. The world of to-day needs the same
adaptation of the pulpit to its wants. We preach to a
struggling and suffering humanity. Tempted men and
sorrowing women are our hearers. Never is a sermon
preached, but to some hearers who are carrying a load
of secret grief. To such we need to speak as to "one
whom his mother comforteth." What delicacy of touch,
what refinement of speech, what tenderness of tone,
what reverent approach as to holy ground, do we not
need to discharge this part of a preacher's mission ! and
therefore what rounded knowledge of human conditions!

Is it a cynical judgment of the pulpit to affirm that
in our times it has reversed the apostolic *proportions*
of preaching in this respect? It is vastly easier to
denounce rampant sin than to cheer struggling virtue.
Preaching to the ungodly is more facile than preaching
to the church. And in preaching to the church it is
less difficult to reprove than to commend, to admonish
than to cheer, to threaten than to help. Hence has
arisen, if I do not misjudge, a disproportioned amount
of severe discourse, which no biblical model warrants,
and which the facts of human life seldom demand from
a Christian pulpit. Look over any large concourse of
Christian worshipers, number the stern and anxious
faces among them, — faces of men and women who are
in the thick of life's conflict. Where shall the cunning
hand be found to reach out and keep from falling these
weary ones? Very early in life, commonly, does the

great struggle of probation begin.   The buoyant joy of youth is short lived.

> " Shades of the prison-house begin to close
>   Upon the growing *boy*."

Probation, more than any other word in the language, tells the story of every human life.   With this one feature of human experience the mission of the pulpit has chiefly to do.   Above all other things, therefore, in the clerical character, this world craves the power of helpfulness.   The Master walking on the sea in the night, and stretching forth his hand to the sinking Peter, is the emblem of that which a Christian preacher must be in every age, if he would speak to real conditions, and minister to exigent necessities.

Intelligent laymen are often sensible of *waste* in the ministrations of the pulpit, growing out of the want, either of knowledge, or of tact in adapting them to the facts of human experience.   The conversation of such laymen will often disclose this.   Their criticisms, it is true, are to be received with caution, as are all the popular criticisms of the clergy.   They are sometimes thrust upon our notice by vain men, by men who ignore the real claims of the pulpit upon their respect, occasionally by men whom it is not uncharitable, and may not be unwise, to rebuke for their unconscious envy of ministerial prerogatives.   It is generally to be presumed that the clergy, like masters in other professions, know their own business better than such critics know it. But, with all reasonable deductions, it will be found that this sense of waste in the pulpit is felt by men of sufficient character, and in sufficient numbers, to deserve attention.   They believe, whether truly or not, that the

failure of the pulpit to reach certain classes of society
is attributable to a distance between the pulpit and the
pew which a more thorough knowledge of men would
do away with.

Said one of these lay critics, speaking of the sermons
of a certain pastor in Massachusetts, " Mr. B—— always
seems to me to be just about to begin, to get ready, in
prodigious earnest to do something; but the something
never looms in sight." The criticism was true. The
radical defect in that pastor's sermons was not want of
culture, not want of piety, not want of power innate;
but, relatively to the character of his hearers, it was an
excess of scholasticism. He commonly preached, either
from or at the last book he had read, often at the last
thrust of skepticism from " The Westminster Review."
This he did to an audience made up chiefly of tradesmen
and mechanics, and operatives in a factory, who never
heard of " The Westminster Review" outside of their
pastor's sermons. To them he seemed always to begin
a great way off.

LECTURE III.

8. CONTINUING the train of thought introduced in
the preceding Lectures, I venture upon another suggestion, which to some may seem questionable. Let it pass
for what it is worth. It is, that we should be watchful
of the ministries of certain eccentric clergymen.

In every age of religious awakening, there is a class
of preachers who break away from the conventionali-
ties of the pulpit lawlessly. They trample upon time-
honored usages. They are apt to handle irreverently
the opinions and the policy of the fathers. As a consequence, they originate new methods of preaching. In
many respects they do evil. Whether the average of
their influence is evil or good may be an open question.

Such preachers, though not safe models for imitation,
are valuable subjects of homiletic study. Though they
may be heretical in doctrine, they furnish instructive
hints to sounder men. Specially they are apt to preach
as men coming down to and into the homes of men.
They have the knack of making men believe that preaching is a reality to them. The impression they make is
that of a business of real life. Better men and wiser

33

preachers looking on may learn things from them which
shall both broaden and deepen the reach of the pulpit.
Those most dissimilar to them may be roused by them
to feel the inanity of some things which were invaluable when they were original, but which the world has
outlived, and which are now effete. The tendencies of
the clerical mind to live upon routine are sometimes
checked by one such comet in the clerical firmament.

A popular critic, a few years ago, observed that not
one in twenty of the newspapers of the week before
had failed to make some allusion to the Rev. A——
B——. When that can be said of any clergyman who
has not committed forgery, and said after he has been
in the public eye for twenty-five years, it is a sign of
power in the man. Such a ministry as his is worth
studying. It is an egregious folly to imitate him: his
sermons no other man can reproduce. But it is impossible that they should not contain elements which can
be transfused into the preaching of other men with
advantage. We may well give time and thought to
the ministry of any man who holds together by thousands, and for years, keen, clear-headed laymen in the
church, and who reaches a corresponding class of minds
outside of the church. The ministry of any such
preacher is a legitimate object of homiletic study, whatever we may think or suspect of the man.

On the other hand, we have reason to be anxious
about any ministry which is visibly producing no impression, — no evil, no good, perceptibly. I do not say
that such an appearance is always real. But it should
cause anxiety: it should set a preacher to searching for
the facts, and to the righting of errors. That is never
the normal attitude of the pulpit in which it barely

holds its own. In such a state of things it will generally be found that something new in the methods of the
pulpit is practicable and wise. We should keep our
minds, then, in a receptive mood towards the apparent
successes of preachers unlike ourselves. Prove those
successes, hold fast only that which can be proved;
but study them. Be sure that you reject nothing that
is proved.

An objection to the views here advocated deserves a
moment's notice. We are said to be living in an age
of unnatural excitements; and the pulpit, it is believed,
ought not to cater to them. "Safe men" tell us that
we must not be whirled out of the old orbits of the
planets by cometary and centrifugal attractions.

To this it should be observed, in rejoinder, that the
charge may be true, without damage to the clerical
policy here commended. It may be that we are living
in an abnormal current of social changes. It may be
that we are passing through a period of transition in
history in which one sea is pouring itself through a
narrow channel into another, like Erie into Ontario.
Niagara, therefore, may be the fit emblem of our modern
life. We may be approaching very near to the last
times. The world may be moving with a rush which is
its ultimate momentum. But one of the first principles of Christianity is to take men as it finds them and
where it finds them, and thus and there to adjust itself
to them. Its mission is to do for men all that it can do
under the disadvantages which sin or any other invincible fact creates. A Christian pulpit can not wait for
men to come into a state in which they can receive its
ministrations gracefully, tastefully, in a scholarly way,
or even contemplatively and candidly. Least of all

has the pulpit any right to refuse to be received in any other way.

A preacher's first business is to find men, to go where they are, and then to speak to them as they are, and speak so as to be heard. We must speak to them anywhere and anyhow, so that at the least we get a hearing. That is not wisdom, it is not piety, it is not reverence for venerable things, it is stagnation, it is timidity, often it is mental indolence, sometimes it is a refined but intense selfishness, which holds a preacher still in ancient ruts of ministration through fear of ministering to unnatural excitements. We had better do some things wrong than to do nothing.

9. An educated ministry needs to consider the study of men for rhetorical culture by the side of another fact; which is, that the literature of the world is not constructed for the masses of society. This is true of the great body of literature in any language. Books for the masses are comparatively a modern idea.

(1) The old theory on which national literatures have all been founded was, that readers must inevitably be few. The chief popular forms of any classic litera- ture are the ballad and the drama. Prose literature has not had till recently much of the popular element in any language. In the main, it has never been de- signed either to represent the common mind, or to be read by the common people. The ballad and the drama also have not been created for readers. They were designed, the one to be sung, and the other to be witnessed on the stage. This was for the very neces- sary reason that they grew up at a time when the people did not know how to read, and were not expect- ed to become readers. It was a time when in England

it was sufficient to save a man from the gallows that he knew how to read. This was English law till the time of George IV. Therefore select classes of mind have been the object aimed at in English literature.

(2) The reading classes have been select not only in numbers, but in character. They have been exclusives. They have been contracted fragments of nations. Their distinction has been, that they were unlike the bulk of the people, and not in sympathy with the people. Their exclusiveness was their glory. Their own social position demanded the popular ignorance as a background. Authors treated them as a superior class. They were cajoled by an obsequious recognition of their caste. Both authors and readers held themselves as retainers of the nobility with an abjectness which often intensified the contempt they all felt for the herd of the people. It is a humiliating fact; but such were the soil and the atmosphere from which the bulk of modern literature grew.

(3) The English literature has a larger infusion than any other of the popular element; but it is not and never has been thoroughly popular. Such a literature is yet to be created. Look into the prefaces of the standard books in our language, turn to the correspondence of authors, peruse the books themselves, and you will discover how oblivious authors have been of the actual numerical majority of the nation. Read John Foster's essay on "Popular Ignorance." In the dialect of the English press the "reading public" and "the nation" have never been synonymous, nor approximately so. Even so late as when Addison and Swift were delighting a select public of readers, the masses of the English people never heard of them. The masses

at that period found their chief excitements at country fairs and boxing-matches and dog-fights and bull-baitings. The only gleam of literary thought which found its way to them, aside from the pulpit, shone from the footlights of the strolling theaters.

John Foster records the following fact as well authenticated to his judgment by direct testimony from that golden age of English letters: On one Sunday morning, in one of the rural churches, the service was read with unusual rapidity, and every legal expedient adopted to shorten the time during which the people should be detained in the house of God. At the close of the service the officiating clergyman gave publicly his reason for thus abbreviating the duties of the hour. He said that "Neighbor B——" was about to bait a bull in the afternoon, and he wished to give the people ample time to prepare for the enjoyment of the scene. So distant from the enjoyment of the literature of England were the masses of the English people.

One reason which has made the poetry of Homer the favorite of English scholarship is the intensely aristocratic spirit which breathes through the Iliad and the Odyssey. Not a trace of the democracy of literature is found in Homer, nor indeed, so far as I know, in any ancient poetry, except the Greek drama and the poetry of the Hebrews: hence the English aristocracy intuitively exalt Homer in their estimate of libraries. English noblemen translate Homer, and write laudatory criticisms upon him. It may reasonably be doubted whether the intrinsic merits of the Odyssey and the Iliad would ever have lifted them to the rank they hold in English criticism, if they had not chimed in so harmoniously with aristocratic tastes in English scholarship.

(4) In the history of English literature the readers who stood between authors and the people at large did not by any means stand midway between. They were much nearer to the guild of authors than to the level of the nation : therefore they were not good conductors of intellectual stimulus from the upper to the nether regions. A gulf as impassable almost as that which separates Dives and Lazarus shut off the masses of the people from the privileges, the occupations, the sympathies, and the ideas of the authors. The project of sinking a shaft of intelligence from above down into the torpid strata of the national mind was never originated by the old standard productions of our language. No trace of it is to be found in the general conception of the mission of literature, even so late as a hundred years ago. Publishers are yet living who remember when such an idea was in its infancy. They can recall the time when a sale of five thousand copies of any thing was deemed a prodigious success in their trade. The sale of Walter Scott's works in his own lifetime — and Scott died in 1832 — was deemed a miracle of literary achievement, and it bankrupted his publishers, after all. When the process of stereotyping plates was invented, it was thought by the more conservative publishers to be of doubtful value, because the sale of so few works would justify the expense of plates. But now a publisher hesitates to accept a manuscript which is not worth stereotyping. Books the sale of which is less than five thousand copies are regarded as the small enterprises of the press.

The facts here noticed should be taken into the account in judging of the limited rewards which some of the most illustrious English authors have received in

their own lifetime. Critics are fond of contrasting the
contemporary with the posthumous fame of authors.
We are reminded, as if it were an anomaly, that no
collected edition of Shakspeare's plays was demanded
during his life; that Milton received but five pounds
for " Paradise Lost; " that Bishop Butler, the most profound of English prelates, was not known outside of
his own diocese; that Spinoza's works, though they
played an important part in revolutionizing the philosophy of Europe, brought no income to the author. Mr.
Froude says that it is only by accident that a work of
genius becomes immediately popular. I doubt this assertion. What is there, what has there ever been, in the
great works of our literature which is fitted to make
them popular? They are not addressed to the people,
not fitted to the popular taste or comprehension. To
this day the actual readers of Milton are few. Those
who heartily enjoy Shakspeare are but a fragment of
the reading public. Even on the stage, no manager
succeeds in resuscitating the great dramatist for any
long period. Let a work of genius, like " The Pilgrim's
Progress," be *made* for the people, and the people recognize it. But the great bulk of our literature is made
for the few; and it has its reward in being appreciated
by the few.

A change is in progress. A popular literature, good
and bad, is in the process of growth. But the old
standard literature of our language, that which has
grown venerable with centuries, that which contains
the classic models of English thought and speech, and
that to which, therefore, all scholarly minds turn for
literary stimulus and refreshment, is a literature, which,
for the most part, has known no such thing as the peo-

ple in the process of its creation. It does not represent the people; it is not of the people; it has never lived among the people; it is not dear to the people; it is not known by the people.

(5) The exclusive character of national literatures exposes the clerical mind to obvious peril in respect to clerical sympathy with the people. It is clear, on the face of things, that such a literature must be in some respects what the Christian pulpit ought not to be, and that a successful pulpit must, in some other respects, be what such a literature is not. Yet it is equally plain that a mind formed by such a literature alone is in danger of acquiring tastes which are averse to popular modes of thought, to popular habits of feeling, and to the study of popular necessities. A preacher may so study such a literature as to be dwarfed in his aptitudes for the pulpit. If he forms his mental character by the study of such books alone, he will inevitably reverse the process of his education for the ministry. Disintegration may take place in his natural tastes for the popular service. Culture itself may unfit him for the pulpit, except as an arena for literary achievement.

I have known instances in which this disorganizing process has been fatal. A student's clerical tastes have been demoralized. He has become disinclined, and therefore unfitted, to the work of the ministry, by an abuse of the very process which was designed to fit him for it. He has shrunk back on approaching the practical labors of the pulpit, through the force of acquired tastes which had the tyranny of instincts over his moral purposes. Such a revolution in the character of a candidate for the pulpit is usually irremediable. The best thing we can do with him is to make a pro-

fessor of him. The inspiration of the pulpit has gone
out of him to return no more.

We need to face this fact squarely. The very discipline of literary culture to which we subject ourselves
in a course of collegiate and theological training is attended with this incidental peril. Like all other great
benefits of culture, literary discipline is gained at costs.
It becomes us, therefore, to know that the danger exists,
and that, for full growth in fitness to the pulpit, we
need a study of men to which no extant literature
invites us.

(6) We should never lose sight of the fact, that, while
there is a literature *of* the pulpit and *in* the pulpit,
the pulpit still has objects which no other medium of
literary expression has. The pulpit is identified with
the people in the very groundwork of its construction.
It stands in among the people. It exists for the people.
It depends for all its legitimate uses and successes upon
the sympathies of the people. It reminds one of the
Pantheon at Rome, which stands down among the shops
and hovels of the poorest poor, partly buried in the
rubbish of ages, but, for all that, a symbol of the history
of a great people for ever.

The pulpit is not designed for select audiences. Its
object is not to furnish entertainment to luxurious
minds, or scholarlike enjoyment to tranquil minds. Its
object is to meet the necessities of minds, which, for the
most part, must be engrossed in a care for their necessities. The pulpit addresses chiefly the millions who
are struggling for a living, and who find the struggle so
severe, that books are as dreamlike a luxury as a coach
and livery. A man of books ranks in their minds with
millionaires. On this great low-ground of society the

pulpit stands alone. Literature has no other department, which in its very nature, as growing out of the
aims for which it exists, is so intensely popular as that
of the pulpit. The modern newspaper, even, does not
bear comparison with it in this respect. The newspaper does not strike so deep as the pulpit does in its
theory of popular necessities. It can not, therefore,
reach so profound and permanent a style of thought.

(7) The only thing I can recall which deserves to be
termed literature, which is at all suggestive of the pulpit
in the ideal on which it was constructed, is the old
Greek drama. The Greek drama was oral in the form
of its communication: so is the pulpit. The Greek
drama discussed the profoundest problems of human
destiny: so does the pulpit. The Greek drama expressed the ideas which lay deepest in the most enlightened theology of the day: so does the pulpit. Above
all, the Greek drama existed for the people; and so
does the pulpit.

In this respect the Greek drama was exceptional to
almost all other ancient literature. The people of the
ancient cities of Greece were the auditors and the
judges of the drama of their times. The entire body
of the free citizens of Athens — not a literary *coterie*
alone, not the members of a university alone, not the
pupils of a school of philosophy only, not a set of
pleasure-seeking idlers, but the entire citizenship of the
metropolis — heard the plays of Sophocles and Euripides. The accomplished professor of the Greek language
and literature in Amherst College is of the opinion
that probably Grecian women were permitted to attend
the exhibition of the tragic drama on the Greek stage,
and that even the slaves were not forbidden to attend.

The most magnificent triumphs of Grecian genius were popular festivals. This department of Greek literature grew up with the Greek people. Their minds awakened it; their demands stimulated it; their tastes passed judgment upon it; their sympathies made it what it was. So far as any Pagan literature could foreshadow a Christian institution, the Greek drama foreshadowed the Christian pulpit. It did so with an approach to resemblance which has never been equaled by any subsequent literature of equal dignity.

This idiosyncrasy of the pulpit, in comparison with the great mass of the literatures of the world, should, therefore, never be forgotten in the ardor of our literary pursuits. The pulpit exists for the people. It depends for its existence, in any broad growth, upon its union with the popular sympathies.

10. The relations of the pulpit to the people are affected, further, by the fact, that, in the moral history of the world, great popular changes often take place independently of the educated classes of mankind as such.

This is a phenomenon in history which is exceedingly prolific of suggestion. I am not confident that the philosophy of it is wholly intelligible, nor that it represents abstractly the normal method of the progress of the race. But of the fact there can be no question in the mind of any thoughtful observer of real life. The fact is most obvious, in respect to changes for the better, in popular sentiment. Evil works most frequently from above downward, — from the head to the heart of society. The bulk of mankind are more receptive of evil than of good from their superiors. A licentious court can make a people licentious more readily than a moral court can make a people moral. An infidel aristocracy can make a nation infidel more easily than a Christian aristocracy can make a nation Christian. The most destructive forms of evil do, in fact, usually begin in high places, and work downward. On the contrary, it very frequently happens that profound moral movements for good begin low, and work upward.

(1) Let us group the cultivated classes of mankind for a moment, and observe how the fact stands. First we have the class of royal and aristocratic birth, — the class represented by the crown and the court. Then comes the military class, represented by the sword. Then we have the literary class, strictly so called, — the class represented by the university and the library. Then follow the clerical, the legal, and the medical classes, represented by the three liberal professions, to which must be added, in our day the fourth profession, the journalists, represented by the most powerful of all printed literature, — the newspaper. To these succeed the small but very influential class of artists, represented by painting, sculpture, and music.

Finally must be appended a class peculiar, for the most part, to our own times, so far as it is distinct from the rest. It consists of those whose chief distinction is their wealth, and whose culture springs from the consciousness of power which wealth creates, and from the leisure which wealth renders practicable. This last class have a refinement which is often diverse from that of court, or school, or camp, or studio, or profession. It is a refinement in which manners take the precedence of mind. These several classes are all of them, in some sense, educated. The idea of culture is prized among them. We may, without essential error, speak of them as the cultivated portions of mankind. Beneath them, in respect to educated thinking and whatever else that implies, lies the great bulk of the human race. Numerically estimated, these cultivated classes are but insignificant fragments of the whole.

The point I wish now to emphasize is, that often great changes of moral sentiment take place in that vast low-ground of society, with which not one of these educated classes, as such, has any visible connection. Individuals from the educated classes are reached by such changes, but not the classes as classes. Religious awakenings of vast reach often start down there before they become visible in the aerial regions above. Advanced ideas of liberty and of national policy, which are rooted in moral principle, often exist in the popular feeling down there, long before they have worked up high enough to find the general voice to speak them from the cultivated strata of thought.

(2) We have a notable illustration of this truth in the history of the antislavery controversy in this country. Looking back to it, now that the main question is determined, do we not discover that the masses of the people have been generally in advance of their leaders on that subject? Where both classes lagged behind the purposes of Providence, have not the many been less distant in the rear than the few? Have not the intuitions of the people been, at almost any time, more far-seeing than the statesmanship of the Senate? Have not the people been, at almost any time, ready for progress which our wise men thought unsafe, but which God at length hurled us into, as if in the anger of his exhausted patience?

The masses of the people never heartily supported the *compromises* which made up nearly the whole of our statesmanship on the subject for half a century. Compromise — that miserable burlesque of wisdom where moral principles are at stake — was the sum total of the vision of our wise men through all that period; but the instincts of the people were never genial to it. When President Lincoln said, "If slavery is not wrong, nothing is wrong," the conscience and common sense of the people responded, "So say we all." President Lincoln himself was a child of the low-grounds. His ideas of political economy and of social rights he got out of the woods. His nearest approach to metaphysical culture was splitting rails. His knowledge of books was almost limited to the Bible and Shakspeare. All that he knew of history he learned from Abbott's histories for children.

If the cultivated mind of our country had been more childlike in its wisdom, and had followed the intimations of Providence more swiftly, it would have had no difficulty with the common mind in executing peaceably the plans which God at last thrust upon the nation in carnage. Carnage is not the normal and necessary instrument of great revolutions. In this also the masses of our people were right in their convictions. "Slavery is wrong," said they, "and it must die; but it *can* die by peaceful means." In this conviction they were nearer to the ultimate principles of God's government of nations than were the few fanatical leaders who ignored the reformatory potency of time. They were nearer to the old Mosaic wisdom on the subject, — that marvelous system of jurisprudence, to which we owe so many germs of the world's latest and wisest statesmanship. History in future ages will tell this story more truthfully than living chroniclers are now doing it.

Even up to this hour, is it not the rude instincts of the people which are taking the lead of political opinion in the solution of those problems, consequent upon the civil war, which have a moral and religious basis? The cultivated classes as a whole are not leading this people: they are following. The real leaders are men of the people, as distinct from, and to some extent opposed to, the men of culture. Such, at least, is the horoscope as I read it. How, otherwise, could the phenomenon ever have been possible, which we have witnessed within the last decade, — that the government of a great nation hung in suspense upon the votes of a few negroes in the backwoods of Louisiana and the everglades of Florida, who could not write their own names, nor distinguish their ballots from circus-tickets?

One is reminded often, in observing such phenomena, of the declaration of the apostle, "Not many mighty, not many noble, are called." It appears as if men of culture did not generally read Divine Providence aright till they are needed as leaders of great movements which have, in the main, been originated without them. After a certain growth of reforms we must have the leadership, either of high intelligence, or, in the absence of that, of miraculous inspiration. God does not permanently abrogate the law by which the superior governs the inferior mind; but temporarily, and when inspiration and miracle can not be interpolated into the system of affairs, he does suspend that law by making the low-grounds of society the birthplace of great ideas.

LECTURE IV.

RELATIONS OF THE CLERGY TO REVOLUTIONS OF POPULAR OPINION, CONTINUED.

(3) THE views already presented suggest, further that sometimes popular revolutions of opinion become distorted and corrupt for the want of an educated Christian leadership. Then come mutterings of anarchy. These, if not heeded, swell into bellowings of revolution. It is my conviction that ponderous questions of right and wrong are now seething among the masses of the nations, which have been started by truthful ideas. They are, at the bottom, legitimate problems of Christian inquiry. They are such questions as socialism strives frantically to answer. Among them are the social problems which are chafing some of the Southern States of our republic. In all the great nations of Christendom questions of this nature are threatening to turn the world upside down. A blind sense of wrong is buried under the enormous inequalities of our civilization, which the first influence of Christianity tends to lash into frenzy over the first principles of government and social order, with a recklessness which breeds civil wars. Looking at the facts as they are known and read of all men, and as they are suffered by the great majority, human nature cries out against them. It declares, that, if Christianity

means any thing, it means something very different from this. Then follow, the world over, the questions, " What and why and how and wherefore," down to the roots of things.

Yet this entire volume of popular questionings of the drift of our civilization might be answered so as to promote the peace of nations and the brotherhood of races, if the educated mind of the world would accept them as questionings which ought to be answered, instead of beating them down by a repressive conservatism, by pride of race, by the tyranny of wealth, and by bayonets. Because those questions are ignored, or falsely answered, by the educated classes, they continue to inflame the unsatisfied mind below. That low-ground of humanity, ignorant and debased as it is, can not rid itself of them. It surges around them angrily and blindly. The more obstinately the mind above crowds them down, or holds still in contempt of them, the more tempestuously, often deliriously, and in the final result demoniacally, the mind below clamors for a settlement of them. At length, in the fullness of its times, the mind below breaks loose from established institutions. The laws and usages of centuries give way. Rabid diseases of opinion take the place of healthy and quiescent faith, — all for the want of a dispassionate, scholarly, Christian leadership.

(4) At the root of almost all the intoxicated developments of popular opinion, there is a truth. It is a truth distorted, but still a truth; a truth tainted by error, but a truth nevertheless; a truth bloated by intemperate defenses, but a truth for all that. A mysterious power has set it fermenting in secret in the inexpressible intuitions of ignorant minds, as if in the

bowels of the earth, where the sun never shines. It must work its way up to light and air. If there is no other way for its ascent, if the repressive forces above are so ponderous and so compact that it can not lift them off gently, then it must spout up volcanically. It will not be smothered passively. A man buried alive will beat the coffin-lid. So these undying truths, pent up in the souls of ignorance and debasement, will struggle for egress. They will find their way out wherever they can discover the weakest spot in the shell with which conservative society becomes crusted over. The Providence of God certainly works sometimes in this seemingly anomalous neglect of the educated powers of the world.

I say "anomalous," because it is not the normal way of Providence to ignore culture, or to work without it. But sometimes, when culture, as represented in the upper classes of great nations and ruling races, is false to its mission, and treacherous to its origin, God starts great truths into life in the hearts of the masses, not in the heads of the few. He lets them work a long time there, in a half blinded way, before the few discover and embrace them.

An episode illustrative of this in literary history was witnessed in the origin and early fate of the "Pilgrim's Progress." Who wrote the "Pilgrim's Progress," and where? A tinker in Bedford jail. By whom, and why, was the tinker shut up in Bedford jail? The upper classes of a great empire put him there to prevent his preaching other such things as the immortal allegory. And how was it received by contemporary opinion? Thousands of colliers and peasants and humble tradesmen read it, and admired it, and loved it, long before the literary and social magnates of England found out that it was literature, and that a great prophet was born among them.

God's method of working is marvelously democratic. If there is one idea which takes precedence of all others in the divine choice of times, localities, instruments, and methods, it is not the idea of rank, it is not the idea of sect, it is not the idea of birth, it is not the idea of culture: it is the idea of *numbers*. To an aeronaut, at a very little distance above the earth, mountains and valleys are indistinguishable. So, it should seem, to the eye of God, distinctions of class are invisible. Humanity is spread out as a plain. The most attractive spots to the divine eye are those where are to be seen the densest clusters of being. The apostolic policy in laying the foundations of Christianity is the divine policy through all time and the world over; " beginning with Jerusalem," and advancing thence to the conquest of the great cities of the world.

11. The object for which I dwell, perhaps at needless length, upon this peculiarity in the divine method of procedure, is to observe specially that the natural leaders of these movements of the popular mind which are started by the first principles of religion are the Christian ministry. The legitimate teachers of the people in the ground-principles by which such movements should be regulated are the ministry. Christianity has conservative as well as quickening and progressive bearings upon social order, which it is the province of the ministry to teach. The wisest statesmanship of nations does not teach them in forms such that the popular mind can take them in, and appreciate the truth of them. It falls to the clergy to represent

them in moral rather than in political principles, tending to the regulation of progress and the moderation of change, and thus to the prevention of sanguinary revolutions. The divinely chosen friends of the people to do this service for them are the ministry. It is theirs to win popular confidence, to calm popular passions, to restrain popular vices, and to teach neglected virtues. It is theirs to teach popular *rights* as balanced by popular *duties*. These duties find almost none to proclaim them among the political leaders of the people. They are such as these, — respect for superiors, obedience to authorities, charity to evil-doers, patience under wrongs, freedom from envy, intrusting government to intelligence and virtue, election of superiors rather than equals to high places of trust and power. These things, so vital to republican life, political chiefs, for the most part, ignore. The only order of men who will or can teach the people this divine balance of rights and duties in self-government are the Christian ministry. Yet to perform this mission wisely, or with any chance of success, the ministry must know the people, must sympathize with the people, must recognize the rights and wrongs of social life; and to do either of these they must study the people.

Probably there is not a country-village in the land, which has any considerable history, in which there is not some mind, or group of minds, which represent the kind of mental inquiry here described. They may be within the church, but more probably are outside of the church, yet are superior material for the growth of the church. The pastor of such minds should be beforehand with them. He may be assured that they represent a movement which extends to other minds in adjacent villages. The pulpit should be brought down and planted alongside of them. The geographical locality of the church should be in the midst of their homes; and its structure should be such as to seem homelike to them. But, most of all, the pastor should be able to win them by his obvious knowledge of their condition, and his friendly appreciation of their wants.

12. These suggestions naturally introduce another in the same line of thought. It is that a certain portion of the clergy of every generation seem either insensible or hostile to popular movements of inquiry which have their origin in Christian ideas.

(1) This, it should in justice be observed, is not true, generally, of those portions of the clergy which are free from State control. History will make distinction in this respect between the ministry and the priesthood of Christendom. Still, in the ministry of free churches, the exception occurs frequently enough to indicate a peril to clerical character and a hinderance to clerical usefulness. It is not a very rare exception that the clergy is represented by a man who suffers popular inquiries, which are rooted in the gospel which he preaches, and which therefore, as a Christian teacher, he ought to understand and to answer, either to go by him unheeded, or to encounter from him an unqualified hostility. He thus permits the activity of the common mind to outrun him in new channels of thought.

(2) Delay in assuming leadership of popular inquiries often results in consigning the people to an infidel leadership. Infidelity in this respect is often enlightened, and to some extent, vitalized, by Christianity. While the clergy are busy, as in the main they ought to be, with teaching and applying the gospel in its

spiritual relations to individuals, infidel lecturers and writers, knowing nothing and caring nothing about the salvation of souls, do detect the bearings of the gospel on social questions. They often advance ahead of the clergy in the public declaration of those bearings. Hence comes to pass that phenomenon which history repeats over and over, and which is so perplexing to a candid observer; viz., that the infidelity of a country or an age seems to be wiser than the Christian ministry, and more successful in obtaining the leadership of reforms which owe their origin to the gospel, yes, to the preaching of the very men, some of whom fail at last to assume their natural right of leadership in those reforms.

(3) Sometimes the leadership of reforms which were Christian in their origin becomes so identified with skepticism in religion, that to follow it is to be treacherous to Christ and to his church. Then, for a time, the clergy are constrained by their religious convictions to stand aloof from such reforms, lest they should degrade the pulpit into an auxiliary to anarchic infidelity. That is a fearfully false position in which to place the Christian ministry. Yet it may come about from a want of alertness in the clerical mind to see the wants of the popular mind seasonably, and to supply those wants by assuming promptly the leadership which is the clerical prerogative.

More than once, for instance, in the religious and political history of Germany, popular liberty has been so identified with infidelity, that the best Christian minds throughout the empire have felt compelled to range themselves on the side of despotic re-action on the part of the government. The "Liberty party"

were "Red Republicans," sympathizing with the Social-
ists of France, and the Carbonari of Italy, and the
Nihilists of Russia. They taught, as many of them
who are now refugees in this country are teaching, the
tyranny of property in land, the usurpation of marriage,
the inhumanity of the Christian religion, and the necessity of abolishing the idea of God. In defense of these
monstrosities, they believed in no silken power of free
discussion, but in the musket and the guillotine. Law,
from God or man, was despotism.

The consequence has been, that such men as Trend
lenburg and Hengstenberg, and with them and after
them the most eminent leaders of German thought in
both the Church and the State, have been driven, in
defense of social order, to sustain the government in the
establishment of, with one exception, the most rigid
military despotism in Europe. In this they have done
only what we should all have done in their place.
When things have come to such a pass that liberty
means anarchy, and the abolition of despotism means
the abolition of God, there can be no question where
Christian and clerical authority ought to stand.

Where, then, lay the mistake of the religious leaders?
I answer, It probably lay farther back, in not watching
and detecting the popular restlessness in its beginnings,
instructing its infancy, and creating ideas of liberty
which were scriptural and rational, and thus aiding
in building up a public opinion which should have
deserved the sympathies of Christian men. Probably
it was once in the power of the Christian thinkers of
Germany, clerical and laical, to control the popular
inquiry on the one hand, and the policy of the government on the other; for it is well known that the

government of Germany has been largely in the hands of kings, emperors, and statesmen who personally have been religious men.

But that time, once passed unimproved by the clergy, left them no alternative afterwards but the wretched choice between despotism and atheism. They chose, as they ought to have done, the lesser evil; but in so doing they threw an immense weight into the scale of infidelity. German atheists to-day have this to say for themselves, that all the religion they know any thing about is a religion of aristocrats and bayonets. Who can compute the dead weight which Christianity must carry in such an unnatural alliance of truth with error? Christianity, in its normal working, never creates a state of things in which the best that good men can do is to make a choice of evils. Where that is the situation, something has always been wrong in the antecedent management.

The question is often asked in this form, " Ought the clergy to lead, or to follow, in the agitation of moral reforms?" In my judgment, it does admit of compact answer in this form. The question of leadership is a question of *dates*. It is in the beginnings of such movements, before they have reached the stage of agitation, that the work of the clergy is required. When reforms are in their germination is the time for the clerical hand to insert itself in methods of wise and temperate control. That *then* the clergy should be leaders, not followers, does not admit of question. The people have no other leaders whose prerogative is so sure.

(4) This leads me to observe, that, if the clergy wait in inaction till the popular mind is so profoundly agitated on a great moral reform that it will hear

nothing else, it is then often too late for the pulpit to be a power of control in that reform. A preacher then seems to speak in self-preservation. The current has rolled in around him, and has risen to the level of his lips, and he speaks because he must speak. His speaking then is the sputtering of a drowning man.

Moreover, the *status* of the community is then fixed. Opinions are settled, prejudices are full grown, the stream is set immovably, and probably some new fountain of opinion is already opened. Popular opinions of the kind now in question do not become popular till about the time when new opinions are forming underneath. A man who wakes to the discovery of a truth at the last moment of its general adoption is still behind his age. That truth is still green in his hand, when it has ripened, and shed its seeds, in the hands of others. Its fruit is germinating in other forms, which are likely to meet from him the same hostility or neglect with which he encountered their forerunners.

Have you never known a pastor whose entire ministry had the look of a losing race? He was not only not in advance of his age, not even abreast with his age, but a little, and only a little, behind his age; so near that he could always be in at a victory, but never there in the fight. A clergyman subjects his professional prestige to a heavy discount, if he permits any popular excitement which is rooted either in Christianity, or in hostility to Christianity, to escape his knowledge, or to advance to its results without his care. To be a power of control in such excitements he must lay a magnetic hand upon them in their beginnings.

(5) The principles here affirmed are not limited in their application to moral reforms technically so called.

They have a much broader range. To illustrate this, let several things be specified to which they are germane. A revival of religion, for instance, ought never to take a minister unawares. Dependent as revivals are upon the sovereignty of the Holy Spirit, they do not come without premonitions; that is to say, signs of their approach are visible to eyes which are open, and watchful for them. There is nothing in the philosophy of a revival which locks it up to occult causes. It will commonly foreshadow its approach in certain spiritual experiences, either within the church, or in Christian families, or in sabbath schools, or, it may be, in spiritual changes in a preacher's own soul. A wise pastor, studious of the laws of the Holy Spirit's working, will often discern tokens of his special presence on the eve of a work of special power.

Again: a renewal of popular inquiry upon any doctrine of our faith ought never to be ignored by the pulpit. A few years ago the doctrine of retribution started a wave of popular interest in many sections of this country, which is still in progress. Believers and unbelievers felt a fresh desire to investigate that doctrine. In a multitude of cases, opinions have been revised. Conflicting opinions upon it have agitated many communities. Theories have been broached respecting it which were locally new. Old errors have been revivified, and re-adjusted to suit modern tastes. Believers in universal salvation have become believers in a non-eternal retribution through their faith in modern necromancy. In some localities Restorationism is thus intrenched in the popular faith to-day more strongly than it was twenty years ago.

What, now, should be the policy of a Christian pulpit

during such a decade of revived inquiry? Evidently it should not be a policy of reticence. The pulpit should not ignore such a revival of popular interest in one of the standards of the faith. We should not retire from it in disgust at its origin. What if the wretched flummery of Spiritualism is in some cases at the bottom of it. That is no reason why the clergy should hold themselves aloof and aloft from it as a thing of degraded birth.

A case to the point occurs to me. In a certain parish in Massachusetts, Spiritualism had stolen a march. Starting with a fortune-teller, it crept into a group of respectable families. An educated physician gave it prestige. *Séances* were held every fortnight. Soon Dr. Channing and Benjamin Franklin began to dance on the tipping tables. The intermediate state and eternal retribution were revised. Several church-members dropped their ancient faith at the bidding of the ghosts of their grandmothers. Their pastor, when inquired of about the still revolution which was going on in his parish, scouted it because of its origin. He was preaching that winter upon the parables of our Lord. He could not descend from so lofty a height to contend with the twaddle of the *séances*. But his people could. Ought he not to have followed them? Ought he not to have known what they were thinking of and talking of, and whither they were drifting under the lead of the skeptical physician?

Christianity never stands upon its dignity. It descends wherever man descends. Its mission is to save the lost. And to save, it seeks: it does not wait to be sought. The clergy are *ex officio* guardians of Christian doctrine. They should claim instant leadership of

popular discussion, and should show by their mastery
of the subject their ability, and therefore their right, to
hold that leadership. Never should such a revival of
popular inquiry upon a Christian doctrine be allowed
to come to a head in a reconstruction of opinion, without the wise and winning voice of the pulpit.

It is on the same principle, and no other, that any
question of practical morals which arouses a community should summon its pastor to the van.   Temper-
ance, the desecration of the Lord's Day, reform of the
"social evil," the ethics of trade, the evils of caste,
the relations of capital to labor, should be watched
narrowly by the clergy whenever and wherever they
are attracting the thinking of the people.   It will
never do to turn these topics outside of the church,
and consign them to strolling lecturers in lyceums
and music-halls, and to wire-pullers in political con-
ventions. If the clergy let these things alone, on the
plea that the pulpit has more spiritual functions, those
spiritual functions can not long hold any leadership of
the people.

13. The relations of the clergy to the popular mind
have still another phase in which they need review. I
refer to that condition of things in which it sometimes
happens that the clergy become identified with the
cultivated classes of society to the practical exclusion
of the lower classes ; and the point to be specially noted
is, that, in such a state of affairs, the pulpit ceases to be
a spiritual power with any class.

The Rev. Dr. James Alexander laments the tendency
of some ministers to seek chiefly "the society of the
rich and the lettered," as he describes them, "instead of
being lights to the world."   He adds, "The democracy

must be reached. People must be made to feel that the
heart of the minister is with *them*. Common people
require this. The age requires it. Young men require
it." He was not the man to put on record even so mild
an expression of the facts as this, if he had not seen
evidence of the need of it, and more, among the clergy
of which he was an honored representative.

(1) But this view is enforced by a deeper principle
than any demand of classes or of the age. Upon it
depends the very existence of the pulpit as a moral
power. Aim at the educated classes exclusively, or
even chiefly, and you lose mastery of all classes. Isolate a Christian pulpit from the sympathy of the uneducated masses, and you forfeit respect for it as a power
of control among the ranks of culture.

You may sometimes detect evidence of this in the
history of individual churches. There are churches
which have allowed themselves to become representatives of the refinement and the wealth of a community
to the practical exclusion of its laboring classes. They
have aimed at the heads of society to the neglect of its
"hands." They forget that to every "head" there are
two "hands." The ministry of such churches are not
respected even in those churches as a power of spiritual
control. They are not recognized as an authority.
Their churches, standing themselves aloof from the
simple feelings and relationships which constitute the
plane of humanity in real life, expect their pastors to
minister to their pleasure, and be guided by their opinions. They expect preaching to meet their tastes rather
than their necessities. Their pastors commonly do as
they are tacitly bidden. Such churches will not long
retain pastors who will not do it.

As a consequence, such a ministry loses all mastery. They lose their liberty as public teachers, and their authority as public leaders. They deserve to lose them. They are in an unnatural position as it respects the masses of the people; and a subtle instinct in the very classes of culture which have tempted them aloft pronounces the position a false one. Nobody looks up to them as men of apostolic power. As men, such preachers may be loved; as social equals, they may be respected; for the truths they do utter they may be commended. Smooth and pleasant things may be said of them for their fidelity in preaching "the gospel," as they call it. In quiet times, in the routine of worship, in pastoral functions, they may fill a place of seeming honor. But they are not revered by their most devoted friends as spiritual superiors. They are not looked up to as men whose opinions are an authority, whose approval is a reward, whose rebuke is feared as carrying the weight of a message from God. They are the very last type of a Christian ministry which the people will feel to be a power in the land.

(2) In further explanation of this phenomenon it should be remarked that the influence of the clergy with the cultivated classes of society is to a considerable extent a moral as distinct from an intellectual influence. The time has long since gone by when the clergy were *ex officio* the intellectual superiors of all their parishioners. They minister now to many who are, in point of intellectual force and general culture, their equals, and to some who are their superiors. The pulpit is criticised now with a freedom which springs from the conscious power, and therefore the right, to say what the pulpit ought to be, and to judge of what it is.

Laymen as a class know less of theology than they did
a half-century ago, but they know more of some other
things. They do not listen to preaching as conscious
inferiors to the man who is addressing them, so generally as they once did.

As a consequence, the influence of the pulpit with
the cultivated classes is pre-eminently a religious influence. It is the influence of the man, of his personal
weight, of his devotional spirit, of his self-forgetfulness,
of his eminence in all the passive clerical graces. The
most intelligent hearers are those who enjoy most
heartily the simplest preaching. It is not they who
clamor for superlatively intellectual or æsthetic sermons. Daniel Webster used to complain of some of
the preaching to which he listened. He said it was too
severe a strain upon the intellect to be sympathetic
with the spirit of worship. " In the house of God " he
wanted to meditate " upon the simple verities and the
undoubted facts of religion," not upon mysteries and
abstractions.

The distinction between religion and theology is one
which such hearers prize highly. While they want
thought, not ranting, in the pulpit, they do not crave
abstruseness, nor is it the intellectual character of the
ministry which chiefly wins their respect. That must
not be beneath their respect, but neither is it nor can it
be now an eminence to which they look up with painful awe. This class of hearers think much of the devotional services of the pulpit. They look there for
much which wins and holds their confidence in the
clergy. For their personal help in a religious life they
want a religious teacher whose prayers uplift them.

The Episcopal Church of this country, relatively to

its limited numbers, embraces a larger proportion of
culture than any other sect of Christians. Yet its
pulpit as a whole is intellectually inferior to that of
any of the other great sects of the American Church.
What is it that holds such an amount of educated mind
in its allegiance to the Christian faith? It is mainly
their respect for and attachment to their ancient liturgy.
They know, and it goes to the hearts of thousands of
devout believers among them every Sunday, that the
Litany is the most sublime, comprehensive, and affect-
ing piece of liturgic expression in the language. They
will bear almost any amount of commonplace in the
sermons of a clergyman who so puts his soul into that
incomparable production as to make them feel his
heart in equal pulses with their own.

In our own denomination the fact is not always so
obvious; but the evidences of it are still abundant,
that the culture of our congregations is moved by the
religious more than the intellectual spirit of the pulpit.
The clamorers for sensationalism in our pulpits are
those who really know least about good preaching, and
are the poorest judges of it when they hear it. The
more ignorant a people are, the more fuss they make
about the want of mental gifts and acquisitions in their
pastors. They will dismiss a really learned pastor, and
complain that they are not "fed," when his sermons
have "meat" enough in them to gorge such hearers to
repletion.

It is to be hoped that you will not experience this
evil; but the chances are that some of you will. If you
do, I trust that the council which dismisses you will be
faithful enough to put on record, as one council did in
such a case, " Resolved that our brother, the Rev. Mr.

A——, in our judgment has given to this church and congregation meat fully equal to their digestive powers." Yes, it is the commonplace mind that complains most loudly of commonplace preaching. The black congregations of our cities and the South are notoriously the most censorious critics of simple preaching. They often feel themselves insulted if a man who *can* write preaches to them an extemporaneous discourse.

LECTURE V.

CLERICAL INFLUENCE WITH THE EDUCATED CLASSES,
ITS CHARACTER. — THE CHURCH AND THE WORLD,
THEIR RELATIONS DISTORTED.

(3) PURSUING a little further our review of the relations of the clergy to the educated classes, let us observe that clerical influence over those classes is very largely a reflexive influence. It rolls back over the cultivated heights of society by the force of its accumulations below. Do we not all sometimes trace our first response to a preacher's influence, even our discovery of the fact that he has in him the germs of power as a leader of men, to the fact of his moving others? We feel his power through the medium of our respect for his power over them. No man who is not past feeling any thing great can be insensible to the spectacle of a man moving to their eternal well being the masses of uncultured mind by so simple an instrument as preaching. There is a sublimity in it which all feel who are not imbruted in sensuality. The educated mind will involuntarily extend to such a man a respect to which his culture can lay no claim.

The landed gentry of England flocked to hear Whitefield, not because of any thing in him which *they* discovered: the discoverers of his genius were the uncultivated throngs in the fields and on the commons

67

of England. It was the great field-preacher in the
lowlands whose voice reverberated to the surrounding
heights, and commanded a respect which might never
have found expression in any other way. The refinement, and the culture, and the wealth, and the noble
birth of England, never found the man out till the
rudeness, and the ignorance, and the plebeian tastes,
and the poverty of England, had opened *hearts* to him.
Then the classic *heads* of England came to their senses
about him. Mr. Spurgeon, in our own day, is illustrating the same phenomenon.

One of the most useful of American evangelists,
when he began to speak in public, was advised by a
group of wise men not to expose thus his infirmities of
speech and poverty of thought. For the time they
were right in that counsel. Even now he would not
claim that his right to speak consists in the affluence
of his materials, or the elegance of his diction. Yet
the *élite* of Boston and Brooklyn numbered thousands
in his audiences. Such critics as those of "The New-
York Tribune" found a theme of thoughtful discussion in his work as a social phenomenon.

Why is this? Not, probably, because of any thing
which *they* feel of power in his discourses, but because
they feel the fact that other thousands of lower grade
are moved by him. His power over his superiors is a
reflection of his power over his and their inferiors. A
secret conviction sways thoughtful minds, that such a
man is in many respects a representative of a Christ-
like ministry. His success is one of the natural se-
quences of the preaching of the gospel in ways in
which spiritual power takes precedence of all other
elements of successful speech. The thing which he is

doing is the business of a Christian preacher. The higher classes no less resolutely than the lower withhold their spirit of obeisance from any man who is too good for it, too refined, too scholarly, too gentlemanly, or too indolent and too weak. The preacher, therefore, who has no power with the common people, has, in fact, no power with anybody. The pulpit which has no standing-ground down in the lowlands of society has none anywhere. An exclusive ministry is always a weak ministry.

(4) The weakness of an exclusive ministry is often not disclosed till spiritual emergencies arise. In quiet times, specially in stagnant times, it may pass undetected. But let emergencies come which agitate all classes, and then the hollowness of such a ministry will reveal itself to all classes. The cultivated will be as prompt as those below them to detect it, and to fling it from them. They look around them for a spiritual leader, to some man who has not sought to please them. Over the heads, it may be, of their own pastors, they will look to some minister of Christ whom they descry in the distance, down on the plain, in the dust and the heat of the battle. For such a man, whose spiritual power has been proved by emergencies, the rest of us must fall back to the right and to the left. The Church wants *him*. The heart of the Church has felt the pulsations of his heart; and now the brain of the Church singles him out by a judgment well-nigh unanimous. The Church wants his experience; she wants his knowledge of men; she wants his insight into the popular necessities; she wants his skill in touching the springs of popular sensibility: more than all else, she wants his sympathy with God's spirit in movement

upon the popular conscience. Under such conditions, *vox populi vox Dei*. Such a man always finds his reward even in this world: it is only a question of time.

14. Another sequence of any general deficiency in clerical knowledge of and sympathy with men is the establishment of anomalous relations between the church and the world.

The biblical idea of the church is simply that of an organized body of regenerate mind: the biblical idea of the world is that of the unsaved multitude of unregenerate mind. Two classes of character, and only two, make up the human race as the Scriptures represent it; viz., saints and sinners, friends of God and enemies of God. Much of the power of the pulpit depends on assuming the reality of that distinction. One of the chief objects of church organization is to make that distinction vivid. A living church always fastens that distinction upon the conscience of the world. Apostolic preaching was full of it. Religious reformations always rejuvenate it. Often the first evidence of a religious awakening is a new illumination of that one thought in the experience of the church and in the convictions of lookers-on.

On the other hand, the amenities of Christianized social life tend to obscure, even to obliterate, that distinction. This is specially true in nations of vigorous mental stock. In such nations Christianity displaces barbarism by refinement: it drives depravity out of brutal into aspiring forms; it crowds the savage under cover of the lofty vices. The churchly idea is then in perpetual conflict with its imitations for its own existence. The tendency is often almost overpowering to

confound regenerate graces with ornate and silken forms
of irreligion.

In such a state of society — and it is one which is
inevitable in any nation which has reached the higher
stages of a Christian civilization — very much depends
on the adjustments of the pulpit. The pulpit has an
office like that of "Old Mortality" in Walter Scott's
romance, — to cut over again, and engrave deeper in the
popular conscience, the conviction of the old distinction
between saint and sinner. One of the vital aims of the
pulpit must be to enforce the scriptural ideal of what
the church should be and of what the world is. Any
thing which enervates the pulpit in that work must
tend to fuse the church and the world together in the
judgment even of thoughtful men. The reality of
consecration on the one side and of ungodly living on
the other will grow dim in proportion as each approaches the other in its external signs.

The point, therefore, to be emphasized is, that any
general deficiency in the clerical knowledge of the
world must tend directly to that end: it must tend to
blot out this churchly distinction. It is well known
that the theory of the moral nature of man which has
been taught in some New-England pulpits has resulted,
in some cases, in the abolition of all church organization, and the disuse of the Lord's Supper as the token
of churchly prerogative. To the same result tends
ignorance of the world in clerical ministrations. It
tends to leave the fusion of the church and the world
to go on unchecked by any forcible delineations of the
difference between them. A ministry not knowing
men as they are will not preach to men as they are.
Not recognizing the face of their own contemporaries,

they will not speak to their own contemporaries. Men who do not themselves feel the pulsations of the popular heart can not minister to the real diseases of the popular condition.

Furthermore, the pulpit, under such circumstances, is apt to be full of side-issues. Preaching becomes powerless from overshooting, or shooting at random. Preaching by routine takes the place of original thinking. One is reminded by it of the old rule of English military tactics, by which a platoon of infantry, at the command "Fire," were taught to discharge their muskets on a dead level before them, without aiming at any thing, and then to wheel around to the rear.

Such preachers will often preach against forms of sin which are for the time extinct, and exhort to virtues which are just there out of place, and just then untimely. They may describe fossilized characters, instead of the living men and women. They will depict sinners in the general, and saints in the abstract, instead of American or English Christians and sinners. They will urge proportions of truth which the popular conscience will not respond to as the most pressing need of the hour. They will preach in a dialect which is not abreast with the growth of the language. They will hold on to phraseology which is obsolete everywhere else than in the pulpit. They will betray no insight into the modes of thinking, the types of inquiry, the subjects of interest, the convictions of truth, and the tendencies to error, which are in the living souls around them. They will preach so that many thoughtful men will not believe them: as many more will not believe that they believe themselves. No large proportion of a community will feel their presence as that of a reli-

gious power.   The masses of society especially, who
are immersed in the struggle for a livelihood, will not
come within reach of the echo of their voices.

A church formed under the influence of such a
ministry, it is obvious, can have no power of conquest
in the world.   The sense of distinction between it and
the world must become practically defunct.   Thinking
men will feel, and blunt men will say, that there *is* no
difference between the character and life of such a
church and many of the more respectable forms of
worldliness.   Worldly organizations with religion
enough in them for ornament, associations for reform,
charitable leagues, secret societies, will grow up and
take the place of the church in the estimation of many,
because they see no churchly mission in actual operation, of which they feel the need.

Meanwhile the deepest religious inquiries of men of
profound conscience do not turn to such a church for
an answer.   Those inquiries go on outside of the
church, with no leanings to it, and no listening ear for
its teachings.   A class of thoughtful men arise who
are not in the church, who do not wish to be there,
who can not be persuaded to be there, and yet whose
consciences do not convict them when the pulpit, in
stereotyped phrase, prays for deliverance from "the
world, the flesh, and the devil," and declaims against
"haters of God, and enemies of the cross of Christ."
They form a third class who are not consciously the
one thing or the other.   They do not "profess and call
themselves Christians;" yet their consciences do not
respond when the pulpit addresses them as sinners in
distinction from saints.

You can judge for yourselves of the extent to which

this picture is approximately true in our own day.
The main point which I wish to observe is, that such a
state of things is a distortion of the normal relations
of church and world, and that it results inevitably
from any general sense of clerical unfitness to the
world of real life. It follows as a necessary sequence,
when the popular mind is left in want of a ministry
which is wise in its knowledge of its own times,
thoroughly cordial in its sympathy with its own times,
and vigorous in adapting the pulpit to the spiritual
wants of its own times. This third class of minds
need a living pulpit in order to be made sensible of
the presence of a living church. They need, not a
pulpit of the past, not a pulpit of the future, but a
pulpit of to-day. They need to see a live man at the
head of the elect. Else their response is quick and
stern, "Who are you, that you should claim to *be*
elect?"

As to the material of preaching, they need not so
much new truth as old truth freshened. They want
the ancient substance of the gospel as apostles preached
it, but clothed in the experience of to-day, and coming
out boldly yet winningly in the speech of to-day. They
want the old creeds of the church, which reverent men
and saintly women have chanted, translated into the
dialect of common life. They claim the right to test
those creeds as uninspired productions. They *will* test
them by the common sense of men in the interpretation of God's word. In that process they claim that
the advance which the human mind has been making in
centuries of popular development shall be recognized.
They ask that the Scriptures as represented by modern
creeds shall seem to be consistent with themselves and

with the necessary convictions of the race. They wait, sometimes a long while, for a living pulpit which shall speak out for them these yearnings of their own souls, and help them to understand themselves. No other kind of ministry can ever win them to the visible church of Christ.

Here the inquiry is pertinent for the moment, What would be the consequence of a permanent isolation of the clergy from the popular sympathy? I answer without hesitation, The destruction of the church as a living power. The few whom we now recognize as a third class — not churchmen, yet not reprobates, earnest thinkers and of upright lives — would increase in numbers and in influence. Christianity is too far advanced in its conquest of human thought to be extinguished by the defection of one or two generations of either church or clergy. In other hands Christian thinking would live, and Christian discussion would make itself heard. Now and then platoons of inquirers would fall back into infidelity. Here and there fraternities of them would become absorbed in moral reforms. But the bulk of them would press their way into some form of organization which should express the idea of Christian fellowship, but which, we may be assured, they would not call a church. They would then create for themselves and their children some order of religious teachers which they would not call a clergy. Meanwhile, as it respects power of conquest in the world, by the side of such an organization the church and her clergy would be stranded.

But we need not fear any such result. God does not permit the clergy to fall permanently out of rank into false relations to the world. It is cheering to note how

seasonably divine intervention prevents that disaster.
Religious awakenings on the eve of emergencies are
constantly vitalizing the pulpit anew. Metaphorically
speaking, new blood is put into clerical leadership.
The spiritual anæmia is cured. Preachers are often,
in popular phrase, "reconverted." Men who have been
deficient in consecrated graces, and some of whom have
held theories unfriendly to direct ministrations, are *re-*
formed. They either preach inconsistently with their
theories, or they change their views, and seem to themselves to experience a new baptism from the Holy
Ghost. By some means the end will always be gained,
of securing to the church a ministry which shall be
sympathetic with their own generation, and studious of
the wants of their own times.

The views here advanced I am very sensible are
liable to misinterpretation. It is difficult to state the
truth on the subject forcibly without exaggeration.
Principles affirmed must be qualified, and some of the
qualifications are as important as the principles. State-
ments of fact also must be limited; and often the limitations are essential to prevent invidious comparisons.
I have endeavored to limit and to qualify as the truth
demands; yet I am sensible of the danger of seeming
to judge the ministry cynically.

I beg you to note, therefore, that the criticisms upon
men, implied in my remarks on this subject, I do not
apply to the evangelical body indiscriminately. They
are true of many in some sections of the church, and
of few in others; of many at some periods, and of few
at others. Let me quote here a slip which I take from
one of the secular periodicals of London. I by no
means indorse it. I present it as a specimen of the

impression which may be unconsciously made upon men of the world by an educated, refined, scholarly clergy representing one or more of the historic denominations of Christendom.

The editor in question classifies the clergy of England thus: " We have first the mild, school-visiting, weak-eyed, tea-drinking, croquet-playing curate, with a strong conviction that he stands in need of feminine sympathy; then the pet parson, who finds his way into the drawing-rooms of fashionable watering-places, as a fly into a sugar-basin; then the comical parson, who is great in organizing archery clubs and bazaars, as well as in enacting the part of social buffoon on every possible opportunity; then the dancing parson and the hunting parson; and lastly the parson who is denominated *par excellence* 'fast.' "

You will observe here, that no place is found for apostolic ministers of Christ, in numbers sufficient to form a class, in the whole body of the English clergy. Nothing limits it absolutely to the clergy of the Establishment. The picture is, of course, a caricature: more, it is a libel upon very valuable branches of the church of Christ. Yet even as a caricature it is instructive. Caricatures do not spring up like mushrooms. This one could not have existed if the classes which it satirizes did not exist in sufficient numbers to suggest it, and to be suggested by it. It could not exist if there were not a considerable minority of the clergy who are making on the world the impression which it exaggerates. They are men of the world in all that makes up its artificial life, and yet are not feeling after and ministering to the profound necessities of the world as a world of lost sinners for whom Christ died. I repeat, therefore, that, in some sections of the church, the criticisms I have made are true of many, and in others of few. My belief is, that in all they are applicable to a minority, and that, relatively, a small one. In some periods of history, also, these criticisms are more obviously true than at others.

But at all periods, in all sections, under all conditions of real life, the *peril* which they suggest exists. This is the point which I wish to impress. The tendency to the disastrous state of things which they imply is always attendant upon the preaching of the gospel in a world like this by such instrumentalities as even the best that human nature furnishes. The tendency lies deep in our civilization to subordinate moral distinctions to social distinctions, and therefore to be swayed by whatever is found afloat on the surface of the so-called "upper classes" of society.

Let that tendency become dominant in the ministrations of the gospel, and it betrays itself in such phenomena as these; viz., the organization of churches by social affinities chiefly; the erection of church edifices so costly and ornate that the poor can not feel at home in them; the crowding together of such churches in fashionable localities, in which "society" lives, and "the people" do not; the consequent adjustment of an educated pulpit to educated hearers only; the gradual separation of the poor from the rich and of the ignorant from the cultivated in religious worship; the gradual concentration, therefore, of the wealthy and the refined into one or two denominations of Christians; the usage in those denominations of acting upon the poor and the ignorant, if at all, by methods which create a sense of social distance between the superior and inferior; the

sequence that success in winning the inferiors to Christ
is made impossible, and the effort to do it under such
conditions farcical; and finally, as the result of all these
things, a worldly ambition among the clergy to be magnates over magnificent churches whose secret pride is
that they have no poor, no ignorant, no rude worshipers in their gorgeous temples, and whose fixed
purpose it is not to tolerate such worshipers under
the same roof with themselves.

It is this peril which I have wished to portray
temperately yet truthfully. I think there are facts
in the present drift of things in our own denomination,
specially in our cities, which should set us on double
guard against it. Calvinistic denominations are all
giving evidences of its existence. The rise of Methodism was a revolt of spiritual forces against it. But
now, even Methodism gives signs of its encroachment
upon the ancient discipline.

The establishment of mission-chapels in our large
cities by the prominent evangelical sects is, in my
judgment, a very questionable experiment. It has not
the right *look* for the working of a Christian church.
I am not prepared to say that it may not be the best
thing now practicable, things being as they are. Human nature must be taken as we find it, in the higher
classes as in the lower. In such a reform of Christian
usage as these remarks suggest, we must begin by
working as we can. We must cherish the patient
virtues with which the apostles trained the imperfect
graces of the early church. But the first thing we
have to do is to see our existing policy as it is. We
should mark its inevitable tendency to foster a classification of Christians by mutual repulsion of classes

from each other. Its tendency is directly to falsify the apostolic principle which lies at the very foundation of a church of Christ: "We, being many, are *one* body in Christ." Whatever may be said in defense of it, it is just what Christ did *not* do when he entered Jerusalem as a preacher. It is just what the apostles did not do at Corinth and at Ephesus. Is it not what neither of them would do to-day if they were to itinerate among our American churches?

To illustrate the temptation to which a pastor *may be* exposed by the spirit of caste in our metropolitan churches, let me relate a single case which occurred in one of our Eastern cities. A certain preacher of considerable local popularity had gathered a large and wealthy and intelligent congregation, not surpassed, if equaled, by any other in the State. Not a pew was unsold in the church, and not a seat often vacant on the Lord's Day. Applications for pews were made months in advance of a supply. Every thing that could minister to the pastor's worldly comfort or ambition he had at his command. For salary, voyages to Europe, increase of library, long vacations, he had only to ask, and he received. The social eminence of his congregation created an eminence for him on which he was seen and sought after from afar. Yet he was not content. He felt himself restrained from the work of his life by the very luxury of his position, and this from the fact that he had none of God's *poor* among his people. Not one family worshiped in his church from the humbler walks of life. It could not be said of his ministry, "To the poor the gospel is preached." They could not shun a pest-house more cautiously than they did his church-door. The long row of private car-

riages before it, some of them with liveried drivers on
the boxes, on a Sunday morning, was a grief to him.
He had no agrarian sympathies; but he felt himself
called of God to preach to the drivers as well as to
their masters.

He at length sought a consultation with the leading
men in his society, and told them his affliction. He
told them frankly that he had done all he could do for
them and their families, conditions being as they were,
and now he wanted an increase of his congregation of
a different social rank. He asked them to put galleries
into their church edifice, hoping by that means to
achieve his object. They heard him respectfully, but
blandly refused his request. He reasoned and pleaded
with them, to no effect. They thought he was hypochondriac, and offered to send him to Europe. But to
go to Europe would be only to " change the place, and
keep the pain." He was an hypochondriac of the class
to which our Lord belonged when he wept over Jerusalem. He must preach the gospel to the poor, or he
could not be content with his life's work. His people
argued that galleries would injure the architecture of
their beautiful temple; but he reasoned them out of
that fear, so far at least as to silence them.

At last they plainly told him that it would be dis-
agreeable to them and their families to have a crowd
of the poor thronging the same place of worship with
themselves. They belonged to the high classes of
society, and wished to remain such. They would not
have galleries over their heads. One of the saints told
him plainly that he did not believe that God meant to
have the rich and the poor worship under the same
roof. He had ordained the distinction, and was re-

sponsible for the consequences. The pastor, with grief
and indignation, at length told them that it was more
than he could bear. Much as he loved them, grateful
as he felt for their kindness, he must leave them.
Preach to the poor somewhere he must and would, if
he had to go into the streets to do it. And they let
him go into the street. They found a successor who
was not "hypochondriac." All honor to the man!
But what of the church as a spiritual power in the
world? How soon would such churches, though as the
stars of heaven in multitude, be successful in the conversion of the world? Indeed, how much better would
the world be than it is now, if it were converted to the
type of Christianity which such churches represent?
Give me rather the philosophy of Socrates and Plato,
and the faith of Cicero, than such a Christianity.

LECTURE VI.

THE STUDY OF MEN, CONCLUDED. — PRACTICE OF LEADING MINDS IN HISTORY.

15. THE theoretical consideration of the study of men as a means of rhetorical discipline invites us to observe further, in concluding the discussion, that the study of living men as a source of discipline is commended by the general practice of leading minds in history. The remarks I have to make on this point will not add much to your note-books. Yet they are necessary to illustrate the reality of the views I have presented, as proved by experience.

The truth is, that the majority of us have passed through our courses of collegiate training, under erroneous impressions, probably, of the proportion in which books have contributed to the making of controlling minds in real life. The cases have been exceptional in which power of control has been gained largely in any department of life without this practice of the study of men as distinct from the study of libraries.

(1) Much is signified to the purpose here by the ancient curriculum of education. The ancient systems of education included provision for extensive travel. The Greek and Roman schools of learning were never considered adequate to the complete training of men for public life. The training of the schools, it was

assumed, was to be followed by travel in other lands.
No man would then have regarded his literary culture
as finished, even in its foundations, without the appendix of travel to the scholastic discipline.

This was the ideal of a liberal education throughout
the middle ages. It has always been the English ideal,
to this day, of the most perfect educational training.
The idea of deriving the whole of a young man's mental
discipline from schools of learning is a modern, and
specially an American idea. Here it has arisen from
the extension of scholastic privileges to multitudes who
have not the means of travel, and also from the fact
that the early entrance of young men upon public life
here in part takes the place of travel in pressing them
into some knowledge of the world.

Plato was thirty years old when Socrates died. He
spent eight or nine years under the instruction of
Socrates, and then he spent ten years in Megara,
Magna Grecia, and Sicily, before he returned, and entered upon his public life in Athens. In this country,
six of the corresponding ten years in a young man's
life are spent in the first experiments of professional
duty. Practically those six years are a part of his
professional discipline. We all find it such in fact.
We depend on the first years of our public life for that
part of our training which the early systems of education derived from travel.B ut, come from what source
it may, it comes from some source in nearly all the
cases in which a power of control is gained largely in
any department of public life.

(2) Not to rest with general assertion on a point of
so much interest as this, let me recall to you certain
biographical facts in the history of literature, and of

government, and of the arts. These embrace specially, among others, some which relate to the habits of distinguished speakers.

But first let me recall the one man who illustrates almost every thing in literary history. The point in the history of the English drama which Shakspeare marks most vividly is that in which it ceased to be scholastic, and became popular. Shakspeare disowned the tyranny of literature, and defied the tyranny of criticism. He became what he was to the English drama simply by being what he was to the English people. Critics have tried hard to make out for him a large acquaintance with books; but that is the very thing of which the evidence is least in his history.

On the other hand, nothing else is so certain in the meager knowledge we have of his personal career, as that he acted his own plays, lived in the world which he sought to entertain, studied the tastes of his own companions, and wrote for the people of his own times. Never was man more intensely a man of the present. From the latest researches in Shakspearean literature, it appears that he seldom or never wrote a tragedy till some one else had first tried the public taste on the same subject. M. Guizot, who, though a Frenchman, has written the keenest criticism upon Shakspeare's works which I have met with, finds nothing else in them so characteristic, and so philosophically explanatory of their success, as the fact that they evince a most masterly knowledge of his own age and country, and that he wrote in a spirit of ardent loyalty to them both.

The next illustration is Raphael. Says one of the most intelligent critics of this prince of painters, " His paintings seem as if he had gone about the streets, and, whenever he found an expressive face or attitude, had daguerreotyped it on his brain, and gone back to his studio to reproduce it." The point of interest in the criticism is the fact that such was precisely the fact in Raphael's professional habits. His most celebrated faces are almost all of them portraits. His personal friends, the celebrated women of his age, some of the courtesans of Rome and Florence, still live on his canvas. Such was the extent to which he carried this fidelity to real life, that some critics even question his originality of conception.

A third example is Edmund Burke. One of his critics, speaking of Burke's writing, says of the man, "He was a man who read every thing, and saw every thing." The key to his success as an author — an author, I say, for he was no speaker — is to be found in his own criticism of Homer and Shakspeare, of whom he said, "Their practical superiority over all other men arose from their practical knowledge of all other men." Burke respected the popular mind. In his appeals to it he laid out his whole strength. Some of his most profound reflections on political economy he embodied in his "Letter to the Sheriffs of Bristol." And what was the "Letter to the Sheriffs of Bristol"? Nothing but a political pamphlet written to carry on a political campaign in a single shire. His "Essay on the Sublime and Beautiful" was the product of a period of recreation. The hard work of his life was expended on the practical affairs of England. He was one of the most ardent and original of theorists; yet such was his subjection of theory to fact in his knowledge of mankind, that his was the first leading mind in Europe which recovered from the intoxication of the French Revolution, and detected the drift of it towards anarchy.

A fourth illustration is Curran, the Irish orator. His mother used to say of him, " O Jackey, what a preacher was lost when you became a barrister ! " The old lady was right if Curran would have carried into the ministry the same methods of self-discipline which he practiced for the bar. He laid the foundation of his success as a barrister in the coffee-houses of London.

The London coffee-houses of that day were what the " London Times " and other metropolitan newspapers are now. Curran used to spend two hours every night in them for the purpose of studying the politicians whom he found there, observing their ways, their speech, their opinions, even their dress. He would go from one to another, selecting those which he said " were most fertile in game for a character-hunter." In this respect he represented almost all the public men of his day who became eminent in the public life of England. Lord Macaulay says that the coffee-house was then a national institution, so general was the resort to it of men whose public efforts of speech and authorship ruled the realm.

Fox and Mirabeau I name as men of great power in speech without great learning. As students of books they were too indolent to accumulate the materials of their own speeches : each had his fag. But as observers of men they were indefatigable : therefore, in spite of their deficiencies in the knowledge of libraries, they became masters in parliamentary debate. These men represent a class of minds which spring up in every country of free speech.

Napoleon is a seventh example. He founded libra-

ries, but never entered them. But that was no boast
when he said, " I know man." He used to visit in dis-
guise the seaports of France to converse in person with
the fishermen and sailors and smugglers. He illustrated
the way in which a man of the world will often spring
at a bound, in religious argument, to results which a
scholastic mind would have reached, if at all, with slow
and wary steps. Thus it was that the superhuman
nature of Jesus Christ revealed itself to him. When
he formed the celebrated " Code " which bears his
name, he gathered around him the first jurists of the
empire, including those of the old monarchy; and he
astonished them all by the practical wisdom with which
he fused the conflicting materials which they furnished
him, into one consistent and feasible system of organic
law. His method of studying any subject which the
welfare of the empire required him to master was to
summon a group of conflicting living authorities on
that subject, and set them to arguing with each other
in defense of their respective opinions.

Another instance to the point is Walter Scott. He
lived with the multitude. His official duties kept him
a large part of the time in a Scottish court of quarter
sessions. Hence it has been so often said that his
fictions read like histories, while the histories of other
men read like fictions. In his school-days Scott was a
dull boy and an inveterate truant. He would entice
one or more of his companions to run away with him
to Calton Hill or Arthur's Seat, and there he would
practice upon them his art of story-telling. He was an
unwearied conversationalist: nobody was too high, and
nobody too low, for him to talk with. In the " Fortunes of Nigel " he represents one of the characters as

saying that a man of active mind can not talk with the
boy who holds his horse at a watering-place, without
obtaining some new thought.   He used to go to the
fish-market at Billingsgate to study the dialect of the
fishwomen.   He has been known to pause in the street
to jot down on a scrap of paper, or on his thumb-nail, a
word which he caught from a passer-by.

In his novels he draws so largely upon real life that
they are not properly called romances.   He deals with
living characters, employs living dialects, records as
fictions actual occurrences.   His own henchman, Tom
Purdie, is described in the "Red Gauntlet."   The
death of the Templar in "Ivanhoe" was an exact copy
of a death-scene which occurred to a friend of Scott
while pleading a cause in his presence in a court-room
in Edinburgh.   The localities of most of his stories he
describes from his own sight of them.   He visited the
Continent to see for himself the localities of "Quentin
Durward."   The best guide-book to the lakes of Scotland is said to be Scott's "Lady of the Lake."

Aristocratic as he was in his aspirations, he still
enjoyed the common people more heartily than the
society of his equals.   The professors of the University
of Edinburgh complained that he chose the society of
men of business rather than their own.   He held to
that choice deliberately.   He said that he found the
conversation of men of the world to be more original,
and more fit to feed a literary spirit, than that of literary
men themselves.   In a moment of petulance he declared
that the dullest talk he ever listened to was that of a
group of literary men at a dinner-table.   "I love the
virtues of rough and round men," he says: "the others
are apt to escape me in sal-volatile and a white pocket-
handkerchief."

Again he writes: "I have read books enough, and conversed with enough of splendidly educated men in my time; but I assure you I have heard higher sentiments from the lips of poor uneducated men and women than I ever yet met with out of the pages of the Bible." On another occasion, when his daughter condemned something for being "vulgar," he replied, "You speak like a very young lady. Do you not know the meaning of the word 'vulgar'? It is only 'common.' Nothing that is common, except wickedness, can deserve to be spoken of in a tone of contempt. When you have lived to my years, you will agree with me in thanking God that nothing really worth having in this world is uncommon."

A ninth example is Patrick Henry. His bankruptcy in a country store in Virginia was a foregone conclusion because of the way in which he spent his time. His habit was to collect a company of villagers in his store, and give them a subject of conversation, and then fall back and listen to their talk. Popular modes of thought, popular ways of argument, popular styles of illustration, popular sophistries, popular appeals, he studied thus month after month. That was his university, his school of oratory, his library. The principles and methods he learned there he adopted and imitated in his subsequent political career. He was the orator of the rabble all through life. He talked like the rabble, lived like the rabble, ate and drank and dressed like the rabble. He did this designedly for the sake of swaying the rabble in his public speeches.

One witness testifies to this from Mr. Henry's lips: "Mr. Chairman, all the larnin' upon the yairth air not to be compared with naiteral parts." Yet to studies and abuses of this kind he owed at last his power to send the House of Burgesess rushing from their seats at the close of his description of a thunder-storm, or rather his adroit *use* of one which occurred near the close of one of his addresses. He was a representative of the whole class of public speakers who are so delusively called "natural orators." There are no natural orators. They all study oratory in studying men.

Passing now to the pulpit, I name but one other illustration, George Whitefield. His name is often adduced as an example of untaught, spontaneous eloquence. He was no such thing. No man was ever further from it. For patient, laborious, painstaking, lifelong study of the art of oratory, give us George Whitefield as the prince of students. Long before his conversion, when he was a tapster in his mother's tavern, he studied the English dramatic writers till he knew large portions of them by heart. He personated some of their female characters amidst rounds of applause from the villagers. Though sometimes intoxicated, he composed sermons, and tried the effect of them on the crowd around the doorposts. He stole hours of the night for the study of the dramatic portions of the Bible. Thus was it that the great field-preacher was made.

One effect of these experimental studies on his own mind was to create such a sense of the difficulty of preaching well, that, after his conversion, he says he never prayed against any corruption in his life so much as he did against being tempted into the ministry too soon. "I have prayed a thousand times," he says, "till the sweat has dropped from my face like rain, that God would not let me enter the ministry till He thrust me forth to his work."

In this spirit of reverence for his work, he became through his whole ministry a student of his audiences. He was incessantly trying experiments upon his congregations. The same sermons he preached over and over, till they were crowded with variations and improvements. Garrick, who himself owed much to his study of Whitefield, said that Whitefield never finished a sermon till he had preached it forty times. He preached from thirty to forty thousand sermons, but only about seventy-five have found their way into print. This is some index to the extent to which he must have carried repetition of the same discourses.

The pulpit is crowded with illustrations, either of the neglect, or the use, or the abuse, of this study of men as a source of homiletic culture. They might be multiplied indefinitely, but it is needless.

(3) I proceed, therefore, to remark that the same view is confirmed by the opinions of a class of writers and speakers derogatory to the value of rhetorical culture.

Oratorical study has to contend with the expressed judgments of certain orators and writers who say that it is useless. They have succeeded, as they imagine, without it. They have refused to be hampered by it. They have trusted to the instinct of speech and the cravings of a full mind for utterance. They have but filled the mind with thought, and then let it express itself. They have followed the counsel they so often give to young preachers, "Find something to say, and then say it." They therefore dispute the value of all conscious effort for oratorical discipline. Cicero, after writing the "De Oratore," condemned books on rhetoric. Macaulay, though the author of criticism enough to make volumes of rhetorical suggestion, decries con-

scious study of rhetorical science. George William
Curtis in this country has reproduced Macaulay's judgment with approval. He sums up the whole argument
by saying that rhetoric makes critics, but never orators
nor writers.

These men represent a class of writers and speakers,
themselves successful, whom every flourishing age of
literature has produced, and who have no faith in the
scientific culture of oratory for any other purpose than
that of mental gymnastics. Its direct practical value
they doubt or deny.

Test, now, these opinions by the actual experience of
such men, and what do they amount to? Simply this:
they are comparative opinions, in which abstract rhetoric is weighed against the literary discipline of real
life. Such critics have profited so much more from the
study of men than from the study of rhetorical treatises
that the latter sink into insignificance in the comparison.
Is it conceivable that Cicero's orations grew out of
innate, unstudied eloquence alone? His own confessions contradict this. Is it imaginable that Macaulay's
style was the fruit of unconscious ebullition of power?
A thousand years of criticism could never convince the
literary world of that. Is it possible that Mr. Curtis's
"Easy Chair" was never manufactured? If the styles
of these writers are specimens of spontaneous generation, the world does not contain any thing which is not
such. The immortal columns of Greek architecture are
no more made, studied, elaborated things than are such
styles as theirs. Those styles have been originated,
compacted, adorned, polished, by laborious study of
speech and authorship in real life. Their authors have
studied rhetoric in embodied forms. They have prac-

ticed it, as literary journeymen, in the mental collisions
and abrasions of public life.   They lived it many years
before they could command their facile pen.

All opinions, therefore, of successful writers, derogatory to the study of oratory, are to be taken as only
practical testimonies to the value of the study of it as
embodied in living men.   Whatever may be the bearing of them upon the scholastic culture of rhetoric,
they are the most emphatic witness possible to the
value of its practical culture through an elaborate and
lifelong study of mankind.

To recapitulate, then, the several aspects of the subject which we have considered : we have observed that
every preacher may obtain much oratorical culture
from the study of his own mind ; that he has a similar
source of culture in the study of other men ; that this
study is often undervalued, because of a factitious reverence for books ; that this study should be stimulated
by that which is well known to be the popular idea of
a clergyman ; that the need of it in some quarters is
indicated by the idea of a clergyman which is most
common in literary fiction ; that the absence of it discloses itself, not only in the unfitness of the pulpit to
its mission of reproof, but also in its unfitness to the
mission of comfort ; that we may learn something to
the purpose from the study of eccentric preachers ; that
the study of men is specially needful to educated
preachers, because the literature of the world is not
constructed, in the main, for the masses of mankind ;
that the need of it is enforced by the fact that often
great changes of popular opinion occur independently
of the cultivated classes as such ; that in such popular
changes the clergy are the natural leaders of the peo-

ple; that a certain minority of the clergy are found to
be insensible or hostile to such changes; that, when the
pulpit becomes identified with the cultivated classes
alone, it loses power of control over all classes; that,
when the pulpit betrays a want of knowledge of men
as they are, the result is the creation of anomalous relations between the church and the world; and that the
study of men here recommended is supported by the
practice of leading minds in history.

You will not understand me as decrying scholastic
discipline in the comparison. On that subject I have,
in the sequel, other things to say. But I have wished
to establish at present this as one part of a preacher's
necessary and perpetual discipline for his life's work:
that he must be a student of men, himself a man of
his own times, living in sympathy with his own times,
versed in the literature of his own times, at home
with the people of his own charge, observant of the
movements of the popular heart, and aspiring in his
expectations of controlling those movements by the
ministrations of the pulpit.

That was a confession which no minister should
oblige himself to make, as a late professor in one of
our theological seminaries did in the last year of his
life, that for half a century he had read more Latin
than English. That was the mark of a mind whose
roots were in an obsolete age, and whose culture was
chiefly in a language, a literature, and a style of thinking, which never can again be dominant in the civilization of the world.

LECTURE VII.

THE STUDY OF LITERATURE FOR CLERICAL DISCIPLINE. — OBJECTS OF THE STUDY.

II. WE have observed in analyzing the sources of our oratorical knowledge, that, while there is but one original source, an auxiliary source is found in the study of models, and that in the term "models" we include all successful and permanent literature. This extension of the term is essential. Our primary notion of a model is limited. When a painter speaks of a model, he means by it a painting, or the thing which is to be transferred to canvas, and nothing more. When a sculptor speaks of a model, he means by it the human form, or a piece of statuary, and nothing more. In criticism of poetry a model is a poem, and nothing more. In military art a model is a historic campaign, or the plan of a battle, and nothing else. That is to say, a model has primarily a professional limitation.

When, therefore, a preacher conceives of a model, he is apt to think only of a sermon, or at most of an oration. Consequently he is in danger of limiting his reading for homiletic discipline to sacred or secular *speech*. The point, therefore, needs to be emphasized as a preliminary, that we should not restrict our idea of models to any such professional range. The advice often given to young preachers in respect to their reading is narrow, in that their attention is directed exclusively to oratorical literature. In my judgment, that is not even the chief source of homiletic culture derivable from books. In the broader view, all successful and permanent literature is a collection of models to an educated mind.

The culture which a preacher needs from books is substantially that which any other professional man needs. Excepting the necessities of the profession, the less his culture is narrowed by professional affinities in its range, the better. Nearly the most meager preparation you could acquire for the pulpit would be the reading of the whole mass of English sermons, and nothing else. Every book which *is* a book is a model of something to an educated mind. By a preacher, every book he reads should be read as a model of something. Whatever has achieved success, specially whatever has been long-lived, we may be sure contains something, which, if intelligently studied, will be to a preacher's culture what the *torso* of Hercules is to sculptors.

Moreover, our conception of a model to a professional man should not be limited to literature as distinct from philosophy or from science. There is a distinction here ; but it is not so important to a professional man as to one whose life is made up of literary pursuits. A mind moving in the orbit of a great practical profession must be open to culture from any thing in our libraries which represents the world's past or living thought. Every such volume is a model to such a mind, in the sense that it contains something helpful to its discipline or its furnishing for its life's work. One young preacher I knew, who found the most effective awakener

of his own mind to original production in the study of
La Place's "Mechanique Celeste." Such are the occult
affinities between literature and science, that there is
a mental appropriation of them both by an alert mind,
in which the distinction between them vanishes.

Bearing in mind, then, the principle that the range
of a preacher's possible study of models opens to him
all standard libraries, the remarks I wish to make
upon the subject arrange themselves naturally under
the objects of the study, the selection of authors, and
the methods of the study.

1st, The Objects of the study of books: what are
they? I answer, in the general, The object is discipline
as distinct from accumulation. Its results, when properly conducted, will never be the mere conglomeration
of knowledge. Its aim is discipline; its process is
discipline; its result is discipline. A certain mental
growth is the sum and substance of it. A man knows
nothing of the rudiments of the culture to which it
belongs who has not begun to be conscious of mental
growth under that culture. One of the first and most
profound impressions which the study of books should
make upon a man is that of the distinction between
literary labor and literary leisure. No habits like those
of a literary amateur can accomplish the object in view.
The aim is never a luxury, except in that stage which
mature discipline at length reaches, in which labor is
itself luxury. But, in particular, the chief objects of
a pastor's study of literature are four.

The first is a *discovery* of the principles of effective thought, and its expression in language. We all
come to the study of books with minds uninformed as
to what is excellence, and what is not. No man's lit-

erary instinct is at the first a sufficient guide to his literary judgment. What are the principles of effective literature is a question to be answered by an after-process to that of feeling the power of literature. It is a process of reflection upon a previous experience. It is as purely a process of discovery as a search in a gold-mine.

Novalis said that painting was "the art of seeing." So the true study of books is the art of seeing what is and what is not there. You read, for instance, an author who moves you. He stimulates your intellect; he arouses your sensibilities; he delights you, fascinates you, elevates you to an unwonted height of mental and moral excitement; he becomes therefore a favorite with you; you feel grateful to him for his disclosure to you of a new world of thought and feeling. At first you have no disposition to any process of reflection. You only feel, as Dr. Franklin felt his first hearing of White-field. But by and by the time of reflective study comes. You ask, What is it in my favorite author which makes him what he is to me? What are the roots of his productions which make them such a vital and vitalizing power to me? The answer, unless your experience has been factitious, will disclose to you one or more of the elements which make all vital literature a power to all minds.

Until our minds go through that reflective process of discovery, we know nothing of books as an object of criticism. We have no intelligent tastes in literature. We have no culture of scholarly judgment. We are, in respect to libraries, in that inchoate state in which a man often is in respect to painting, or sculpture, or music, in which he honestly confesses, " I do not know

what is artistic excellence, I only know what I like."
Exactly thus we might express our state of culture in
literature before the critical taste is formed in us by an
introversion of mind upon our own instincts, and by
thought upon the objects which have pleased or roused
them. We do not know what is excellent in literary
creation : we only know what we like. Whether our
taste is true to any lofty ideal we do not know : we
only know what we like. A savage knows as much
when he struts around in his adornments of beads and
peacock feathers. A child knows as much when his
tears are dried at the jingle of nursery-rhymes.

On the other hand, the faculty of good taste under
high culture becomes one of superlative excellence.
It is an instance in which an acquired faculty rivals
original endowments of mind. We should not be
deceived by our associations with the word " taste." It
is the only single word by which our language expresses
the thing in question. Yet the word is unfortunate in
the multiplicity of its uses. We connect it so much
with millinery and upholstery and *bijouterie*, if not
with the pleasures of the table, that we often carry it
into literature with degrading associations. We need
there to enlarge and ennoble it. It expresses there one
of the last and noblest results of mental discipline.
I can not call it virtue : usage calls it taste. " Virtue "
is reserved for a class of conceptions totally distinct.

Yet taste does express lofty intellectual character,
not moral character, but a development of intellect
which stands over against moral character, and corresponds to it in dignity. By it we distinguish what is
true from what is factitious in letters. We penetrate
by it to that which is deepest in thought. We reach

that which, in literary expression, corresponds to integrity in morals. We discern, therefore, that which is and must be long-lived. Taste under high culture gives to a scholar, not only knowledge, but foreknowledge, of literary history. He learns to look into the future with as much confidence as he feels in his knowledge of the past. He pronounces judgment on certain works with the confidence of an oracle. He says of them, "These must fade: there is in them that which dooms them to decay." Of other works he says as confidently, "These will live: these express the soul of man and the voice of God in forms which the world will not willingly let die."

This finished taste represents a state of mental conquest. A man's own insight into the life of literature becomes a law to him. He is an independent thinker, reader, scholar, author, preacher. His own insight, if it conflicts, as it sometimes will, with a popular taste, gives him repose, while that taste lasts, in the assurance that it will be ephemeral. He can work on calmly in his own way. He is like an eagle in his eyrie: he knows that he sees farther than his contemporaries, he knows as surely that he must succeed in the end. Wordsworth expressed grandly this vision of the literary future, when he replied to the outburst of hostile criticism with which "The Excursion" was received at the first. "This will never do," said Jeffrey in "The Edinburgh Review." "It must do," responded the poet, as if inspired. "I very well know that my work will be unpopular; but I know, too, that it will be immortal."

The second object of a preacher's study of literature is that *familiarity* with the principles of effective thought and expression which gives one a working knowledge of those principles as distinct from a critical knowledge. We need such an inwrought possession of them, that, in our own productions, we can apply them unconsciously. In the act of composing, the mind can not pause to recall by sheer lift of memory a principle of good writing, and then apply it by conscious choice. This is specially true of select hours of composition. All writers have such hours. Our best work is done in such hours. The mind then is lifted by the impulse of original invention. Thought is ebullient. An act of creation is going on. The creating mind then must seize involuntarily upon the forms of language which lie nearest, and which come unbidden. Lawlessly, rudely, arbitrarily, it uses those forms, so far as any conscious selection is concerned.

If, therefore, we have not so learned the principles of power in speech as to be able to apply them unconsciously, we can not apply them at all. Therefore we need to acquire such familiarity with those principles, that our command of them shall be what the unconscious skill of the athlete is to muscle and sinew.

In this view it is obvious that the familiarity of unconscious use of principles of literary expression marks a high state of mental discipline in respect to executive skill. We have observed that the object of literary study is discipline, not accumulation. We have observed also that a full discovery of the principles of taste marks a high discipline in respect to criticism. The point now before us indicates an advance upon the discipline of criticism. It contemplates discipline in respect to executive skill. Such possession of the principles of effective writing as that involved in the unconscious use of them marks power of execution.

No man can have listened to Edward Everett or
Rufus Choate, for example, without being sensible of
the fascination of some of their prolonged and invo-
luted passages. They are marvelous phenomena of
executive discipline. Pages could be selected from
their writings in which the processes of reasoning, of
judging, of analysis, of comparison, of combination, of
imagining, of memory, of abstraction, and of invention,
all interlace each other in one marvel of expression.
The mental strain of producing the wondrous network
seems like torture to a critic who is looking on; yet
those processes embrace each other with a kindliness
which makes them seem, to one who feels only the
naturalness of their evolution, like the play of spiritual
beings at their ease. We obtain a new conception of
the susceptibility of discipline which is in every mind
from such specimens of high art in discourse.

This view is confirmed by the fact that exquisite
taste often exists without executive skill. Eminent
critics are often not superlative writers. This is only
saying that they know more than they can do. The
reason is found in the distinction before us, between a
discovery of the principles of effective speech, and such
a possession of them as would secure unconscious obedience to them in one's own productions. It has been
said of Lord Brougham, that in his own writings he
violates nearly all the rules which in his criticism of
others he prescribes. The critical study of books
tends to prevent such anomalies as this, by giving us
the principles of good writing in illustrated forms. We
most readily become familiar with them, if we have
them exemplified. The example which we enjoy will
tend to fix in our taste the principle which otherwise

it would be a drudgery to remember. Like all other knowledge, that is most homelike to us which comes through the medium of an experience.

This attractive knowledge of rhetorical principles comes to us but very slightly from rhetorical treatises. Some minds, it is true, may be fascinated by rhetoric in its scientific forms, and for their own sake. Dr. Arnold could honestly speak of Aristotle, after years devoted to a study of his works, as "that dear old Stagyrite." But very few minds are so affectionately constituted. Few, therefore, attain to such passionate love of abstract science in their studies. The large majority become fascinated by such studies only through the medium of example in favorite authors.

A fine illustration of this is found in the literary discipline of Dryden. Dryden is one of the acknowledged masters of the English language. In his day he was an autocrat in criticism. Nobody presumed to question a decision by Dryden. Yet he says of himself, "If I have gained any skill in composition, I owe it all to Archbishop Tillotson, whose works I have read many times over." One can not but marvel at his choice of a model; but it illustrates the power of any choice which a man makes with enthusiasm, and therefore enjoys.

The same truth is illustrated in an interesting fact in the literary history of Edmund Burke. I know of no fact which furnishes a more instructive key to the structure of Burke's mind. When he was about seventeen years old he conceived a passionate fondness for the works of Milton. In a debating-club of which he was a member, in Dublin, his Miltonic taste still exists on record. Among other examples of it the record states that Burke rehearsed the speech of Moloch in the " Paradise Lost," and followed it with his own criticisms upon it. Thus it is that literary models which attract us fondly to themselves plant within us the principles of effective speech which underlie those models, and make them what they are. We much more cordially, and therefore successfully, aim at resemblance to a living character than at obedience to an abstract law. This is as true in literary as in moral discipline. An example is worth more than a rule. An illustration has more authority than a command.

This view suggests a third object of a pastor's study of books; viz., *assimilation* to the genius of the best authors. There is an influence exerted by books upon the mind which resembles that of diet upon the body. A studious mind becomes, by a law of its being, like the object which it studies with enthusiasm. If your favorite authors are superficial, gaudy, short-lived, you become yourself such in your culture and your influence. If your favorite authors are of the grand, profound, enduring order, you become yourself such to the extent of your innate capacity for such growth. Their thoughts become yours, not by transfer, but by transfusion. Their methods of combining thoughts become yours; so that, on different subjects from theirs, you will compose as they would have done if they had handled those subjects. Their choice of words, their idioms, their constructions, their illustrative materials, become yours; so that their style and yours will belong to the same class in expression, and yet your style will never be merely imitative of theirs.

It is the prerogative of great authors thus to throw back a charm over subsequent generations which is often more plastic than the influence of a parent over a child. Do we not feel the fascination of it from certain favorite characters in history? Are there not already certain solar minds in the firmament of your scholarly life whose rays you feel shooting down into the depths of your being, and quickening there a vitality which you feel in every original product of your own mind? Such minds are teaching you the true ends of an intellectual life. They are unsealing the springs of intellectual activity. They are attracting your intellectual aspirations. They are like voices calling to you from the sky.

Respecting this process of assimilation, it deserves to be remarked, that it is essential to any broad range of originality. Never, if it is genuine, does it create copyists or mannerists. Imitation is the work of undeveloped mind. Childish mind imitates. Mind unawakened to the consciousness of its own powers copies. Stagnant mind falls into mannerism. On the contrary, a mind enkindled into aspiration by high ideals is never content with imitated excellence. Any mind thus awakened must above all things else be itself. It must act itself out, think its own thoughts, speak its own vernacular, grow to its own completeness. You can no more become servile under such a discipline than you can unconsciously copy another man's gait in your walk, or mask your own countenance with his.

A fine example of assimilation as distinct from mannerism is furnished by the literary history of Coleridge's "Christabel." That poem on its first appearance produced a profound impression. It was circulated in manuscript among the scholars of England several years before its publication. It is believed by good

critics to have exerted a powerful influence upon the
subsequent writings of Byron and Shelley and Scott.
A casual reading of it in a little circle in which Shelley
was present affected him so deeply that he fainted.
Some of his poems published afterwards bore traces
of the poetic stimulus which his imagination then
received. Mr. Lockhart says that it was the hearing
of "Christabel" from manuscript which led Scott to
produce the "Lay of the Last Minstrel." It gave to
all those poets a conception of the possibilities of the
English language in freedom of versification, and specially in the expression of supernatural imagery, which
was new to them. Their minds drank it in, and appropriated it, as flowers do light. Yet what critic has
ever thought to charge them with imitating "Christabel"? Assimilation of it in their poetic culture rendered mannerism in copying it impossible.

Further: it should be observed that identity of opinions with those of a great author is no evidence of
assimilation to his genius. It no more follows that a
man has a Platonic or an Aristotelian mind because he
adopts Platonic or Aristotelian opinions than that his
body belongs to one or another of the molluscan species
because his digestion craves a molluscan diet. Assimilation goes deeper than the plane of opinions. In any
broad culture it will be generous to diverse models.
From the fountains of conflicting opinions it will derive
the fluids of its own life, and they shall be all the more
pure and the more vital for the mingling.

It is a mark of a narrow culture that a man feels no
sympathy of resemblance to widely different characters
in the history of thought, even to those whose opinions
are in flat contradiction. Great minds are more nearly

alike in their genius than in their opinions. Great and
sincere minds tend always to unanimity in their final
influence. A student of their works may become more
sensible of this than they themselves were. You may
derive from them a more generous growth than they
had. You may feel the identity in spirit of the very
works in which, perhaps, they fought each other as
champions of rival factions.

Among the recent discoveries in Athenian architec
ture, it has been found that the lines of a Doric column,
which have for ages been supposed to be vertical, and
parallel to each other, are almost imperceptibly con
vergent as they ascend from the pedestal; so that, if
projected to an immense height above, they would meet
in a point. It is believed that the Greek artistic mind
adopted this model, not fortuitously, but with design,
to express thus the ultimate oneness of all ideas of
beauty.

So it is with the aspirations of great minds as ex
pressed in their works. They seem to run in grooves
of eternal parallels, in which they can never come
together. They might traverse the universe apparently,
and come around to the point of their starting, as defiant of union as ever. But the great Architect of
mind has not so constructed them. An appreciative
student of their works may discern, what they could
not, — a point in the upper firmament of thought in
which the lines of their influence converge, and they
become as one mind in their projection upon the world's
future.

Do not all generous minds already judge thus of the
two great lines of thought represented by Aristotle and
Plato? Do not such minds feel the same ultimate

sympathy between the life's work of Leibnitz and of
Bacon? Do we not often catch glimpses of the same
destiny of union between Kant and the Scotch philosophers? Let a scholarly mind keep itself open and
receptive in its study, and it can not fail to experience
this consciousness of the convergence of the great
thinkers through the blending of them in its own
culture.

One advantage, therefore, of literary study, is that
it tends to liberalize mental culture in those lines of
thought in which culture is most profound. By such
discipline we become disinthralled from partisanship.
Be it in philosophy, in theology, in æsthetics, in art, a
partisan spirit is sure to be outgrown. Positive as
our opinions may be, we spurn bondage to schools of
opinion. One of the most striking evidences often of
a young man's growth under such discipline as I
am advocating is, that he outgrows a school of something in which he was once an enthusiast, and unconsciously a servitor. As we approach maturity of
culture, we become conscious that we have a culture
which lies deeper than our opinions, and which runs
under opposing schools.

Our expressed opinions may often be governed by
the wants of our own age or the business of our own
profession. They may represent but a fraction of the
entire circle of our beliefs. But a perfect culture
might master the beliefs of all ages, so as to hold all
the truth that was ever in them. Assimilation to the
loftiest in literature may give us a vision of truths
which minds of narrower discipline will ignore. Thus
expanded in its culture, a scholarly mind becomes
eclectic in its opinions in every thing. It becomes

calm also in the utterance of them. It will be generous
to opponents in proportion to its trust in itself. It can
afford to cherish both these qualities of a liberal mind.

One other remark upon this point of assimilation to
the genius of literature is that from its nature it must
be the work of time. All mental discipline is such,
but this peculiarly : no man reaches it at a bound. A
sudden appearance of it in a man's professions is sus-
picious. He is probably self-deceived. His enthusiasm
for the great authors is probably not a genuine growth
into their likeness, but an upstart fancy for them, — for
their defects, it may be, rather than for their excellences.
It may be even so poor a thing as an affectation of
sympathy with their reputation, instead of a genuine
reverence for their character. In the nature of the
case, like all other enduring growths, a true assimilation to the noblest ideals is the process of a lifetime.
A collegiate and professional education can do little
more than to plant the germ of it, and fertilize the soil
which shall nurture it through life.

LECTURE VIII.

OBJECTS OF A PASTOR'S STUDY OF LITERATURE, CON-
  CLUDED. — THE ADJUSTMENT OF SELF-ADAPTA-
  TIONS.

To the three objects of literary study already considered should be added a fourth, which is to facilitate
a man's knowledge of his own powers and adaptations
to professional labor.

It is unsafe to trust incautiously the early fascina-
tions of books or men over a young mind. Our earliest tastes may give us false ideas of our own capacities.
Specially do we need to study our favorite authors with
reference to our adaptations to our life's work. We
are not supposed to be mere *literati* by profession. We
do not study literature for its own sake and that only :
we have a laborious profession in prospect. Our studies
must fit us for that, or they may become a hinderance
to our life's work. We need to know our own adaptations ; and that literary enthusiasm is a woful blunder
which misleads us in that self-knowledge.

The theory of Jesuitism in one respect is most instructive. The whole Jesuit policy turns upon the
adaptation of men to work, and work to men. The
Jesuit theory is, that every man is better fitted, or may
be made so, to one thing than to another ; and that
every work requires one man more imperatively than

111

another. It assumes to fit the man to the work, and the work to the man, as precisely as Nature fits together the brain and the skull. Jesuitism is wise so far as this, that it lays the study of adaptations at the basis in building an order of public men. That study must lie at the foundation of the liberal professions, if they are to be powers in the world.

The study of adaptations must form the clergy. Under a free system, every clergyman must perform that study for himself. For the want of it men have often entered the ministry under a mistaken self-estimate. Is it not one of the most obvious and pain ful facts of clerical life, that men have entered the ministry who would never have done so if they had known seasonably their own natural qualifications? Such men fight the air, through life it may be, because they do not understand their own mission.

The importance of the error here indicated justifies a consideration of it at some length, at the expense of an *excursus* from our main-line discussion. The peril of a wasted life in the ministry, through errors in self-estimate, will be best illustrated by a case in hand. A graduate of this seminary once came to me asking advice respecting his abandonment of the ministry for some other profession. He had been a pastor two years. He was pleasantly and usefully settled. He made no complaint of his people, nor they of him. He did not wish for a different parish. But he thought he had better leave the pulpit. Why? The reason lay wholly in the mental make and culture of the man. He had inveterate tastes for a different line of mental activity from the one which the ministry opened to him. By natural constitution those tastes were pre-

dominant in him. His collegiate training and his reading had intensified them. He had denied them, and
chosen the ministry as a profession from convictions
of religious duty, as Pascal did under similar circumstances, but with no such mental rest in his choice as
Pascal experienced. He found that the practical duties
of the pulpit were a drudgery to him. He felt no intellectual elasticity in them. To be a guiding mind to
others in the office of a religious teacher did not draw
out his aspirations. He seemed unable to make himself
what the Scriptures call "apt to teach." He had
struggled with himself two years in silence to force his
mind and body to do the bidding of his conscience, and
to do it joyously; but the effort was undermining his
health. A nervous headache had become the invariable
consequence of a morning's work in the writing of a
sermon, and an afternoon given to chemistry or flori-
culture was the only remedy. He dragged himself
through another year of purgatorial fidelity to his
ministerial vows; and then his health was so seriously
affected as to leave no question as to the path of duty.
He left the ministry, studied for three years another
profession, and is now contented, healthy, happy, and
useful in it, and as a layman is pronounced by his
pastor to be the most devoted and useful member of his
church.

One thing is certain of this case: it is that a woful
mistake was made at the outset for the want of a thorough study of the man's own aptitudes. At least six
years of his early manhood were, not lost indeed, but
extravagantly expended on an experiment which a more
thorough self-knowledge would have prevented.

A similar experience, I think, in less degree, befalls

some men who remain in the ministry. Are they not
found in all denominations? They work at cross-pur-
poses with Providence, because it is a long while before
they accept themselves for what they are. They attempt things which they can not do, or as often they
fail to do things which they might do, because they dare
not attempt them.

The late Dr. Griffin used to say that he thought
Providence designed him for a metaphysician. I suppose it is very certain that no other man who knew
Dr. Griffin, thought that Providence would have been
wise in any such designation of a man who was so
eminently an orator by nature and by training.

Dr. Chalmers expressed the opinion, that, as he said,
"Nature had cut him out for a military engineer." In
the public life which he afterwards led, he, too, thought
that his specialty of talent for public influence lay in
the department of intellectual philosophy. He probably stood alone in both those opinions to the day of his
death. Chalmers was by nature a statesman. In the
Church his great power lay in the discovery and the
use of administrative principles. The reach of his mind
in this respect was marvelous. He was in the Church
the counterpart of Edmund Burke in the State. The
thing in which consisted the greatness of both would
have prevented either from taking the first rank as
metaphysicians.

Professor Stuart believed, that, when he began his
public life, he had no special taste or aptitude for
sacred literature, or any department of philology; but
no one else believed this of him after it was found
that the youthful pastor in New Haven, though crowded
by the care of the old "Center Church" in a powerful

revival of religion, still kept his Hebrew Bible within reach of his dinner-table, that he might devote to it the fragments of time stolen from that meal.

Providence is often very kindly in pressing men into a service which they would never have been wise enough in self-knowledge to choose for themselves. Yet often the wisdom of Providence is not regarded, or the finger-point is not seen. Perhaps, like Nelson, men turn their blind eye to the telegraphic order. Then comes a long history of wasted ministerial energy.

Ministerial energy, when it is not all a waste, is often most extravagantly expended on the results it achieves. Do you not know men in the ministry who have been sailing obliquely all their lives? All that some accomplish in the ministry is accomplished laterally to their conscious aims. In their deliberate aims they fail; in incidentals to those aims, which Providence always seems to be on the watch for in ill-regulated lives, they succeed. The sum total of their work, when it shall be tried as by fire, may be this, — relative uselessness in the things they have aspired to, and relative success in the things they have undervalued. To them is fulfilled the promise. "Thou shalt hear a voice *behind* thee, saying, This is the way; walk ye in it." "The door into life," says a living writer, "generally opens behind us. A hand is put forth which draws us in backward." This is eminently true of the professional life of a certain class of ministers.

Here, for example, is a man who honestly thinks that poetry is his birthright, while in fact his very make is prose personified. The Muses were slumbering at the hour of his birth. He wastes himself in rhymes which

are "published for the author," — that rose-colored
gauze by which is covered the polite negative of publishers. This is literally true of one of the early graduates of this seminary. Rather, it *was* true; for I am
grateful, for his sake, that he has found rest in a world
where even he can aspire to no such poetry. He had a
wasted ministry here, so far as man could judge of it,
because he was for ever puttering at verses which could
command no circulation except by the anxious assiduity
of a blind man who made a pittance by their sale. Another man for several years sent to me by mail, as often
as about once a quarter, his poetic deliverances, printed
on tinted sheets at his own expense. Of their quality
what shall I say? The old couplet in the Primer —

> "In Adam's fall
> We sinned all" —

is a gem in the comparison.

There is a man, who, like Dr. Griffin, because he
knows the difference between metaphysics and psy-
chology, imagines that intellectual philosophy is the
forte of his brain and the end of his creation; while in
fact the elements of a popular orator are the constituents
of his nature, and those he despises. He wastes himself in attempts to settle the problems of the ages.
His book — the labor of his prime, and the darling of
his soul — is for sale at the bookstalls, on that shelf
which is so sad a monitor to aspiring authorship, the
shelf placarded with "Fifty Cents." Yet the pulpit,
if he would but lift his downcast eyelids to see it, would
be a throne to him.

One of the most successful preachers now laboring
in a city of the interior, when he left this seminary,

endeavored earnestly to convince me that philosophical study and authorship were the department in which lay prospectively the design of his creation. Not one of his instructors shared that opinion. His scholastic life had thrown a glamour around that group of studies, so that, for the time, he saw nothing else. He did not begin to be himself till the spell was broken by a religious awakening among his people.

Again: a man conceives that literary criticism, or the study of languages, is his *forte;* while in fact his most valuable talents are colloquial. He wastes himself in struggling after a place in reviews, or pining for a professorship, when the place of honor for him, because the place of richest usefulness, would be the pastoral routine of a parish.

Another is persuaded, that, if he has any specialty of fitness, it is to advance the Christian culture of the more thoughtful and educated classes; while in fact he is only on a level with such classes. This deserves to be noted as the most frequent error in self-estimate by a certain minority of educated clergymen. Many such preachers have culture enough, backed by natural force enough, to go into classes of society below them, and make their power felt there like a hydraulic engine. But some of them waste themselves by aims at that which they suppose to be the standard of pulpit eloquence in cities. They do not understand why they are not more thoroughly known by Providence, and by committees of vacant metropolitan pulpits. It is astonishing how many secret enemies such men have. Great is the mystery of their life's trial. But the truth is, that the church of a factory-village or a farming-town would be more than the temple of Jerusalem to them in an eternal estimate of their lives; because, working on a level below them, they could work with *downright* power.

The mistake here indicated is one of the perils peculiar to an educated clergy,—peculiar in degree, if not in kind. No judgment is more hollow, none betokens more ignorance of the philosophy of ministerial success, than that sometimes cherished by a youthful preacher, that, because he is an educated man, therefore he must minister to educated men; because he has acquired cultivated tastes, therefore his parish must consist of families of cultivated tastes; because he has become familiar with refined society, and has acquired the manners of a gentleman, therefore his pastoral charge should be in refined society, and his manners should have gentlemen to appreciate them. If Providence does not order his lot by the law of intellectual and social affinity, the cause of Christ suffers a mysterious waste of ministerial usefulness, and he suffers a mysterious eclipse. The man has not found his place, nor the place its man, till each is adjusted to the other by the satisfaction of mutual similitude. Like must minister to like. This is what it amounts to when we put it into the most charitable form of plain English.

I speak of this as a frequent error among young preachers, the most frequent of all that concern the topic before us. I am glad that my observation enables me to testify, that, with rare exceptions, it is but a youthful folly, outgrown in the tug of real life and under the pressure of eternal things. I have known but one instance in which it extended into a preacher's middle life.

The truth is, that the error is oblivious of one of the

plainest principles of ministerial success; viz., that, to achieve any thing worthy of the clerical office, a minister must work from above downward. The ministry is something more than a profession in which a man is struggling for a living, and a position among his equals. It is a grander thing than all that, — a thing of God's making. It is a power from God, or it is nothing to the purpose. Its work is that of a superior on an inferior mind. The law of gravitation bids a laboring man to work down hill with his spade and his wheelbarrow, if he can. That law is not more imperative than the spiritual law which bids clerical influence to flow from above downward. Thus regulated, all culture is available in a preacher's work. Nothing else is like it in the range which it gives to the worker. The highest culture finds its use in the lowliest labor. Often the richest fruits of culture will be discovered in despised spheres of effort. Mental discipline of the rarest finish will find its reward in the exhaustion of its resources upon ignorant and debased materials.

One of the most accomplished of our American missionaries spent her life in Africa. Her education, her refinement, her tastes, her manners, would have graced and elevated any metropolitan society. Yet her testimony was, that she found use for them all in the Christianizing of savages. She was not conscious of one wasted gift. She had no regrets over useless acquisitions. Not a single accomplishment of her beautiful youth — her drawing, her painting, her music — ever lay idle. She was right in her judgment of herself and her life's work. It will bear the test of eternity, whatever this world may say of it.

The same principle applies to ministerial labor everywhere. Locality and surroundings have very little to do relatively with its prospect of results. No other work is so absorbent in its power to appropriate to itself all the resources which culture can bring to it, even in its rudest and most unpromising forms, provided only that culture be wise enough to be humble, and to labor on something below its own level. The clerical hand, if it is a cunning one, will be always reaching downward in its activity. There is an infinite sadness in the sight of a minister of Christ turning from the level he stands on to lift himself into the air above him, or struggling horizontally on a stream that is level with his lips, instead of being content to stand where he is sure of his footing, and to work down upon the strata beneath him. Any ignorance of himself which leads a man to this inversion of his life's work may doom him to a barren and disappointed ministry. If in exceptional cases this result does not follow, it is because the providence of God sometimes compassionately provides an inferior work for the man when it is impossible to develop the man to the best work of his opportunities. But such adjustments are adjustments to the man's infirmities, not to his strength. He is never all that he might have been. He is like the patriarch Lot, to whose whining over the risk of climbing the mountain his guardian angel gives way.

Details might be specified, if it were necessary, in the work of the pulpit, in which there is sometimes a certain proportion of waste, because energy is expended in methods of preaching and styles in preaching (sometimes imitated methods and styles) which the preacher can not execute well. It is a great thing for a man to know what *he* can do. It is a greater thing to do *that*, and not something else, to aspire to it if a man is self-distrustful, to come down to it if he is self-conceited, to be content with it and grateful for it when he finds it out.   To have done *any thing* in such a service is a thing to be grateful for for ever.   " Permitted to preach the gospel seven months " is the epitaph on the tomb-stone of an alumnus of this seminary, who died before he had a parish of his own.   It was placed there at his dying request.

It is not always, I do not think it is generally, any unusual defect of piety which leads to these distortions of clerical life.   It is chiefly the want of self-knowledge. I mean that this is the weight which turns the scale adversely to a man's usefulness.   Whatever be his moral delinquencies, if he is a man of genuine consecration at heart, they will give way if they are not protected by honest intellectual misjudgments.   The moral growth, on the other hand, is greatly expedited by the mental rectitude, when once gained.   Therefore I say, that, in respect to the point before us, the chief want is the want of a correct self-estimate.   No matter how it is gained, whether through the heart or through the brain, the critical need is that of a full measurement of self in comparison with other powers in the world, like that which life in the business of the world very soon forces upon a man of sense in reference to capacities for suc-cess in the business of the world.   For the want of this gauging of one's self skillfully, the early years of min-isterial life are often like those of a young landsman before the mast.

Returning, now, from this *excursus*, and applying these views to the main topic before us, let us observe the bearing of a study of books upon the discovery of a

man's own adaptations.   We have already given ample
space to the study of men as one expedient for a minister's culture.   We have now to observe, as tending
to the same result, the self-discipline which comes from
literary pursuits.   Until a man knows a certain amount
of the work of the great minds in literature, he has no
adequate standard by which to gauge himself.

It has become a truism, that self-educated men are
but half educated.   They are apt to blunder into errors
which the educated mind of the world has long ago
exploded.   They announce as original discoveries that
which the history of opinion long ago recorded and as
long ago refuted.   They seem to themselves to be original in processes of mind which a better knowledge of
libraries would teach them are the common property
of thinkers.   Much as a man gains from actual conflict
with living minds, he may gain much even of the same
kind of knowledge, though different in detail, from the
accumulated thinking of the past.   No living generation can outweigh all the past.   If books without experience in real life can not develop a man all around,
neither can life without books do it.   There is a certain
dignity of culture which lives only in the atmosphere
of libraries.   There is a breadth and a genuineness of
self-knowledge which one gets from the silent friendship
of great authors, without which the best work that is in
a man can not come out of him in large professional
successes.

Disraeli says, "The more extensive a man's knowledge of what has been done, the greater will be his
power of knowing what to do."   He adds substantially,
that those who do not read largely will not themselves
deserve to be read.   This is doubly true in view of the

effect of reading upon a man's criticism of himself. The whole class of romantic ambitions which have been illustrated will almost surely disappear from a young man's mental habits, if he gains the consciousness of thorough scholarship in even one line of study. The juvenility of such ambitions is discovered in the process. The cost of their indulgence to a man's executive force in a great practical profession takes its proper place in his estimate of them. He learns the magnitude of that which must be done to realize them by adding any thing to that which has been done. One of the unerring signs of this mental growth in a young man is a certain sobering of tone in his judgment of himself, which springs from an expansion of his studies. It is to character what the ripening of colors is to painting. The character is enriched by the very process which subdues its exuberant confidence. This view is too well known among educated men to need further expansion.

But there is another view, not so often recognized, which deserves more attention than it receives. It is that the study in question stimulates self-appreciation, as well as represses self-conceit. You may learn for the first time of the existence of certain powers within you, from the awakening of those powers in response to the similar gifts of other minds distinguished in literature. Your own enthusiasm awakened by good models may disclose to you susceptibilities and powers which you never conjectured as existing within you.

Sir James Mackintosh gives it as the result of his experience as an educator, that, with all the evils of self-exaggeration among young men, the evils of self-depreciation are greater. Among Christian young men this certainly is true. Many young men are not sufficiently aspiring. They do not aim at labors which are within their reach, because they are not immediately conscious of power to perform those labors. Nor will they be conscious of it till some inspiration from without awakens it in them. That inspiration often comes from a simple extension of literary study. Give to yourself a hearty, affectionate acquaintance with a group of the ablest minds in Christian literature, and, if there is any thing in you kindred to such minds, they will bring it up to the surface of your own consciousness. You will have a cheering sense of discovery. Quarries of thought original to you will be opened. Suddenly, it may be, in some choice hour of research, veins will glisten with a luster richer than that of silver. You will feel a new strength for your life's work, because you will be sensible of new resources.

There is no romance in these assertions. The only peril in making them is, that the class of minds who need them, and of whom they are true, are not the class who will most readily appropriate them to themselves. Still they express a truth, which, with all its perils, we do right to accept, and apply with inspired adroitness, saying, " Let him that readeth understand."

A very striking illustration of this kind of mental awakening, on a large scale, from the study of literary models, is found in the transition of European mind from the middle to the later ages of the Christian era. The dark ages, as we call them, followed the entire loss of the Greek and Latin classics. The effect of that loss was an almost entire oblivion of good models of literary expression. The mind of the middle ages strove to work alone : it began *de novo* the history of letters. The consequence was the suppression, for the time, of the natural genius of those ages. It never rose from that depression till the ancient literatures were recovered.

Gasparin of Barziza, one of not more than three or four minds to whom is due the credit of starting the revival of the ancient classics, says that he gave himself to the study of Cicero till his own instinct was developed within him, by which he could judge of the Latin language, and till his own power to use the language grew to maturity under that single discipline. The study of one author developed him to his maturity. It was the recovery of the Greek and Roman treasures which stimulated the awakening of the genius of the middle ages, as it was the loss of them which had originally depressed it, and enslaved it to vitiated tastes. What is true of national minds is as true of individuals and of orders of public men. Let the ministry be ignorant of the best authors of the past, and their own powers will lie undeveloped in proportion to the depth of that ignorance. Lift them out of such ignorance, and their own powers receive an original impulse in proportion to the extent and the depth of their scholarship.

It is one object, then, of a pastor's study of literature, to reduce and to elevate his estimate of his own powers. The object is to restrain and to stimulate, to check and to cheer. If a man is inclined to see himself at either end of the telescope, the right study of models of literary excellence will act as a corrective, and give him his natural eyesight. I know of nothing else that is better fitted to give temper to a young man's criticisms of his own productions, so that his judgment shall be calm and clear, as keen as steel, and yet as true, than a large acquaintance with those works which have become monumental in Christian literature.

To recapitulate, and to distinguish clearly the four objects which we have now considered, I observe that the first, the discovery of the principles of taste, will tend to make a correct writer; the second, the familiarity with those principles, will tend to make a natural writer; the third, assimilation to the genius of the best authors, will tend to make an original writer; and the fourth, a just estimate of his own powers, will tend to make both a modest and a courageous writer. In other words, the first develops a man's literary perceptions; the second, his literary skill; the third, his literary genius; the fourth, his good sense in literary aims.

LECTURE IX.

2d, WE have thus far considered the objects of a pastor's study of literature. The second thing to be regarded in that study is the selection of authors.

Rogers the essayist remarks that "a very useful book might be written on the art of reading books, if we could get a Leibnitz or a Gibbon to compose it." True: yet the reading of the majority of educated men must be governed so much by circumstances which can not be controlled by any theory of scholarship, that I think the hints which are necessary on the subject must be susceptible of very flexible application. Scarcely any subject of professional inquiry is less capable of rule. Of the principles which concern it, two preliminaries need to be first remarked. The first is, that in practice these principles will cross and qualify each other. Any one of them alone would be one-sided and impracticable. They must be considered singly, yet applied collectively; and each must be subjected to limitations by the others. Otherwise, as literary advice, they would be nonsense.

The second preliminary is a repetition, for the sake of emphasis, of a remark already made in the preface of this volume, and which will be treated more at length in the sequel, — that, at the best, scholarly principles of selection can suggest only an ideal of a pastor's use of books, which must be in many cases theoretic, but out of which each man may obtain the elements for forming his own. Some can use more of it than others.

I have hesitated whether to venture at all upon the question of a pastor's *selection* of books, I am so well aware that practically that selection can seldom, if ever, satisfy a scholarly ideal. But to make any selection wisely, of even a few volumes, a pastor must *have* a scholar's ideal in mind : therefore I attempt it, trusting to your good sense to see the limitations and qualifications which the condition of your life's work render necessary. One book which deserves a scholar's reading is worth for a pastor's discipline a dozen of inferior quality.

(1) With these preliminaries in mind, let it be first observed that we must put out of our account of literature vicious and worthless books. A book may be vicious in literary influence, which is not immoral. It may foster false principles of taste, and minister to degraded conceptions of scholarship. A book may be worthless, which has no positive power for evil. A book which is a negative quantity in the sum total of our acquisitions is a worthless book. Menzel, in his history of German literature, says, "Bad books have their season, as vermin have. They come in swarms, and perish before we are aware. How many thousands of books have gone the way of all paper, or are now moldering in our libraries ! "

We make a stride of advance into the heart of a seemingly unconquerable library when we have accus-

tomed our minds to the reality of bad books in that
which goes by the name of literature. Books false in
principle, corrupt in taste, effeminate in influence, or
negative in all that respects high culture, are to be
found in all our large collections. There are books
which once had some force for good or ill, but which
the world has outlived. A man has no more use for
them now than for an Arabic work on alchemy or
magic. Hundreds of such volumes are to be reckoned
in all libraries which are reckoned by thousands.
There are folios of commentary on the Scriptures,
works in criticism, works in philosophy, which have
been displaced bodily in the living thought of mankind,
and which will never be resuscitated except by antiquarian curiosity.

That which De Quincey calls the "knowledge-litera-
ture" of the world, as distinct from the "power-litera-
ture," is incessantly changing: it is constantly retiring
to the attics and lofts and inaccessible shelves of libraries, unread and forgotten. Later knowledge must
for ever crowd back into oblivion the earlier. Such is
the law of progress. If a displaced literature is restored by antiquarian research, it is of no use; for, as
Horace Walpole says, "What signifies raising the dead
so often, when they die again the next minute?"

We need, then, to begin our studies with an agile
effort of good sense to distinguish between books which
are living literature, and books which are dead. Do not
revere every thing which appears between two muslin
covers. Remember Charles Lamb's demand for "books
which are books." It is a partial relief from the night-
mare which one feels in the vision of a huge library, to
remember that there is a vast multitude of volumes, as

comely as any to the eye, and as tempting to the bibli-
ographer, which are not living literature in any scholarly
sense of the term or for any scholarly use in real life.
We can no more use them for the purposes of a living
civilization than we can use mastodons and ichthyosauri
as beasts of burden.

Further : we need not adopt any very limited range of
the term " literature " in order to rid ourselves of them.
We need not be so chary of the title as to withhold it,
as Professor Henry Reed does, from professional and
technical and sectarian books. A much more liberal
policy than this will serve the purpose ; for the works
to which I refer, as related to scholarly culture, are
useless to us in any way whatever. No profession, or
art, or sect is served by them. They are not models
of any thing but ignorance, or vicious taste, or self-
conceit, or puerile fiction, or exploded and superannuated science. They are the paralytic literature of the
world. It mumbles to us in thickened speech, and
with distorted visage. Let us cover up its deformity
compassionately, and pass on.

I do not pause to specify more narrowly what these
volumes are, because practically our exclusion of them
is necessitated by other principles of selection, even
more imperatively. It is essential, however, that this
principle be firmly lodged in our minds at the threshold
of our advance, — that we must not read, even in a
cursory way, every book we happen to lay our hands
on, nor look with awe upon every volume we have to
strain our eyes to see in our libraries.

(2) A second principle of selection is, that we must
abandon the idea of universal scholarship. The Hon.
Mr. Toombs of Georgia is reported to have once said

that he could carry the treasury of the Confederate States of America in his hat. Probably it could have been put into less space than that. So, I suppose, the time must have been when all extant literature could have been committed to memory, and covered by one hat. But it is a truism which we often seem to forget, that no man can perform that achievement now.

The idea of literary omniscience long ago became a fable. It was true when foxes talked with hares, and frogs were erudite philosophers. Comparatively speaking, no very large portion of the literature now stored in the world's libraries can be known to any one mind. It is the cant of literature which makes pretensions to the contrary. Division of labor is nowhere more imperatively demanded than in scholarly reading. The wisest scholar of the age must be content to die in ignorance of the greater part of what other men have known, and to possess an equal proportion of that which he does know only at second-hand.

It is the right of every pupil in any branch of learning to receive cautiously the oracles which professors are apt to give, I must confess, more authoritatively than their own acquisitions justly warrant. A single fact speaks more than a homily on this point: it is, that the mechanical process of reading those books which are or have been the standard literature of their times would require more than three thousand years. Such is the estimate of a respectable English critic. If Homer had begun the labor at twenty years of age, and read till this time, he would still have had two hundred and fifty years of it before him. If Plato had been set to the task by the immortal gods of Greece, he would not by this time have got beyond the discovery of America.

Dante and Racine and Goethe and Shakspeare would still be unknown to him; and Wordsworth and Bryant and Longfellow he would never have heard of.

It is evident, then, how little of the wisdom of the past any living man can know within the limits of one lifetime. This conviction forces itself upon extensive readers sooner or later. It is well to admit it " sooner " rather than " later." Robert Southey, one of the most voluminous readers that England has ever produced, at the age of fifty years writes: " After all, knowledge is not the one thing needful. Provided that we can get contentedly through the world, and to heaven at last, the sum of all the knowledge which we can collect by the way is infinitely more insignificant than I like to acknowledge in my own heart."

What, then, should be the influence of this impossibility of universal scholarship upon our literary plans? I answer in three particulars. One effect of it should be to prevent our wasting ourselves in impracticable plans of study. Every young man should take the measure of his time, his physical health, his degree of independence of other avocations, and specially his power of mental appropriation. Then his plans of reading should be adjusted accordingly. No other one habit is so unproductive to a student as that of omnivorous reading. The space which such a reader traverses in libraries is no evidence of his culture. The most useless men living are the bookworms who are nothing more. There are men who devour books because they are books. They read as if they fancied that the mechanical process of trotting doggedly through libraries were the great business of a life of culture. Such men can not possess sound learning.

A writer in "The Edinburgh Review" very justly satirizes them as "entitled only to the praise of being very artificially and elaborately ignorant. They differ from the utterly uncultivated, only as a parrot who talks without understanding what he says differs from a parrot who can not talk at all" You have made a great discovery when you have found out what is and what is not practicable to yourself. Carlyle, addressing the students of the University of Edinburgh, said to them : "It is the first of all problems for a man to find out what kind of work he is to do in this universe." So is it the first of problems in the details of a scholar's life to find out what he *can* do. To attempt impracticable plans of reading is one of the most discouraging of literary mistakes. It leads many young men every year to abandon all hope of a scholarly life.

Another effect of the fact before us should be to prevent our minds from acting feverishly under the necessary limitations of our reading. We should submit to the literary privations of our lot gracefully. No man will do his best in literary effort till he can work contentedly. Our early efforts are often inflamed by a certain heat of blood which indicates a chafing of the spirit against the restrictions of time and sense and finite faculties. That is a bad absorbent of literary energy. We must rid ourselves of it. We must abandon the ambition, which Fontenelle says he indulged in early life, "of driving all the sciences abreast." At the basis of our culture, in this respect as in others, we should lay our religious principle. By prayer, if need be, bring your mind into a state of contentment with the limitations of human knowledge, and of your own in particular. You have made some progress in the culture

of a manly habit of study, if, with an earnest sense of
the dignity of an educated life, you can spend an hour
alone in a large library, and can come out of it with a
perfectly equable and happy resolution in your own
life's work.

Says the late Professor Reed of Philadelphia, "It is a
bewildering thing to stand in the midst of a vast concourse of books. It is oppressive to conceive what a
world of human thought and human passion is dwelling
on the silent paper, how much of wisdom is ready to
make its entrance into the mind that is prepared to wel-
come it. It is mournful to think that the multitudinous
oracles should be dumb to us." Who of us does not
understand this mourning over inaccessible knowledge?
Yet we have no reason to mourn. The restrictions
upon our knowledge are a part of our discipline; and,
as we have seen, discipline, not accumulation, is the
great object of a scholarly life, as it is of every life.

Gibbon was one of the most laborious of readers; yet
he says, "We should attend, not so much to the order
of our books as of our thoughts. The perusal of a
work gives birth to ideas. I pursue those ideas, and
quit my plan of reading." Gibbon in this remark hits
the vital point. A book is valuable for the ideas it
starts *in* the mind, rather than for those it puts there.
The book depends more on what you bring to it than
on any thing you take from it. No knowledge is of
vital moment to a man, which is not thus reproductive
within him, which does not, in some sense, work itself
into character. Of knowledge we need so much, and
only so much, as we can assimilate to ourselves in some
form of character. If to possess less than that is a
misfortune, to possess more is no blessing. The mind's

capacities can be no more than full. We have no more reason to mourn over unconquerable departments of knowledge than over inaccessible planets and angelic travels. Contented with our literary limits, we can advance to our life's work buoyantly.

The third effect of the view we have taken should be, that we should regard a choice selection of volumes as the first step to success. This is obvious. We should make an elaborate selection of the best only. If we can read but one volume in a year, let that one be worthy of a scholar's ideal of good reading, all the more so because it is but one. Our chief peril is that of allowing ourselves to be impelled by the pressure of our professional avocations down an inclined plane, from the scholarly upland to which our collegiate training lifted us, to a level so low that no scholarly eye can recognize us fraternally. Read only the best, therefore. Then the whole remaining literature of the world should be as irrelevant to any purpose of ours as the cinders of the library of Alexandria.

(3) The third principle of selection should be, that we rank first in our estimate those authors who have been controlling powers in literature; not necessarily first in the order of time in our reading; not, indeed, that we must read all of them at any time; not, as we shall see in the sequel, that all of us must read any of them outside of our own vernacular, but that we should mentally give them the first rank, in point of intrinsic worth, as models of the noblest culture. What we do read we should select and read under the elevating influence of this recognition of what *is* the best.

In stating this principle, I purposely speak of our *estimate* of literature, rather than of our personal study

of it, because the exigencies of professional life will
not permit every pastor to read largely in this regal
literature of all the ages. Because Homer was in one
sense the father of all poetry, it does not follow that
every pastor in Oregon, and every missionary in Africa,
should read Homer. We shall return to this qualification again in a future lecture : at present it is sufficient
to note that we should rank the authors in question as
the first in our scholarly judgment.

Taking the standard literatures of the world together,
there is a group of names which all scholarly judgment
has placed at the fountain-head of the streams of thought
which those literatures represent. They are the originals of all that cultivated mind has revered in letters.
They have been powers of control. The world of mind
has recognized them as such. Their names, therefore,
float on the current of all times. In any enlightened
age and country they become known to schoolboys.
Several suggestions respecting them deserve notice.

First, They are not numerous. In any one of the
standard literatures of the race you can number this
order of imperial minds on the fingers of one hand. In
the Hebrew literature, not more than three ; in the
classic Greek, not more than three ; in the Hellenistic
Greek, only two ; in the Roman, possibly two ; in the
Italian, only one ; in the French, less than that ; in the
Arabic, the Spanish, the Scandinavian literatures, none ;
in the German, only three ; and in the English, but
four.

Of course, opinions would differ in the assignment of
individuals to groups so small as these ; but they would
not differ as to the main assertion. I do not assume to
speak *ex cathedra* on this matter. I have sought to

enlighten my own judgment by correspondence with scholarly readers in several departments in which they are acknowledged experts. I discard, also, as I have remarked before, the technical restriction of the term "literature" by which philosophy and science are excluded. That restriction is not germane to the purpose now in view. An original philosopher, for instance, may give character to a nation's thought for centuries with such authority that no technically "literary" author shall equal or approach him as a national power. It is the great *powers* over national thought that we seek to discover in such an estimate as the one now before us. As the result, therefore, of the means of judgment which I possess, I should reckon the world's royal names in literature as follows; viz., in the Hebrew tongue, Moses, David, and Isaiah; in the classic Greek, Homer, Plato, and Aristotle; in the Hellenistic Greek, St. Paul and St. John; in the Roman, Cicero and Virgil; in the Italian, Dante.

In the French I have said, "less than one," because no mind among French scholars has, so far as I can discover, exerted a formative and permanent influence outside of France itself. Some critics would name Voltaire among the first class of authorship; but his influence outside of France has been short-lived. Even among his own countrymen, I am informed that few French authors of equal eminence are so little read to-day. Scarcely any works of solid French literature find so poor a sale as those of Voltaire. His fame and his influence were at their height among his contemporaries, and have been steadily declining ever since his last triumphant entrance into Paris, shortly before his decease. The ruling influence of France in modern civilization has been in politics more than in literature. If Descartes deserves a place in so select a group as I have in mind, I confess that my imperfect knowledge of his writings and of the opinion of experts about them does not qualify me to affirm it, and perhaps I ought not therefore to deny it. Let my impression pass for what it is worth.

The Arabic, the Spanish, and the Scandinavian literatures have all of them fallen into the second and third ranks of authorship. In the German I should follow the general voice of German critics in selecting the names of Goethe, Schiller, and Kant. In the English, after much hesitation, I assign the first rank to Chaucer, Shakspeare, Bacon, and Wordsworth, — to Chaucer as the historic head of English poetry, to Bacon for his influence on the national mind of England in all departments of thought, to Wordsworth as having revolutionized English poetic tastes, and to Shakspeare as the "myriad-minded," the poet of all times and nations. I hesitate in excluding the name of Milton; and many would dissent from the position which I assign to Wordsworth. But for this I have the authority of Coleridge. It may interest you to know that one of the most accomplished critics in our own country, to whom this classification has been submitted, added to the English quadrilateral the name of Hawthorne as being an absolute and solitary original in English letters.

The main point, however, to be noted, is that all scholarly opinion would limit the authors of the first rank in literary influence upon national mind to very few in number. The marvels of genius are like century-plants. Ages of mediocrity often separate them. They are elect spirits, and generally they are given only to elect nations.

This suggests, further, that these authors of the first class claim their rank by virtue of their power over other literature. They have given to national literatures their great impulses of development. Their names mark epochs of growth. They have been awakening powers. Multitudes of other great minds, who but for these would never have been great, have been aroused by these the greater. We can not appreciate the other literature of the world without knowing the creative power of these few originals. No man knows well the Greek development of mind, who does not know Homer and Plato. No man knows the Italian graft upon the Latin stock, who does not know Dante. No man knows the ripening of Christian civilization in the English mind, who does not know Chaucer and Bacon. And no man can judge profoundly of all the existing drifts of culture, who does not know, or who refuses to recognize as literature, the writings of David and Isaiah and St. Paul. This historic position of a very few names along the line of the world's advancement would be sufficient to attract attention to them, as the first in rank of representatives of what the mind of the race has thought and felt and expressed in literary forms.

Again: these authors of the first order claim their position by reason of the perpetuity of their influence. They live while others die. All poetry feels to this day the impulse of Homer: all philosophy feels the impulse of Plato. German literature abounds with commentaries on Shakspeare, and calls him inspired. No Italian scholar becomes eminent in any department of thought, without paying tribute to Dante. No modern thinker in Europe or America climbs to pre-eminence as a power with his contemporaries, except on the ladder which Bacon has erected. Everywhere those minds which represent most prophetically the literature of the future are those which are most profoundly imbued with the literature of the Hebrews. Wordsworth, speaking of the ancient classic literatures, says, "We have appropriated them all;" and of Milton he says, "He was a Hebrew in soul."

This immortality of the few royal minds of the past is the ultimate test of their authority. Nothing else *proves* a thing as time does. Nothing else gives authority like the unanimity of ages. It is not safe for a young man to dissent from such authority as this. It is virtually the voice of the common sense of mankind. Says Coleridge, "Presume those to be the best the reputation of which has been matured into fame by the consent of ages." If there is any truth in universal convictions, every mind that is intent on scholarly culture will sooner or later seek its most enduring impulses, directly or indirectly, from those few ideals which the common consent has pronounced the grandest, the most symmetrical, and the most intense. That is a foolish waste in one's policy of study which leads one needlessly to sacrifice those ideals by expending one's enthusiasm on their inferiors.

Yet it should be observed that in the study of this class of authors, with the exception of the inspired writers, we do not seek direct contributions to our professional labors. We do not seek to appropriate their contents bodily, but their scholarly influence. We are not ferreting out examples for imitation. We are not preparing to quote Homer in our sermons, nor to preach Lord Bacon or Shakspeare. The weakest possible preaching may be that in which our study of these authors is visible. They are to exist in our own work only by the transfusion of their genius into our own mental character. We seek to be mentally uplifted by them. The least significant part of their usefulness to us will appear in the form of quotation. Indeed, one of the perils of extensive reading, to be watched and shunned, is that of excessive extract from other authors. Avoid a mania for quotation: a great deal of literary cant appears in that form. You will soon note in your reading two classes of authors who quote little. They are those who are the most original, and those who are the most profoundly sincere.

Further: the study of this first class of authors has a special tendency to promote independence of provincial narrowness in our culture. The secret of the perpetuity of their power is, that they are universal in their adaptations. They appeal to and they represent elements which are innate in human nature. They are independent of sect, or class, or school. Hence comes their literary autocracy. Schools may have grown out of them, but they were never schoolmen. They did not aim to found schools. No man was ever less of a Platonist, in the sense of a Platonic partisan, than Plato himself; no man was ever less of a Baconian, in the scholastic sense, than Bacon himself. What schools of poetry did Homer and Shakspeare found? Schools grow up with smaller minds. They would be as offensive to those whose names they bear as the apostolic sects were to Cephas and St. Paul.

A preacher, therefore, by drinking in the spirit of such authors, imbibes a constitutional antidote to contracted tastes, to narrow opinions, and to cramped

methods of working. Let a young scholar drink deep
at these fountain-heads of power, or absorb their influence from the atmosphere around him, and he must do
violence to his whole scholarly nature if he becomes a
bigot or a cynic. You will discover, if you take pains
to observe it, that often purely theological extremes
and distortions of opinion are corrected or forestalled
by a purely literary culture. Such are the affinities
of all truth with all truth, that breadth of culture anywhere tends to produce breadth of culture everywhere.
Who, as a rule, are the most liberal thinkers in theology? In whom do you find the most evenly balanced
faith? Are they not the men of profound and enlarged literary sympathies? On the other hand, if you
find a preacher who holds and tries to preach an impracticable dogma which outrages the common sense of
men, can you not affirm safely beforehand that he is a
man of contracted reading? He knows little or nothing of the great creators of the world's thought in
libraries. When, for example, I hear that a celebrated
English preacher has been heard to say that the reason
why God permits the wicked to live is that " He knows
they are to be damned, and is willing to let them have
a little pleasure first," I know without inquiry that that
preacher is not a man of books. I venture to affirm
that he has never read Spenser's " Faerie Queene."
It is doubtful whether he could with a clear conscience
read Shakspeare. Such a ferocious notion in theology
never could survive contact with the regal order of
minds in literature, even the most remote from theologic thought. It is the property of a little mind, fed
by little minds, and sympathetic with no other.

To these suggestions it should be added, that, to

these authors of the first rank, inferior literature should
be largely sacrificed.   The chief peril of a preacher in
his reading is suggested by this remark: it is that he will
devote a disproportionate amount of time to ephemeral
books.   We are apt to sacrifice the great powers of literature, not of design, but by neglect.   The reading
of the majority of educated men, I think, is wasteful.
We read newspapers and magazines indiscriminately.
What do we want to know of the murder in North
Street last night, or the forgery in State Street last
week?   William Prescott the historian used to instruct his secretary, in reading to him the morning
newspaper, never to read about an accident or a crime.
He applied to his newspaper the same eclectic economy of time which he practised in exploring the Spanish
archives.

Stern self-discipline should adjust the proportion of
our reading.   It is well to read such an author as Carlyle; but by what right do we neglect for his sake
such writers as Bacon and Milton?   It is well enough
to know Byron as the representative of a certain phase
of English poetry; but what principle of scholarly
policy justifies our sacrifice to him of such an author
as Dante?   What axiom of economy leads a preacher
to buy Hood's poems, when he is too poor to own a
copy of Shakspeare? or to purchase the works of
Thomas Moore, when he can not afford to own Wordsworth?   Who can, without a twinge of scholarly conscience, spend an hour a day over the newspapers of the
week, when he has never opened even a translation of
Schiller?   If I am rightly informed, merchants in active
business do not feel able to spare half of that time for
their morning paper.   Is the accumulation of money

of so much more value than the accumulation of brains?
In these suggestions, however, I have in mind the habits
of a healthy scholar, not those which disease has demoralized.

I once took up from a student's table a book of three
hundred duodecimo pages on the culture of poultry.
I took occasion to ascertain from him afterwards that he
had never read a page of Spenser's "Faerie Queene,"
and he did not know who wrote the "Canterbury Tales."
On another occasion I took from the shelf of a young
pastor's library a book of nearly equal dimensions with
the other, on the breeding and training of horses. Possibly a cramped salary may compel a pastor to own such
a book, as his wife must own a cookery-book; yet in
the case in question there was no such economic necessity, and I learned from that pastor that he had never
been able to "wade through," as he expressed it, a history of the Reformation. What business has an educated man, not pressed by the necessities of poverty,
to be plodding through the literature of the farmyard
when three-quarters of Westminster Abbey are unknown
to him?

An earnest scholar will sacrifice much that is useful
in inferior literature, if his knowledge of it must be
purchased at the cost of acquaintance with names which
must outlive it a hundred years. Dr. Arnold says,
"As a general rule, never read the works of any ordi-
nary man except on scientific matters, or when they
contain simple matters of fact. Even on matters of
fact, silly and ignorant men, however honest, require
to be read with constant suspicion; whereas great men
are always instructive, even amidst much of error. In
general, I hold it to be certain that the truth is to be

found in the great men, and the error in the little ones."
Pascal said that he had left off reading the Jesuits,
because, if he had continued it, he must have "read a
great many indifferent books."

Once more: not merely worthless literature should
be sacrificed, but, for the sake of the best, we must
sacrifice much which would be very valuable to us if
we had not the best. Pliny said that no book had ever
been written which did not contain something profitable
to a reader. Leibnitz and Gibbon, both of them vora-
cious readers, expressed the same opinion. One of the
most rapid and voluminous readers and writers of our
own day once told me that he had never read a book
which did not give him some new thought.

These judgments, with qualifications, are true; yet
they do not justify that bibliomania which leads a man
to seize upon the book which lies nearest to him, because
it *is* a book, and because something or other can be got
from it. We must sacrifice a great many good books.
We must let go our hold upon much which would be a
model to us if we had no better. We must force our
way grimly through the heaps of them which bestrew
our path in order to reach the smaller but weightier
heap which lies beyond. Otherwise we shall be very
large readers of comparatively small thought. Our
culture will suffer from a plethora of little books. The
after-clap of their reading will be more distressing than
that of the little book in the Apocalypse.

LECTURE X.

BEFORE proceeding to consider other principles bearing upon a pastor's study of books for homiletic culture, let a moment be given to a plausible objection to the principle already advanced, that we should exalt to the first rank the few controlling minds in the world's literatures. It is urged that that principle would practically doom a pastor to reading nothing but the ancient classics, or at best to waste himself on dead or foreign languages.

I have in the sequel much to say of the practicability of literary study to a pastor. But for the present, and in application to the point in hand, I answer, The objection is often a valid one. Therefore I have said that we should rank first in our *estimate* of literature the authors of first rank. Then we should read them, if we can. This is the practical summary of the principle before us. But, further, it is not impracticable for the majority of pastors in active service to know the leading authors in foreign literatures through translations. The prejudice against translations is not sensible. It was originated when literature was less voluminous than now. Ralph Waldo Emerson reads translations, and respects them. His reading would have been

146

restricted vastly, if he had not done so. Who sup-
poses that he gets his quotations from the originals of
the Veda and of Confucius?

It is not impracticable, then, for the majority of pastors to read translations of Homer and Plato. It is
not impossible to own, and to read in some vacation, so
readable and so portable a book as Carey's "Dante."
For the intrinsic value of Dante's "Inferno," let me
cite the opinion of Mr. Prescott the historian. He
says that he deems it "a fortunate thing for the world
that the first poem of modern times should have been
founded on a subject growing out of the Christian religion, and written by a man penetrated with the spirit
of its sternest creed. Its influence on literature has
been almost as remarkable as that of Christianity itself
on the moral world." It surely is an irreparable loss
to the culture of a preacher to remain through life ignorant of such a poem. So of Goethe's "Faust" and
Schiller's "Robbers." Coleridge's translation of Schiller's "Wallenstein" and the "Piccolomini" would promote a double purpose by giving you German classics
in splendid English poetry. One might select twenty
or thirty volumes of English translations which would
give to a hard-worked pastor, not by any means a masterly knowledge, but a very useful and usable knowledge, of the best authors in the great literatures of the
world outside of the English tongue.

Again: it is not impracticable for all pastors to
exercise the *spirit* of this principle in the selection of
authors of our own language. Every educated man
can read and enjoy the great writers in English literature. We can spend our time on these rather than on
the little ones. In doing this we may really imbibe

much of the best literary culture of all times and countries. The great authors of England have fed upon
the ancient and the modern continental literatures of
Europe. Wordsworth was right when he said, " We
have reproduced all that." He was right to this extent, that English literature has reproduced in Christian
forms the best of all that Pagan literature ever was.

(4) The principles of selection in literary study
already discussed need to be qualified by a fourth
principle, which is, that, in our choice of authors, the
literature of the English language should predominate.
You have no reason to think meanly of your acquisitions, or to apologize for them, if they are limited to
your mother-tongue. In the majority of cases a pastor's reading will be limited thus, be his theory of reading what it may. In such a case he has no reason to
be ashamed of the necessity. This view is contested
by good critics; and I approach it with a sense of the
difficulty of expressing to you what I believe to be the
exact truth, without being misunderstood. Yet my
conviction is the growth of years, that, if there is one
peril greater than another to our scholarly habits, it is
that of doing injustice to the literature of England.
Intense as our national spirit is in other respects, it
does not rise to the level of the birthright we possess
as inheritors of the treasures in the English tongue.

In a discussion of the subject, we have to encounter,
in the first place, a prejudice which attributes superiority
to whatever is foreign. The distant, the strange, the
unknown, the half-known, awes a cultivated mind often
as it does the rudest. We are apt to stand agape at
the wisdom locked up in a foreign speech, as children
do in listening to foreign conversation. Did you never

experience this? I must confess to having stood momentarily in speechless wonder, in my first efforts to acquire the German language, because a German truckman in the street could talk the language so much more volubly than I could, and a dray-horse, in understanding him, was my superior. Yet as senseless as that is the feeling which underlies much of the preference often felt for foreign literatures above our own. If indulged with equal knowledge of the literatures brought into the comparison, it is literary cant. This is the ground of the pre-eminence given to the French language in some schools for the education of women.

Then, in approaching the question of the worth of the English literature, we encounter the atmosphere which is created by our system of training in the ancient classic languages. Our collegiate system we have taken chiefly from the English universities. Those grew up at a period when England had no literature of her own. The reverence then paid to the ancient classics was normal and necessary. Generally speaking, there was no other literature which deserved reverence. The revival of the ancient learning created for the modern mind the only models in existence which were of superior finish for the purposes of liberal culture, except the sacred models of Palestine. The new enthusiasm for learning must have looked to Athens and Rome, or nowhere. Hence arose that profound reverence for what is called classic study, which tinges the university system of England, of which the American college is an offshoot. That reverence is not a whit too profound absolutely; but it is, by a vast proportion, too exclusive relatively.

Our usage by which we designate the ancient litera-

tures by the term "classic" is an evidence of the depth
to which the preference of the ancient authors over
every thing English is embedded in our scholarly inheritance. It is as if nothing English could deserve the
title of a classic, i.e., of a model for the education of
mind. English authorship has been compelled to contend for its right to the name in its own language. A
youth of to-day is at first confused when he hears the
phrase "English classics."

Our collegiate discipline — and here lies the precise
point of its defect, in my judgment — preserves no just
proportions between the ancient and the English classics. The English literature is a fact to which it does
no justice in its theory of the education suitable to an
English or an American pupil. This literature is now
the accumulation of centuries. It is expanding with
every decade of years. Yet who of us ever obtained
in our collegiate experience any very exalted conception
of it as compared with the Greek and Latin models?
I think I speak the experience of a majority of educated
Americans in saying that a sense of the classic rank of
the English literature is a discovery, which, for the most
part, they have to make for themselves after they have
left our collegiate and professional schools. It dawns
upon us as a novelty when we begin to extend our English reading. When we do admit it, when the glory of
our native literature forces it upon us, we feel a sense
of regret that the discovery has come to us so late in
our mental history. We turn to our own language,
then, with something of the rebound with which we
spring to a long-neglected virtue.

Again: the presumption is always in favor of the pre-
eminence of the literature of one's vernacular tongue in

one's culture, if that tongue has a literature. If a language has no literature, the mind to which it is vernacular is so far a barbarous mind. Culture, in the high sense of the term, is impracticable to it in its native tongue. But, if a language has a literature, that literature is an expression of the national mind. It is a product of that mind. Of that mind, the man himself is a fragment; his own mental structure is a part of the growth which has made the literature. He sustains to it, therefore, a relation which he can not sustain to any embodiment of foreign thought. It is a relation of sympathy and kindred. The very life-blood of thought flows to and through him by means of the vernacular arteries, as it can not by transfusion from any foreign fountains.

Says Dr. George P. Marsh, "Deep in the recesses of our being, beneath even the reach of consciousness, or at least of objective self-inspection, there lies a certain sensibility to the organic laws of our mother-tongue." He elsewhere adduces two facts in proof of this. One is, that a man's vernacular language, though forgotten, "can never be completely supplanted or supplied by another;" and the second is, that those who grow up speaking many languages very seldom acquire complete mastery over any one of them. That which is true of linguistic acquisition is doubly true of literary culture. The secret sympathies of mind with truth in the vernacular speech more than realizes Wordsworth's fancy of the communings of the seashell with its native ocean. No man can do violence to those sympathies without a loss in the breadth and naturalness of his own development. The confusion of tongues bears every mark of a curse upon the race. It

is an evil of incalculable magnitude, that we must
derive so much of our mental training through other
media of expression than that which we grow up with,
and grow into as our minds expand from childhood.

Experience in the conducting of foreign missions
confirms these views. The original idea of foreign
missionary work, and the one which first roused Christian enthusiasm most profoundly, was that the heathen
world must be Christianized mainly by the agency of
preachers sent from Christian lands. I heard in my
boyhood the claims of foreign missions urged on American Christians' and students for the ministry, on the
ground that thousands of preachers must be sent from
Christian countries, outnumbering by multitudes the
whole Protestant clergy of the world. "How shall
they hear without a preacher? and how shall they
preach except they be *sent?*" was the text. Inspired
authority for it seemed to be given at the outset.

Experience has corrected all that. It has proved
that heathen nations are not to be reached, any more
than Christian nations, in the large masses, by a ministry which to them is foreign, trained in a foreign civilization, pervaded by foreign modes of thought, and
using *their* vernacular under the embarrassments created by the mixture of the idioms of a foreign speech.
It has long since become trite that the great bulk of
the work of Christianizing the heathen world is to be
done by a native ministry trained originally by foreign
teachers, but ultimately taking the work into their own
hands. Minds created under the influence of the language spoken by a people are needed to become controlling powers in the Christian civilization of that
people. The secret sympathies with vernacular speech
run very deep. We are all ruled by them.

Applying this principle, then, to our own preparations for the American pulpit, I contend that if a Greek or a Latin, or a German literature, or all combined, have for us claims superior to those of our English speech, it is a thing to be proved. Perhaps it can be proved; but the presumption, in the nature of things, is against it.

Further: the utility of a man's culture, other things being equal, requires the ascendency in it of the literature of his native language. Culture is for use, not for display, not for literary enjoyment mainly. The weakest education is that which is aimed at display. The highest homœopathic trituration of the educational ideal is that of a modern French boarding-school for young ladies. It is worthy of the "nugiperous gentledame" whom the "Simple Cobbler of Agawam" describes as "the very gizzard of a trifle, the product of a quarter of a cipher, and the epitome of nothing."

But the most selfish education, and therefore the narrowest of all educational ideals which may be respectable for strength, is that which is directed to literary pleasure.

The danger from this source to the integrity of a pastor's studies justifies a brief *excursus* at this point upon the selfish ideal of a scholarly life. No conception of life, not grossly sensual, can be formed, which is more odious for the intensity of its selfishness than the life of a man of letters who is that and nothing more, with no aims in his studies but those of an amateur student. A studious man in dressing-gown and slippers, sitting in the midst of a choice library which is adorned with works of art and costly relics of antiquity, yet from which not a thought goes out to the intel-

lectual or moral improvement of mankind, is a model
of refined and fascinating selfhood. Under certain
conditions it may do more evil than the life of a
libertine. Walter Scott's ideal of life, as expressed in
the building and furnishing of Abbotsford, was not
the true ideal of a Christian scholar. For their influence on the tastes of educated men, give me rather the
drinking-songs of Robert Burns. These are the less
seductive to such men, and carry their antidote on
the face of them. Prescott the historian pronounces
the mental luxury of successful composition one of the
two most exalted pleasures of which man is capable;
the enjoyment of a reciprocated passion for woman
being the other.

Conceive of a man so constituted, or so trained to
literary enjoyment, that he can honestly say, as Buffon
did of his hours of composition, "Fourteen hours a day
at my desk in a state of transport!" It is not difficult
to see that such a man's life *may* become as selfish in
its literary enjoyment as that of another man in his
sensuality. Is there not, indeed, a class of literary
men who suggest to us the doubtful query whether
they have any large, generous sympathy with their
kind? Their studies are conducted with a stolid indifference to the questions which are agitating the masses
of mind underneath them. At a sublime altitude above
such problems as those which involve the salvation, the
liberty, the education, the bread, of the millions, these
favorite sons of literary fortune dwell in an atmosphere
of rarified selfishness, from which comes down now and
then a sneer at the boorishness, or a fling at the fanaticism, of those who are humbly striving to feed the
hungry, and clothe the naked, and save the lost.

Give us rather the literary spirit of Milton, who returned from his tour in Italy, and gave up his projected visit to the Acropolis of Athens, "because," said he, " I esteemed it dishonorable in me to be lingering abroad, even for the improvement of my mind, when my fellow-citizens were contending for liberty at home." Dr. Arnold was so sensible of the peril of literary selfishness, that he held firmly to the opinion that literary pursuits " should never be a profession by themselves." They should be an appendage always to some business or profession which should keep a man's mind healthy by interesting him in the questions of real life and in his own times. Speaking of Coleridge's " Literary Remains," he says, " There were marks enough that his mind was diseased by the want of a profession. The very power of contemplation becomes impaired or perverted when it becomes the main object of life." Mr. Froude the historian has been heard to say, that, if his son sought to make literature his profession, he would oppose it as he would an imprudent marriage. Yet Froude speaks from experience of the error which he condemns. A pastor's life meets precisely the conditions which such critics deem most healthfully conducive to success in literary study. Literary labor held by the necessities of a profession in adjustment with the real world we live in, and made tributary to great and unselfish uses, — this is the Christian ideal of a scholar's life.

Yet, returning to the main point before us, this is one of the most cogent reasons that can be urged for giving pre-eminence in our culture to the literature of our own language. We belong to the English-speaking stock. With the exception of foreign missionaries, the American clergy must find their life's work among an English-speaking people. If heathen preachers were prepared to carry on the Christian work efficiently, they would do it among their own countrymen more efficiently than you can do it.

It is not merely the accumulations drawn from our vernacular, and applied to direct use in our labors, which will fit us most effectually to influence the minds of our countrymen. It is more than these: it is the very breath of mental life which we take in from the literature of our vernacular. It is the very essence of all there is in us which gives us claim to be called educated men, and which qualifies us for intellectual and moral leadership. We must derive this chiefly from our vernacular literature to fit us to influence most effectively those who speak our vernacular language. That literature is an expression of their minds as it is of ours. That language is a medium of more than speech between us and them. It is a medium of magnetic currents of brotherhood. Speak English, and they understand you. Think in English, and you think their thoughts. Feel the pulsations of an English culture, and you feel the throbs of their heart. Live in an English literary atmosphere, and you live near to their level,—far enough above them to insure their respect for you as their superior, yet near enough to them to feel yourself at home with them, and make them feel at home with you.

Let me, in passing, notice one phenomenon in the history of theological education which I do not entirely understand, but which illustrates the peril into which an educated preacher sometimes falls. It is that foreigners educated for the pulpit in this country are seldom inclined to spend their professional life among their own countrymen. A German educated here seldom wishes to preach to Germans; or a Jew to Jews; or a Swede to the Swedes of our north-west; or a Welshman to the Welsh churches of Pennsylvania. I have repeatedly known them to struggle with the infirmities of an imperfect knowledge of the English language, and persist for years in the conflict with the adverse influences they encounter among American congregations, rather than to preach in their vernaculars to their own countrymen. Even a black man I have known to throw away the advantages of kindred race to lift himself up into competition with the white race. Such struggles are among the saddest mistakes in professional policy. They are struggles against nature. They abandon invaluable advantages ready to one's hand, for the sake of others which must be gained by years of toil, and which, if gained, never can equal the treasure lost. A preacher, above all men, should never abandon his vernacular if he can help it. As well may a fish leap out of the sea.

Even those contributions to our culture which we receive from foreign sources need to be Anglicized in our use of them. They should be received with English tastes, seen with English eyes, interpreted with English idiom, wrought into our opinions under the superintendence of English discipline, and adjusted to our use with a certain sifting and weighing process conducted with a heavy preponderance of English habits of thought. Every literature which is transferred from its native soil to be used as an exotic in another land needs to be passed through some native mind of that land, which shall act in a spirit of loyalty

to its own language. Otherwise that exotic literature
can not be largely useful there. It will not be useful
because it can not be used. No national literature is
ever dug up, and transported and replanted bodily.
The living forces of a nation's libraries can not migrate
in any such way. Laws of national character represented by diversities of speech forbid such violent
transitions.

Therefore nothing dooms a man to greater sterility
in the pulpit than the attempt to import whole the
spirit of a foreign culture. Sermons to an Anglo-
American audience, founded upon an exclusive or
ascendant German model, expressive of German habits
of thought, clothed in German idioms, though in English words, are useless, — necessarily so, though they
may not contain an error or a distortion. I once knew
a pastor, who, under the pressure of severe pastoral
duties, preached to his people through a winter, on
Sunday afternoons, a free translation of the sermons
of a German preacher. He was dismissed in the
spring. Similar would be the tendency of German
sermons to a German audience expressive of English
culture alone. The same is true if the ancient literatures have predominated in the forming of a preacher's
mind.

Said a clergyman of high repute in the ministry, "I
always fear for the result when I see a very scholarly
man enter the pulpit." The remark was founded on
his observation of the fact that eminently scholarly
men are often alienated unconsciously in their tastes
from the national mind of their own country. They
live so much in dead or foreign languages, among
modes of thought which are alien to those of their

own times and kindred, that they do not sympathize
with their audiences, and therefore have no magnetic
power to move them. No literature is so universal in
its adaptations to the mind of the race as to be absolutely independent of its national history. Even that
of the Bible is not so. It is Jewish in its type and
spirit. We can not use it with power until we Angli-
cize it. We are obliged to bring to it our own minds,
trained in the school of English thought, and to receive
it into our own culture as into English molds, before
we can reproduce it in English sermons to which the
sympathies of an American audience will respond.

De Quincey entertained such strong convictions on
the subject of servitude to foreign languages, that he
said the act of learning a new language was in itself
an evil. "Unless balanced" by other studies, he declared it to be "the dry rot of the human mind." He
expressed more temperately the true principle of culture in this respect by saying to a young man, "So
frame your selection of languages, that the largest
possible body of literature available for your purposes
shall be laid open to you at the least possible price
of time and mental energy." "The largest available
for your purposes: " this is common sense. And to
every man of English or American stock, except a
professional philologist, it requires the subjection of
every thing outside of the English tongue to acclima-
tion in the atmosphere of English libraries.

LECTURE XI.

IN addition to that which has been already remarked of the predominance of the English literature in a pastor's studies, it should be further observed, that, all things considered, the English literature is intrinsically superior to every other. In the preceding Lecture we claimed this superiority for it on the ground of professional usefulness. It is now claimed on the ground of intrinsic worth. I repeat the qualifying clause of the statement, "all things considered." It is a foolish partisanship in learning to decry any of the great collections of wisdom which represent the growth of great nations in intellectual power. That man has one of the elements of scholarship yet to acquire, who is unable to admit the inferiority in some respects of that which, as a whole, may be his favorite language and his dearest resource of thought.

I do not wish to assert extravagant claims, still less to speak magisterially of literatures in which I am not at home. I assume to give you only the judgment which is founded upon that knowledge of our own literature which is current among educated men, and is supplemented by the judgment of other literatures expressed by men whose knowledge entitles them to

160

be received as authorities. In a sober estimate thus formed I must think that our own literature heads the list. The grounds of this judgment are numerous, and they underlie the whole discussion of what is and what is not vital in the current of a nation's thought. We can do little more than to glance at them with remark sufficient to indicate the line of argument.

In the first place, the argument is narrowed in its range by the fact that but few of the literatures of the world can enter into the account at all. There have been but few great literatures in history. You will easily recall them. The only great ones of antiquity are those of Palestine, Greece, and Rome. The Egyptian, the Arabic, the Hindoo, the Chinese, are all provincial. They are all either infantile in character, or *lateral* to those lines of culture which have projected themselves with power of control into modern thought. Those secondary literatures had no power of reproduction. They were eddies in the stream and along the shore of civilization.

Then, of the modern literatures, all that can bear comparison with each other are the English, the French, and the German. No intelligent scholar would place by the side of these the Italian, the Spanish, the Portuguese, or those of the Scandinavian nations. It is at the head of these imperial literatures which have made and are making the deepest grooves in history, that I would place the work of the English mind as a whole, and as a means of culture to be used upon the world of the present and the future.

This is, furthermore, presumptively true, because the English literature is the expression of a *composite* order of mind. Nations, like individuals, are subject to physi-

ological laws. One of these laws is, that virility of
national mind is proportioned to the intermingling of
virile races. Mental power does not flow in the isolated currents of national being which aristocratic
jealousy has kept running for centuries in the channels
of pure blood. In this relation of things pure blood is
weak blood. It runs low, and grows pale. It is what
Shakspeare calls "pigeon-livered." Mental force flows
rather in the crosses and reduplications and interfusions
of diverse and even contrary elements of being. Conquests which bring warring elements into one solution
are essential to the best intellectual resultant. The
best national mind in the history of civilization is what
the composite column is in architecture. It consists
of a union of eclectic forces. We can not designate
it briefly and yet more definitely than by terming it a
composite mind.

Just this the English mind is in its make. The English literature is an expression of such a composite
mind. There is no other spot in the Old World into
which so many diverse streams of life-blood have
flowed as into the British Isles. Not a full-blooded
race in all the northern and central parts of Europe is
unrepresented in the present blood of Great Britain.
Those are the cool regions, where forceful men are
made by the very elements. This is a vital fact, that
the cool zones of Europe have poured their populations,
either for colonization or conquest, into the original
reservoir of the British Empire. Germany and France
have both contributed some vital vigor through the
Angles, the Saxons, and the Normans, to the living
English.

Dr. George P. Marsh finds linguistic evidences, in the

structure of the Anglo-Saxon dialects, of a marvelous commingling of tribes in the early invasions of Britain. He pronounces the linguistic evidence of such a commingling more conclusive than the historic evidence. " Diversity, not unity, of origin," he says, is indicated by the structure of the Anglo-Saxon. There is no evidence that any one people ever spoke it outside of Great Britain. It bears internal signs of having grown up there from heterogeneous elements imported from abroad. Moreover, philologists think they find traces of the same heterogeneousness of origin in the modern dialects still existing around the North Sea, the district from which the early invaders of Britain came. In no other part of Europe, it is said, are there so many forms of language, within the same area, which are not intelligibly interchangeable, as are found there. Such philological phenomena all point to the fact of a most remarkable solution of ingredients foreign to each other in the original compound which forms the basis of the English tongue. And what the English tongue is in this respect, the English mind is, from which our literature has sprung, and of which it is the immortal expression.

It is accordant with all the laws which govern the growth of national minds, that a literature which is the natural representative of such a composite mind in books should be, as a whole, the superior of the literatures springing from the provincial resources which have been tributaries to the stock of that mind. The " Father of Waters," it is to be presumed, has a volume and a momentum exceeding those of any one of its feeders.

The same law which in this respect has made our

literature what it is, is now operating anew in our own country to make our literature what it is to be. Races are intermingling here to an extent unprecedented since the Gothic conquests of Rome. New blood is flowing in from every source on the globe which contains the elements of national vigor. It is borne hither in the veins of the most enterprising and athletic classes of the old nations. Such are always the migrating classes. They are the classes in which family stock has a future. It has not spent itself in the vices and luxuries of a decadent civilization. Such migratory hordes always carry with them the germs of great nations. That virility which first appears in the growth of numbers and of material prosperity will by and by show itself in a new stock of composite mind. This, again, will reproduce and prolong under new conditions the national literature. It must be English at heart, but broadened and deepened to represent the mind of a new world.

The claims of the English literature to pre-eminence in our culture are confirmed by a third fact; viz., that the English as compared with other literatures is pre-eminently a literature of power as distinct from a literature of knowledge only. Turn to De Quincey's "Essays on the Poets." In his essay on Alexander Pope you will find very clearly expressed a vital distinction between the literature of power and the literature of knowledge. The function of the literature of knowledge is to teach: that of the literature of power is to move. "The first is a rudder; the second, a sail." To illustrate, he inquires, "What do you learn from the 'Paradise Lost'? Nothing at all. What do you learn from a cookery-book? Something you did not know

before, on every page. But would you, therefore, put
the cookery-book on a higher level than the 'Paradise
Lost'? What you owe to Milton is not any knowledge,
of which a million separate items are but a million advancing steps on the same earthly level. What you
owe is *power ;* that is, expansion and exercise to your
own latent capacity of sympathy with the infinite,
where every pulse and each separate influx is a step
upwards, — a step ascending, as upon Jacob's ladder,
from earth to mysterious altitudes."

I can not develop this idea further so vividly as you
will find it expressed in the essay to which I have
referred. The whole essay, by the way, is a superior
specimen of criticism. The point I would observe
more particularly is, that, in the judgment of European
critics, the English literature as a whole is superior to
any other modern embodiment of thought as a literature of power. It is a plastic as distinct from a didactic
literature. The most intelligent German scholars concede this respecting English poetry as compared with
that of their own language. German critics write
commentaries on Shakspeare as on one of the prophets.
M. Guizot concedes substantially the same thing to the
English as compared with the French drama.

Our literature is less accumulative than the German,
but more creative. An impulse received from its great
models strikes deeper, and lives longer. The English
mind is constructive, and builds for durability. We
have more numerous poets, historians, orators, whose
productions have become standards and whose influence is of the creative sort, than are to be found in
either of the rival literatures of the Continent. German philosophers and philologists are more numerous

than ours. French scientists are more numerous than ours. But with these exceptions our authors of the rank which De Quincey designates by the word "power" as contrasted with "knowledge," outnumber those of France and Germany together. On such a subject as this, few men can claim to be authorities. But the drift of critical judgment among scholars, if I have not misread it, is in this direction, giving ascendency to the English over the Continental literatures in respect to creative and durable vitality.

Again: the English is pre-eminently a Christian literature. No other is to so large an extent pervaded with Christian thought. No other has so little in its standard works that is adverse to Christianity. No other is so profoundly rooted in the Christian theory of life. No other deals so intelligently with Christian ideas of destiny. No other is so reverent towards the Christian Scriptures. No other owes so much of its own vitality to the literature of the Hebrews.

These features constitute the great distinction of our literature above those of antiquity. No Pagan embodiment of thought can possibly be a substitute for it or an approximation to it. It stands on an upper level, above Greek and Roman culture, in the very fact that it is built on Christianity. It therefore embodies a large experience, which the ancient classic languages had not even words to express, if the ancient people had had the ideas. Coleridge, for example, declares that "sublimity" in the true conception of it is not extant in any production of the Greek literature. He contends that it is a modern idea which was Hebrew in its origin. Yet the English literature is full of it. Moreover, the sterility of the classic Greek language in words expressive of Christian thought is seen in the very existence of the New Testament. But our English tongue is built upon Christian thought.

The English is also a Protestant literature, — Protestant as distinct from a Romish, and equally distinct from an infidel bias. In this it stands above both its rivals on the Continent. Dr. Newman of Oxford says, speaking of the conversion of England to Rome, "The literature of England is against us. It is Protestant in warp and woof. We never can unmake it." This feature of it gives to it a splendid opening into the world's future, if there is any truth in our faith that the world is to be converted to some simple, spiritual, apostolic type of Christianity.

Furthermore: the English is the literature of constitutional freedom. It is not a literature of anarchy, nor of despotism, as so large a fragment of the Continental literatures is, but is an expression of constitutional liberty. I emphasize, it is an *expression* of that liberty. It is not a silent nor an expurgated volume in respect to the ideas of freedom which are upheaving the nations. The body of it has never sprung by stealth from a muzzled press. It has not been obliged to ask leave to be, from the police. Next to the Bible, no other single fortress of liberty in the world is so impregnable as the walls and buttresses of English libraries.

Those libraries are full of outbursts of the love of liberty in poetic forms which stir the passions of nations. The common people sing them in their homes; mothers over cradles; and plowmen among the hills. Our libraries are full of calm and scholarly defenses of freedom in the forms of constitutional argument which create great statesmen for the leadership of nations. They are full of the statute laws of England, which are liberty embodied in good government. They are full of histories of liberty in the great battles and revolutions of England, — a record which a nation never retreats from or dishonors till it falls off from the platform of great Powers.

Other nations can not know our literature with safety to despotic ideas. Men have to expurgate it, as slaveholders did our school-books before the civil war, in order to make it innocent of hostility to despotism. The poetry of England must be riddled with expurgations, before it can be safely taught in the schools of a people who fear the growth of free ideas. The Bible is but a fragment of that mass of thought which Romanism would expel from our schools. The sonnets of Milton and Wordsworth, the speeches of Edmund Burke, the story of Magna Charta, the biography of Wilberforce, the battle of Bunker Hill, must all be expunged or garbled before Romanism is safe in common schools in which the English literature is taught or sung. No poetic fiction is it, but the most prosaic of sober facts in political economy, which Wordsworth uttered : —

> " We must be free or die, who speak the tongue
>   That Shakspeare spake."

This affiliation of our literature with constitutional freedom is a feature of it which must open avenues for it into the world's future. Certain great arteries of life in the great nations run directly into it. The heart of the nations is beating in sympathy with it to an extent not true of any other literature dead or living.

Moreover, the English is a well-balanced literature. No important department of it is meager. In some departments the Continental literatures surpass it in affluence ; but the critic betrays ignorance of the English mind who pronounces it barren in any of the great lines of scholarly thought.

The only department of culture in which England is poor, as compared with the Continental countries, is that of the fine arts. Canova gave the true explanation of that when he said, "It is all owing to your free institutions. They drain away genius from the arts to the bar and the House of Commons. Had England been Italy, Pitt and Fox would have been your artists." In no great department of literature is the English language barren.

Our literature is evenly balanced, also, in the fact of its aversion to extremes of opinion, and extravagances of culture. In philosophy, in criticism, in morals, in poetry, in theology, in politics, the English mind revolts from excesses. As a whole, the literature is healthy. It is full-chested, and walks erect. In the main, it is a liberal and candid literature. It is free, also, from innate inclinations to sentimentality or to mysticism. It is an earnest growth of thought rooted in good sense. If a literary monomaniac happens to spring up, and attract attention by unseemly antics, the reading people of England look on long enough to laugh, and then go about their business.

Opposites are well balanced in our literature. It never surges this way and that, as if a whole nation had run mad for the want of mental ballast. In this respect it is superior to that of France. No single man could ever have had such power to lead the Eng-

lish people on a tramp of delusion and godlessness as
Voltaire had over the French mind. It was not in the
make of the English mind to be thus inveigled into a
volcanic revolution. Both nations had their revolutions. Both executed their monarchs on the scaffold.
But England did it decently, under the forms and in
the spirit of her ancient laws. She did not sacrifice
all her institutions for the sake of doing it. The
conscience of the nation acted in it a great national
tragedy, with no heart for ribaldry and brutality. It
was done under a *régime* marked by days of religious
fasting.

Macaulay says that the two most profound revolutions in English history were that which effaced the
distinction between the Norman and the Saxon, and
that which effaced the distinction between master and
slave. Both were brought about by silent and imper-
ceptible changes. Civil war accomplished neither;
moral causes produced both. It is impossible to fix
the time when either ceased to be. Lord Macaulay
says that the institution of villanage has never been
abolished by statute to this day. With such history
as this in the process of making, and constantly going
on record in her libraries, and taught in her universities,
and fostered by her pulpits, and acted in her drama, and
sung in the ballads of her people, it has never been
possible for England to have a " Reign of Terror."

The literature of this English stock, therefore, excites
trust in its genuineness. It is a grandly equable thing
by which to form a scholar's mind. It cultivates his
powers symmetrically. It exalts intellectual and moral
above material and turbulent causes in his judgment
of events. It creates a predisposition in his tastes

to a moderation of passionate opinions and to an appreciation of opposites both in historic and in living character.

Yet again: the English is the most mature of all the great embodiments of the world's thought. It expresses the results of the longest growth of power in literary forms. It has claims, superior to those of any other, to be regarded as the last and ripest fruitage of intellectual energy that the world has yet seen. The proof of this can only be hinted at here.

In the comparison with the ancient literatures, it is sufficient to say, as we have before observed, that the English has utilized them all. It is in part built upon them. It has absorbed whatever is vital in every one of them. If they were extinguished to-day in their original forms, every idea they contain which is vital to mental culture could be reproduced from the English literature alone. Dr. Johnson said, that, in his day, almost the whole bulk of human thought and learning could be expressed in a vocabulary drawn from the writings of Bacon, Raleigh, and Shakspeare. It is more strictly true that not a thought which is of any value to the present or the future of civilization can be found, in either of the three great literatures which represent the ancient development of mind, which is not extant in English libraries. Consequently no man can thoroughly master the English literature without receiving unconsciously into his own culture the substantial literary life of Palestine, Greece, and Rome.

Large account may fairly be made of this fact in the case which is prominently before us, of a man whose life is given to an arduous profession, and who, therefore, can find little time or mental force for the study

of the ancient classics.   Let him master the classics
of his own vernacular, and he is breathing an atmosphere made up, in part, of the best Hebrew and Greek
and Roman models all the while.

In the comparison of the English with the German
and French literatures, it is sufficient, so far as the point
of relative maturity is concerned, to note the fact that
the English is much the oldest of the three, and yet is
growing abreast with its rivals.   So far back as when
Chaucer, Spenser, Shakspeare, Milton, Hooker, and
Jeremy Taylor had all appeared, the French literature
was barely beginning.   De Quincey says, that, in the
time of Corneille, he was the only French living author
of general credit, and Montaigne the only deceased
author of equal eminence.   The English had an immense bulk of literature long before that, which has
lived to our day.   As to German literature, at that
time it was almost a cipher.   The English literature is
by far the most mature of those of modern growth, in
that it has the longest historical development, and is yet
thriving.   It gives no signs of decadent taste.

Still further: the English is the nearest approach the
world has seen to a popular literature.   Strictly speaking, there is no popular literature in existence; but
ours is an approximation to it to an extent which is
not true of any other which has existed since the time
of the old Greek drama.   Created as it has been
under the influence of free institutions, it is a nearer
approach to the masses of the people than any other
of modern times.   A mind formed under its sway has
less to acquire from other sources in order to fit it for
leadership of the masses of men than if formed under
any foreign culture whatever.

The spirit of the French literature, in this respect, was expressed in the sentiment of Voltaire, that the people should be amused, and have bread, but should never be tempted to reason; for, "if the people became philosophers, all would go to destruction." The literary mind of France, till a recent date, has had no faith in the people. Moreover, so far as French authors do address themselves to the popular mind, it is chiefly to the Parisian mind; and they publish much which is vicious both in morals and in taste. The chief representative of popular literature in France is the French novel, the most corrupt of all modern fiction. It seldom deserves a place in a popular library.

In Germany we find a similar gulf between the people and the national literature. I am unable to say what changes may be taking place there in this respect; but, if I am rightly informed, there is scarcely another body of men living, of equal numbers and intelligence, comprising so many masters of solid learning, who are so far removed from the masses of the people as the scholarly men of Germany. German taste in literature seeks the clouds. My attention has been called to the fact, that, so far as German books are addressed to the popular mind, they are aimed at a lower grade of intellect than the same class of books in this country. They assume that the people are nearer childhood in their tastes. The paternal idea which pervades so largely the German theory of government is prominent in German books for the people.

This involves no disparagement of the German literature in other relations. Palliations of the existing state of things are found in the political distractions of Germany for the last half-century. German govern-

ments have virtually said to German scholars, "Think
and print for yourselves and among yourselves. Do not
set the people to thinking." Consequently, as related
to the English, the German literature is inferior in those
elements which go to make a thinking commonalty.
The English has more of the popular mind and heart
expressed in it, and in forms which can reach and
inspire the popular mind and heart. It assumes the
existence among the people of a more manly mind and
a broader range of thinking. It has more of those
universal ideas which appeal to human nature as such
and in its maturity of development, and which are
seconded by the large common sense of mankind.

Consequently, a mind in whose culture English
thought and taste predominate will, other things being
equal, have a larger capacity of influence over the
popular mind than one in whose growth the German
literature is ascendant. It will have less of the contraction of an exclusively scholastic discipline.

Finally, the English literature contains a rich department devoted to the several forms of persuasive speech.
Eloquence proper is more largely represented in the
English language than in any other in all history. The
forensic and deliberative eloquence of England has contributed standards to libraries which have almost no
counterpart, and can have none, in any other living
language. The senate and the bar on the continent
of Europe have till recently been almost nonentities for
any purpose of oratorical culture. The restriction of
free speech there has doomed the Continental libraries
to sterility in both these departments which are so
essential to the culture of a public man in America.

The strictly professional literature of the pulpit also is

largely represented in our native tongue. De Quincey, by a refreshing departure from his usual contempt for the clergy, admits that the living pulpit of England is uttering a vast amount of unpublished literature every Sunday. The English language has a large contribution from the pulpit of the past also already among its published standards. In the richness of this department it stands unrivaled. The ancient classics contain no word for such a thing as a pulpit. Preaching was an undiscovered art when Plato taught and when Homer sung. Aristotle's rhetoric would be proof, if there were no other, that he never heard a sermon. The vocabulary of Plato and Homer can not express all the ideas which are predominant in Christian preaching.

The French and the German pulpits bear no comparison with the English. They contain no single models which equal Barrow and South and Taylor and Robert Hall. Still less do they contain any such variety as is found in the history of English preaching. The French ideal of the pulpit is too theatrical for profound and long-lived influence. The Germans can hardly be said to have an ideal of it which reaches up to the German ideal of learning. In the German view the pulpit is beneath scholarly criticism. Tholuck, Krummacher, Nitzsch, Schleiermacher, and Steinmeyer are fair representatives of the first rank of German preachers in the last half-century. Not one of them would be placed by an intelligent critic by the side of American preachers of the corresponding rank.

The English language, on the contrary, overflows with the literature of the pulpit. It abounds in material which secular critics admit to *be* literature. This is a concession which secular criticism makes with difficulty. But the fact compels it. We have standards which were created by the pulpit, to which scholars in all departments of thought turn, as among the choicest productions of the English mind. The bearing of this opulence of our literature in the forms of persuasive speech upon the claims of it on the study of a preacher is obvious.

It is not that the ancient or the foreign literatures should be ignored, or estimated lightly, but that they should be subordinated. We should go to them from an English culture, and come back from them to an English culture. Enlarge that culture, expand it, deepen it, elevate it, but let it in the end be English, pervaded by English tastes, controlled by English good sense, and supported by sympathy with English models.

LECTURE XII.

THE PLACE OF AMERICAN LITERATURE IN THE STUDIES OF A PASTOR.

(5) THE views thus far advanced suggest a principle in the selection of authors, by which the principles already named should be modified. It is, that, in our estimate of authors, the just claims of American literature should be recognized. The chief value of this suggestion is felt not so much in the practical selection of books as in the spirit in which a pastor's studies are conducted. Respect for the national mind of one's own country and for contemporaneous authorship is a prime factor in the preparation of a man to minister to his own countrymen. The same law by which a preacher's culture is impaired for professional service by an excessive fondness for the ancient rather than the modern, or the distant above the near, in literary development, holds good respecting a similar preference of the foreign to the national literature.

It must be conceded that one of the dangers to the reading of an American pastor is that he will read disproportionately American books. Our proximity to them, the ease with which they can be obtained, and the fulsome style of criticism in which American periodicals indulge, expose us to the peril of wasting our mental force on works of ephemeral authority. An American library needs frequent weeding to rid it of books which do not wear well in the judgment of mature scholarship. One of the most eminent of our American scholars, at the time of his decease, had hundreds of such discarded volumes in his attic-chambers, where he had hidden them for years, that his eye might not be wearied by the sight of them, and, perhaps, that his vanity might not be wounded by the remembrance of his folly in purchasing them. During the civil war, when manufacturers gave large prices for waste paper, many libraries were reduced in bulk, but improved in quality, by the sale of American books to peddlers.

Still, in this as in more important things, it is a protection against the extreme to see and to trust the mean. The principle is a sound one, that an American scholar should recognize the growth of American mind. In books, as in affairs, that growth demands a scholarly respect. The literature of one's country does not deserve the pre-eminence which belongs to that of one's vernacular. The growth of a language is a more profound development of mind than the peopling of a continent, or the organization of a republic. But there is a literary justice which a preacher should not withhold from the literature of his country in his adjustment of proportions in his own reading. He can not do it without peril to the adaptations of his own culture to professional service.

Our American literature, be it observed, then, claims our recognition on three grounds. One is that of its intrinsic merits in some departments. In *poetry* it must in candor be admitted that we have nothing yet to show which criticism places by the side of the great poets of England. The American is not yet a poetic temperament. Our civilization has not yet reached the poetic stage of its development. Our national history is not old enough to create for itself the poetic enthusiasm. We have, also, in the past of the English mind, so radiant a constellation of poets, that the taste of our own scholars delights in them without attempting to emulate their luster. "Like thee I will not build; better I can not," said Michael Angelo of the dome of Santa Maria in Florence. Such may be the instinct of the American imagination in visiting the "Poets' Corner" of Westminster Abbey.

Whatever be the cause of the phenomenon, we owe it to the integrity of our critical judgment to acknowledge the fact that our literature is not eminent in this department of production. We are a young nation. We have been living poems. Many events in our history are grand themes for poetic story. Says a writer in "The Edinburgh Review," "There is a poetry of the past, of the mountains, the seas, the stars; but a great city seen aright is tenfold more poetical than them all." A Pacific railroad is a poem in act. The State of Massachusetts is a poem. Old Governor Winthrop is a hero beyond Greek or Roman fame. The colonization of Kansas is splendid material for a great epic: so is the war of the rebellion. Magnificent materials have we in our history for poetry which shall by and by rival Wordsworth's sonnets, and Shakspeare's historical dramas. They will give birth to great poems when age has gathered around them the imaginative reverence of scholars. As Carlyle says of "The Mayflower," "Were we of open sense, as the Greeks were, we had found a poem here, one of Nature's own, such as she writes in broad facts over great continents."

In several other departments, however, we have a literature already of which we need not be ashamed. In the department of history America is represented by authors whom European criticism does not hesitate to rank by the side of the great historians of England. Baron Alexander Humboldt thought that there was not in existence a finer specimen of historic writing than Prescott's " Ferdinand and Isabella." In the department of the *essay* we have writers representing in monographs nearly all the varieties of English style as perfectly as writers of the same class in Great Britain.

In *prose-fiction* Walter Scott and Charles Dickens are the only names which deserve to precede that of Cooper. Mrs. Stowe must be credited with having produced a romance which has had a larger circulation, in more numerous languages, than any other book ever published, except the Bible. In *forensic and parliamentary eloquence* the names of Webster, Clay, Calhoun, Sumner, do not suffer by the side of Burke, Pitt, Fox, Brougham. In the department of *demonstrative eloquence* I do not know the name in the annals of any living nation which should stand before that of Edward Everett. For that style of eloquence, Everett's orations are well-nigh perfect.

In the *literature of the pulpit* there certainly are names, of the living and the dead, which must be ranked as equals, at least, of the most powerful preachers of England. In no country in the world has the pulpit proved its power by its effects more conspicuously than in ours. The fear sometimes expressed of the decline of the American pulpit is not entirely unwarranted; yet, all things considered, the evidences of decline are offset by evidences of improvement. Our pulpit has a fluctuating history; but on the whole it has never had a more docile, and at the same time intelligent, hearing than it has to-day. The decline of the pulpit in the sense so much boasted of by skeptical critics is disproved by the very impunity with which those critics proclaim their sentiments. They would be at the whipping-post, and their books burnt by the hangman, if the American pulpit had not assisted by its reasoning habits to enlighten and liberalize the popular faith. On the ground, therefore, of its intrinsic merits, American literature deserves to be recognized in our estimate of the resources of our professional discipline.

It deserves recognition, also, as an offshoot of the literature of England. This is at present its relative position. As we have no American language, neither have we an American literature, which is not a graft upon the English stock. Their literature is ours, and ours is theirs. In this respect our literature partakes of the same character with that of nearly all the institutions which lie deepest in our civilization. Those institutions are essentially English. Our religion, our jurisprudence, our educational policy, our periodical press, our tendencies in philosophy, in a word the make of American mind in all its great expressions of itself, are English at bottom. They are not German; they are not French; they are not derivatives from the ancient republics: they are English. No man understands the American mind who fails to appreciate this, or who does not act upon it in his public life.

Public speakers among us fail to reach the popular

heart, if their own culture is tinged with foreign and
ancient literatures to such extent as to make those
obvious in public speech. The chief defect in senator
Sumner's speeches was the excessive freedom with
which he indulged in quotations from the ancient
classics, and allusion to the ancient mythology. He
was at home in English literature and history. He was
master of a solid English style. For durability and
richness of material, no other speeches in the Senate,
since Mr. Webster's day, were equal to his. Yet he did
not seize and hold the popular mind. Even the United-
States Senate sometimes wearied of him. This was in
part because of the artificialness created by his freedom
in the use of the learning he had derived from the
dead languages. In the real affairs of life, and specially
in the government of great nations, men demand an
intensity, and a homeliness of aim at present realities,
which forbid a very free and very obvious use of
foreign and ancient lore. It chills their sympathies
to quote from an author who has been two thousand
years in his grave. Therefore it weakens a speaker's
grasp of the popular mind.

It is a mystery to many that the English Parliament
should tolerate so much as they do of that which
seems like pedantic use of the Latin, and, to some extent, of the Greek languages in parliamentary debates.
The English House of Commons is said to be the most
prosaic body of men living. Any thing like " fine writing " they put down with their inimitable " Hear,
hear ! " in a tone of derision which a young speaker
never ventures to encounter but once. The style of
their debates is almost wholly conversational. The
prime qualities which command their hearing, if not

their votes, are good sense in talking to the point, and stopping at the end. Yet some of their most eminent debaters interlard their speeches with classic quotations to an extent which seems inconsistent with the parliamentary taste as evinced in other things.

I have never till recently met with a satisfactory explanation of the apparent anomaly. But probably the truth is this, that the great majority of those quotations are relics of the school-days of the members of Parliament. They are almost all of them graduates of the two universities. In the universities, classical study is the central discipline. It overshadows every thing else. It takes largely the form of committing to memory favorite passages from Greek and Latin authors, and imitating their versification. A certain routine of such passages becomes as familiar as the English alphabet to the graduates of Oxford and Cambridge. To a great extent, they all know by heart the same extracts, and know the English of them. When, therefore, twenty years after graduation, they meet in Parliament, and harangue each other, an apt recitation from one of the old text-books of the university, given with the proper intonation and prosody, is instantly recognized and understood by four-fifths of the audience. It comes to them also with the golden associations of their youth. Hence the applause with which such a quotation, if apt, is often received. More than once a ministry has been unseated by the irresistible power of a piece of sarcasm clothed in the words of Juvenal or Cicero.

This explanation, which I have from a trustworthy source, is plausible, to say the least. But it is obvious that an American senator who should imitate in that respect an English leader in the House of Commons would have no such prepossessions in his audience to protect him from the charge of pedantry. In this country, audiences scarcely tolerate a Greek or Roman tinge in the style of public speech. But they bear any thing belonging to our vernacular. With all our hereditary antipathy to English aristocracy, and our rivalship with English prestige, we are still English at heart. We feel in every throb our English origin. We confess our kinship to English modes of thought. We love the old mother-country. We can not help this till we cease to *think* in the mother-tongue.

American literature has furthermore a special claim upon the clergy, in the fact that the theological thinking of this country has been to a certain extent original. In no part of the world in modern times has theological discussion been more vigorous, or more unique in its character. Some of the ablest minds of the last century spent their lives in it. It has also commanded a respect among the laity which it has not received in England or in Continental Europe. Men who in Europe would have been foremost as philosophers and states-men have here been found among our theologians. The ablest contributions of this country to mental philosophy have been made at the instance of theology, and chiefly in direct connection with theology.

The Puritan type of theological thinking in this country, even as compared with the corresponding type in England and in Holland, was largely original. The inquiry is often made, by those who are not familiar with the theological history of New England, whether or not it has developed any thing new in theological science. The controversy between the "Old School" and the "New School" in the religious thought of this country has retired into the shade in consequence of the re-union of the Presbyterian Church. It has given place to a totally different class of discussions. It is worthy of consideration, therefore, in a brief *excursus* from the main theme before us.

Is the orthodox theology of New England an advance upon that of the older confessions? A glance at the character of the early clergy of New England will go far to answer this inquiry. They were remarkably self-reliant men, made such by the force of their origin and condition. They wore no man's livery. They were not predisposed to recognize uninspired authorities in matters of religious faith. It is impossible to read the history of the four New-England Colonies, before their separation from Great Britain, without observing, that, from the very landing at Plymouth, the idea of independence had possession of the colonial mind. In government, in religion, in social civilization, our fathers scented subjection to human authority a great way off. Probably the world has never seen a more intense development of individualism.

In religion, especially, the New-England mind was a law to itself. In religious affairs they saw the extreme of peril to all men's liberties, and their vigilance against authority was sleepless accordingly. It was with difficulty that they recognized the necessity even of the fellowship of churches. A scheme for a "consociation" of churches, which was laid before the Massachusetts Legislature in 1662, never got further than the order that it be printed "for the consideration of the people." The people have had it in safe "considera-

tion " ever since. Independence was in the air. It
pervaded every important subject of colonial interest.
It was the last thought of a true Pilgrim when he
retired to rest at night, and the first that sprang to the
birth in his mind in the morning. No body of men
were ever more faithful illustrations of that "eternal
vigilance " which is " the price of liberty " than the
people of these Colonies.

This feature in the make of the New-England Puritans has given character, down to this day, to the whole
drift of New-England theology. They knew no right
more sacred, and no duty more imperative, than that
of private judgment. At the same time they did not
have the means of forming their theology as a deriva-
tive from other standards than the Bible. They had
not access to large libraries. They were isolated from
frequent correspondence with the old countries. There
was no such intimacy of correspondence between the
American clergy and their Scotch and English brethren
as that which fed the English Reformation from the
fountains of the Dutch and Genevan schools. No such
volume, for instance, as the "Zurich Letters," grew out
of the relations of the colonial ministry of this country,
or their immediate successors, to their brethren in Great
Britain. They had no ecclesiastical ties binding them
as a body to authorities and standards on the other side
of the Atlantic. If they acknowledged the standards
of the European churches, they did so feeling at entire
liberty to modify them, or to attach to their formulæ
an interpretation of their own.

In New England, as matter of fact, the right and
the duty of private judgment were a right and a duty
exercised. Separate creeds for separate churches were

the rule. Each church changed established formulæ at its own pleasure. Even individuals, by the ancient usage of New England, were at liberty to frame their own creeds in their own language ; and their fitness to be admitted to the communion of the church was judged of, so far as doctrinal tests were concerned, by the soundness or the unsoundness of such private creeds. Originality in theological literature was the necessary outcome from the conditions of colonial life here from the very first. If this country was to have any theological thinking at all, it was a foregone conclusion that it must be original. It was predestined to be home-made, like the rye bread upon their tables and the homespun cloth in their looms.

Moreover, the early theologians of America were preachers. Many of them were eminent preachers. Their theology has come down to us largely in the form of sermons. They constructed their theology for the pulpit. It was suggested to them by the demands of the pulpit rather than by the demands of the school as represented in any current system of philosophy. No other type of theology since apostolic days has been so purely the product of the pulpit, aimed at the objects of the pulpit, breathing the spirit of the pulpit, and actually preached in the pulpit, as the theology of New England.

In this respect of its homiletic origin, the New-England theology was widely diverse from the patristic and mediæval confessions. Those were largely the product of the schools. They grew out of the abstract relations of philosophy to a revealed faith. They were in some degree subservient to the philosophies of the respective ages in which they crystallized into creeds. The Puritan theology, on the contrary, and specially that type of it which grew up in New England, was the theology of the pulpit. The men who framed it were preachers, and, either consciously or unconsciously, they aimed to produce a theology which should preach well. The pulpit was their throne, not the school, not the chair of philosophy, not that of ecclesiastical dominion.

Theirs was a theology, also, which was molded by powerful religious awakenings. These, in the peculiarities of their development, were intensely American. As time passed away, they became almost an idiosyncrasy of American religious life. Not in their ultimate spirit, but in many of their external phenomena, they were American. So peculiar were they in some respects to this country, that for a long time they have been regarded in Great Britain and in Germany as the result of some peculiar diathesis of American temperament. Under the dominant influence of religious awakenings, the theology of New England has grown up to its maturity.

All these facts in the history of our theological literature tended to give it originality. It is the work of men who were, by the force of circumstances without and of tendencies within, thrown back upon their own resources. They recommenced theological inquiry *de novo*. They laid new foundations, and erected new structures. For good or for evil, such was the fact. We have no occasion to blink it, and no right to deny it. We unconsciously falsify history, if we try to secure for the New-England theology the prestige of unswerving conformity to the more ancient standards by conceiving of it as a mere reproduction of them. It claimed to be, and it was, an advance upon them. In the direction of truth or of error, according to the prepossessions of the looker-on, it was a *progress*. Its authors claimed for it the title of an improvement in theology as a human science. They called it Calvinism, but Calvinism *improved*. In my judgment, they committed a mistake in theologic policy in clinging so pertinaciously to the name of Calvin. The system they framed was *not* Calvinism, as Calvin taught and preached. They started with the assumption that theology is an improvable science, and they ended with the claim that they had improved it. They claimed thus to have evolved, more completely and symmetrically than Calvin had done, the spirit of the Scriptures, and to have made the scriptural faith appear more reasonable, and more accordant with the necessary beliefs of the human mind.

Yet this fact has been almost wholly ignored by the opponents of the popular theology. Scarcely a trace of its recognition can be found in the writings of Dr. Channing. He almost invariably aimed the shafts of his argument and invective at the theology of Calvin, not at that of his own contemporaries. The same is true of the whole history of that side of the debate which he represented down to our day.

Specially is the originality of New-England theology true of it, as represented in a succession of theologians extending over nearly a century and a half backward from our own times. The leading theologians of New England during this period — beginning with the elder Edwards, and ending with one still living — have done more, in the way of original thinking, for the advance of strictly theological science, than any other equal number of men, within an equal space of time, since Augustine's day.

The theological work of the reformers, as I understand it, was mainly the recovery of a lost theology : that of this *catena* of American theologians has been the establishment of an advanced theology. They have been originators in a sense which can not properly be affirmed•of the great bulk of their contemporaries in this country or in Europe. We do an injustice which history will eventually undo, if we try to throw a suspension-bridge over their heads, and to attach our own work to that of the theologians who preceded them, as if nothing new in theological thinking had been done in the interval. They certainly were originators, if any man ever was. As such they will stand in the final version of theological history. If opprobrium is attached to the fact, New England must bear that; if dignity, she is entitled to this.

The German theologians recognize the same thing whenever they inform themselves of the history of American theological thought. As a rule, I am told, they know very little of it. A solid and useful work remains yet to be done by some American student in Germany, to publish in the German language a history of the American development of theological opinion. But, so far as our most eminent theologians of the last century and a half are known at all in Germany, German scholars detect in them an original vein of thought. The same is true of English scholars. When such a man as Frederick Robertson reads President Edwards, he finds in him the germs, as he says, of an original style of thinking. It strikes him not as a reproduction, but as a discovery.

Resuming the line of suggestion from which we have deviated, let the fact be noted, that this originality of our theology furnishes a peculiar ground of claim for American literature upon the studies of a preacher. You do not know the full development of theological science, if you study it only in the older European standards. The American development, and specially that of New England, as being the earliest and the most adventurous and the most unique, is needed to fill out the programme of the course which theology has actually taken in the history of opinion.

LECTURE XIII.

BEARING OF PROFESSIONAL PURSUITS ON A PASTOR'S
STUDIES. — BREADTH OF RANGE IN SELECTION OF
BOOKS.

(6) SOME of the remarks already made suggest another principle of selection in pastoral studies. It is
that the true ideal of a pastor's reading must be regulated in part by his professional duties; in how great
part, the good sense of each must decide. The principle is vital, that reading for the direct purpose of
homiletic use is a necessity, and as such should be
respected. It not only is not unscholarly, but a pastor's scholarship is radically defective, without it, and
this for two reasons.

One is the necessity of such study to the dignity of
other literary pursuits. That is a degrading definition
of literature which excludes from it professional studies.
We create effeminate conceptions of it when we isolate
it from the tug of real life. It becomes the accomplishment of an idle character, if you limit it to the
amusement of idle hours.

Professor Henry Reed notices the popular use of the
phrase *belles-lettres* as indicating the tendency of a
certain class of minds to this degrading notion. That
phrase was the invention of an effeminate taste, which
sought to hide its own feebleness under the guise of a

foreign tongue. Coleridge remarks it as one of the
disastrous revolutions of England, that "literature fell
away from the professions." For the earnestness, and
therefore for the dignity, of our literary pursuits, we
need to associate them with some regular and necessary
avocation in life. The necessity of labor for a living
is not a hinderance, but a help, to the depth of our
scholarly life. Every important vocation in life has
some literature of its own: at least, it has a history
which a man is the wiser for knowing. The clerical
profession has a literature which no clergyman can
afford not to know.

A second reason for this principle of selection is its
obvious necessity to professional success. There are
two kinds of interest in the clerical office. One is the
direct interest in its objects; the other, interest in *it*
as a profession. Providence has benevolently arranged,
for our assistance in life's labors, that we are so made
as to enjoy, not only the results, but the process to
results. Pleasure is imparted, not only at the end, but
on the way to the end. This professional joy is as
legitimate to a clergyman as to a lawyer.

Not that it is the highest motive to clerical fidelity,
but it is an innocent and a stimulating motive. The
highest success is never gained without it. The possession of it, however, leads necessarily to study of
professional literature. This is as it should be. Our
tastes in reading ought to be tinged with the peculiarities of our profession to a sufficient extent to make
them tributary to it. The two may blend, so that the
one shall never be a drudgery, and the other never
effeminate.

(7) Our choice of authors should cover as large a

range of literature as can be read in a scholarly way.
This as a theory seems self-evident; yet in practice it
is at this point that the hopelessness of the scholarly
life to a pastor appears most invincible. Yet, be it
ever so limited in its practical application, the recognition of the principle is invaluable to a pastor's scholarly spirit.

Observe, in confirmation of this, the uselessness of
variety, if gained at the expense of scholarship, in
reading. Adults in years are often juvenile in culture.
This juvenile period is characterized by three things, —
reading is amusement, the choice of authors is for-
tuitous, and opinions about authors are either an echo
of their reputation, or a wilful contradiction of it. No
profound personal sympathy with authors is yet created,
and no antipathies for which scholarly reasons can be
given. Our collegiate curriculum does not commonly
advance a student much beyond this juvenile period
of culture, unless he is above the average age of collegians, and has read more than they commonly read.

In this juvenile period the first peril encountered is
that of reading too much and too variously. We are
in danger of skimming the surface of every thing that
falls in our way, without penetrating any thing. One
very soon wearies of such reading, if it is directed to
any thing which deserves to be called earnest literature.
To read such literature with any pleasure we must be
ourselves in earnest; and to be in earnest in it we
must penetrate it in spots. The mind, otherwise, is
like a bird always on the wing. This is not scholarly
reading. No man will pursue it long in the use of
serious literature, unless he falls into an affectation
of scholarly tastes.

A second peril to which the juvenile period of culture is exposed is that of literary affectation. Did you never see a freshman in college, in a fit of literary eagerness, carrying to his room a huge folio in Latin, or a set of the Greek classics, under the hallucination that scholarly culture must have some such unknown and unknowable beginning in order to *be* scholarly? Profuse and promiscuous reading often results from such affectation of literary aims.

One of the humiliating confessions which we have to make for educated men is, that there is not a little of affected taste among them. This is of so great importance to a youthful scholar, that it demands notice by an *excursus* from the line of the present discussion. You will discover, as you extend the range of your reading, that there is a class of authors who at first awe you by their prodigious learning, by their glib use of the technical dialect of scholarship, and by their oracular opinions. But they are among the authors whom you most quickly outgrow. The conviction soon forces itself upon you that they are pretentious. Their dialect is not necessitated by their thinking: their reading has been discursive, not penetrative, and their productions are too heavily indebted to their common-place books. You find that other authors, less voluminous, with a less gaudy parade of the tackling of science, and with a more simple style, move you more profoundly, and their influence lives longer in your mental growth.

Religion and religious men suffer often, at the hands of the men of books, from the charge of cant. The charge is too often true. But it is my firm belief, that among any number of plain Christian men and women chosen at random, there will be found less of that morbid affection than can be found among an equal number of literary and scientific authors and literary amateurs chosen at random. What is cant in religion? It is nothing but affectation of unreal virtue; not conscious hypocrisy, but unconscious self-deceit. As a mental phenomenon it is not confined to religion. The same thing essentially vitiates manners in society. It is witnessed in the enthusiasm of travelers, in the raptures of connoisseurs of art, in the patriotism of politicians, and in the conscientiousness of obstinate minorities. It infects as well the aspirations of authorship and the early enthusiasm of readers. It is a ubiquitous infirmity of human nature. Indeed, do we not distrust ourselves more in this respect, the more we know of ourselves? But a fragment of our experience, probably, is absolutely free from affected virtue. That fragment is commonly purified of this taint by the discipline of emergencies. Yet even death does not press it out of some natures. They die as they have lived, deceivers and deceived, or, to speak more exactly, deceived, and therefore deceivers. Authors who make the most showy parade of mental integrity are often guilty of some glaring sign of its opposite. Carlyle has been the severest censor of the English public for its insincerity in every thing; yet Carlyle's style in the very utterance of his invectives is one of the most disingenuous specimens of quackery in modern authorship.

It is no marvelous thing, then, if we find cant in books in which we least expect it. Critics who have an honest culture complain of it in all the great literatures of our day. Addison complained of it in his

contemporaries. It was the butt of Dr. Johnson's
sarcasm ; yet the old elephant was not free from it
himself when he tried to dance. Menzel and Niebuhr
stigmatize it in the German literature. Guizot has
scorned it in one department of the French literature.
Niebuhr flatly charges it upon some of his literary contemporaries, that whole pages of references to authorities were copied from others, a few here and a few
there, with no attempt at verification, but purely to
impose on the reader by a parade of extensive reading.
Such is the jugglery of scholarship.

I could name two celebrated writers of this country
who belong to the class of literary jugglers. In one
case, if he ever read his footnotes in their original
connections, he would have found some of them to be
hostile, and some of them irrelevant, to his own positions. As I do not suppose him to have been consciously a knave, the most charitable construction of
his error is that he borrowed them, and imposed them
on his readers, trusting to their ignorance as he had
to his own. In the other case, a theological controver-
sialist was hard pressed by an opponent more learned
than himself. He "read up," as we call it, for the exi-
gency, and gave to the public a rejoinder in which were
heaped together mediæval names which his readers had
never heard of, and he probably had not heard of till
then. As authorities, some of them were worth little
more than the London "Punch." His opponent saw
through the trick at a glance, and never answered what
he doubtless deemed an affectation which was beneath
him. That is a ruse which is never perpetrated without being discovered by somebody.

Returning, now, from the excursion we have taken

from the point in hand, let us observe, that, if grave and
mature authorship is capable of such affectations, the
taste of youthful readers, till it is chastened by breadth
of culture, may be at least in equal peril. We need,
therefore, to guard ourselves against extent of reading
which would be gained at the expense of scholarly
reading. Variety is not scholarly, if it is not so thorough as to result in symmetrical culture, so far as it
goes. It is unscholarly, for instance, ever to read a
book for the sake of talking of it, or to be able to
say that one has read it, or to be able to quote from it
in one's own production.

The real culture of a man shows itself in his original
thinking, not in that which he prates about, and puts
on parade. Give us your thought, man, your thought!
That is the proof to us of what you have *lived* in your
own mental being. That tells us what you are. Who
cares for any thing else you have to give? Sly hints
of prodigality in the use of books go for nothing. Do
not be awed by them when you encounter them in the
authors you read. You can provide all such pabulum
for yourself, and then you will know what it is worth.
Do not allow an author to impose it upon you for any
higher worth than it would have if it came from your
own pen.

A noteworthy fact in this connection is, that one's
reading, and one's use of reading in one's own productions, will act and re-act upon each other. What the
one is, the other is apt to be. Therefore, freedom from
affectation in your use of books in sermons will tend
to secure the same freedom in the reading of books.
Make no display of learning or of varied culture. The
loopholes through which a hearer can look into your

library should be made as few as possible in your preaching. A thorough-bred traveler does not boast of his travels. He is mindful of Lord Chesterfield's advice to his son, not to begin every fragment of his conversation with, "When I was in Japan." So a genuine scholar does not pry open the crevices through which the extent of his reading can be seen.

A young man has gained one of the prime elements of scholarship, when he has learned the worth of artlessness in his literary dealings with himself. Play no tricks upon yourself. Do not be hoodwinked into an imitation of the tricks of authors. Be honest in your secret literary habits. Keep yourself always on the safe side of plagiarism in your sermons. Be assured that you *will* plagiarize unconsciously quite as much as is consistent with the rights of authorship. As a specimen of the care which should be practiced in this respect, if you quote in your sermon, see to it that you put the signs of quotation into your delivery as well as into your manuscript. In a word, be yourself in literature as in religion. Let your reading be, and appear to be, in your use of it, the symbol of a real life. There is such a thing as intellectual integrity. The price of it is above rubies. If you will plan your reading, and use it with this kind of truthfulness to yourself, the range of your reading and the symmetry of your culture will be exponents of each other. The variety of your reading will grow to meet the wants of your culture. Beyond that, it is of no imaginable use to you or to others.

But, while protection against affectation of literary culture is the first need of a youthful writer, there is, on the other hand, an obvious value in that variety of study which is a genuine index of symmetry. Let the

fact be observed, therefore, that all the excellences of
literature are not to be found in any narrow group of
writers. Every great mind is great by virtue of some
sort of individuality. That individuality represents a
power. But no mind represents all such individualities. The universal genius is a fiction : it can be real-
ized only in a mind of infinite capacities. We speak
of Shakspeare as if he were such a genius ; but it is
hyperbole. If he is the first of poets for his excellences,
he is the first, also, for his faults. Intensity in authorship generally exhibits itself, in part, by violations of
taste.

Only by varied reading, therefore, can we combine
in our own tastes any very wide range of excellences.
We must achieve our object as a bee gathers honey.
Apiarists tell us that no two honeycombs have precisely the same flavor. A bee can not concoct the most
delicate honey from any one species of flora. Diversities of the saccharine element must be distilled from
species which are opposites, some of which are even
antidotes to each other. So the finest culture is the
transfusion of the greatest breadth of literature. Opposites and antidotes in thought may blend in mental
character, and produce a flavor which no other com-
pounds can imitate.

The principle involved here is not impaired in value
by any degree of richness which one may find in a few
favorite authors. There is a virtue in variety for the
sake of variety. The illustrious Literary Club, to
which Dr. Johnson belonged, included, besides him,
Sir Joshua Reynolds and Edmund Burke, the latter
the most profound thinker of the age. But Goldsmith
expressed a practical want, even in the society of such

men, when he advocated the enlargement of the club
by the introduction of new members, "because," he
said, "the original members had traveled over each
other's minds so often and so thoroughly." So it is
with our culture from books, even the wisest and most
quickening. We appropriate from them in time all
that our affinities can appropriate. We must have
fresh food to keep the mind new and progressive in its
tastes.

Further: a certain variety of knowledge is necessary
to the perfection of any one species of knowledge.
An old book often receives a new power to enlighten
or to quicken us from our perusal of a new one. Still
more is diversity of mental character necessary to perfection in any one quality. Culture is sensitively sympathetic: it is a compound of sympathies. Diseased
culture in one respect generates disease in other respects. Amaurosis in one eye may cause the other eye
to weep itself blind: so a contracted culture is, for that
reason, a shallow one. Of two authors, for instance,
we appreciate one the better for appreciating the other
justly. Of two departments of a library, we penetrate
the one the more profoundly for every glimpse of
insight which we obtain into the other. Of two national literatures, we have a mastery of the one in some
degree proportionate to our conquest of the other. In
all nature every thing helps every other thing. In the
ultimate products of mind there are no rival literatures nor antagonist departments: they are mutual
auxiliaries. The history of human thought is a history
of great alliances. Breadth of reading, therefore, pro-
motes depth of descent in any one spot.

Again: it is a calamity to a public speaker to subject

his culture to the exclusive influence of any one author, or group of authors. Mental servitude often follows extravagant enthusiasm for one writer, or for the writers of one school. Individuality of character, then, is sacrificed. Not merely is independence of opinion lost: indeed, that may not be sacrificed perceptibly, and, because it is not, the student may imagine that his mental freedom as a whole is unimpaired. Not so: his culture is literally *sub-jected*. It lies under the hoof of a contracted authorship. Such a mind has no catholicity of taste. It reveres nothing which does not come within the vision of the few minds to whom it looks up as oracles.

Cicero tyrannized thus at one time over a class of Italian scholars. Erasmus describes, in a dialogue which he satirically calls " Ciceronianus," a man who for seven years read no book but Cicero. He had only Cicero's bust in his library, and sealed his letters with a seal engraved with Cicero's head. He had composed " three or four huge volumes, in which he had criticised every word of Cicero, every variation of every sense of every word, and every foot or cadence with which Cicero began or closed a sentence."

Dr. Johnson tyrannized over a class of educated minds in England. Even so robust a mind as that of Robert Hall confessed to having worked through a period of servitude to Johnson in his early discipline. Coleridge has more recently swayed another class of readers with an authority which no man should consciously submit to for an hour.

In the pulpit, Dr. Chalmers, for a time, was an autocrat over a large class of admirers. Few men have appeared in the modern pulpit whose faults and virtues have more frequently been copied entire. I do not say reproduced, but copied; for the spirit of a great mind is never reproduced in us till we have either lived through or overleaped a servile admiration of him, and become consciously independent. Soon after Chalmers published his "Astronomical Discourses," a swarm of little Chalmerians, if I may coin the word, appeared in the pulpits of Scotland and America. The pulpit of Scotland has not entirely recovered from that influence to this day.

Carlyle has given a similar lurch to a class of minds in our own literature. Twenty or thirty years ago American taste, as represented by a considerable group of writers, reeled under the blow of Carlyle's tyranny, from which it has never yet fully righted itself.

In this country one man is to-day exercising autocracy over a class of youthful writers and scholars. Scarcely a year passes in which I do not find evidences of this in manuscript sermons. It is difficult to convince a man by criticism of his subjection to a contemporary author. I often make such criticism when I know that it will be rejected now, but that the subject of it will surely see the truth of it eventually. This is true of the present sway of the author in question over a certain class of minds. Few things appear to me so sure in the future of American literature as that the educated mind of this country will outgrow its adulation of him and his works. His is a diseased mind, and the world is sure to find it out. Some of you will live to witness a change of literary opinion of him not unlike that which has overtaken the literary fame of Byron. In both cases you are safe in assuming the existence of distorted literary tastes from the distortion

of religious faith.   It was not possible for Byron to
be a true literary guide while his rebellion against religious restraint was what it was.   A worse than any
literary bondage inthralled him.   So of the author I
have in mind : pure as his private life is, it is impossible
for his intellect to be a great and true literary seer
so long as he hesitates whether or not to apply to the
being of God the personal pronoun.

Sometimes servitude to authors takes the form of
subjection to one school in philosophy.   Then a young
scholar trusts nothing, reveres nothing, knows nothing,
sees nothing candidly, which conflicts with the school in
which he has been tutored.   He looks at every thing
under the shadow of the school.   He apes the dialect
of the school.   The truths of common sense, which
other men can express in the language of common
sense, he puts into the formulæ of the school.   The
most simple elements of belief he must transmute in
the laboratory of the school.   Nothing seems literary
to his taste, nothing puts on the glamour of literary
associations, so as to excite his respect, till it has been
fused in the alembic of the school.

Such subservience to one or to few models of thought
is a sad folly, an enormous folly.   But one book in
the world deserves such submission of the intellect,
and that book never claims it in respect to literary
taste.   A young man should check the beginnings of
such a folly in his own consciousness.   An amateur in
the cultivation of orange-trees tells me that the fruitage
of the tree depends on the size of the box in which
you pack its roots when it is young.   Cramp them then,
and you can never make other than a dwarf of it.
Give them large room to expand, and the quality, as

well as abundance, of the fruit, will reward your fore-
thought. So it is with a young scholar's early tastes.
By an agile effort of good sense he can rid them of a
narrow prejudice when it is new. Later in life he can
only live it through at the expense of a great deal of
contraction of usefulness, and alloy of pleasure.

Some minds never do live through their self-subjec-
tion to a one-sided authorship. In the weaker class of
minds the effects of such a period of enslavement sink
deep, and become a second nature. They become as
inevitable and involuntary as the distinction between
the right and left hands, — a distinction which physi-
ologists now declare to be entirely unnecessary, if the
physical mechanism could only be started into volun-
tary use without it. It is said that our right-handed
habit of body has the effect, upon a man lost in a
forest, of insensibly twisting him around to the left, to
the extent of eventually moving in a circle, through
the mere instinct of the right side to take the lead
of the left, and that the circle, other things being
equal, will always be described in one way, — from right
to left. Such a monotonous circle does the life's culture of some men become, who are never emancipated
from a one-sided twist received in their early discipline.
They never learn to do even-handed justice, in their
literary judgments, to any broad fraternity of authors.
They never learn to enjoy any wide range of scholarship. They never become, therefore, men of generous
culture in their own development. They are always
lost in the forest, and always tramping in a spiral.
Ruskin says that a false taste may be known by its
fastidiousness. " It tests all things," he says, " by the
way *they* fit *it*." But a true taste, he contends, is

" reverent and unselfish," for ever learning, for ever
growing, and " testing itself by the way *it* fits *things*."
This is as true in literature as in art.

Let us, then, be jealous of the influence of schools
in any thing.   Be watchful of the power of favorite
authors over you.   Professor Reed says he has known
a man " late in life to lose the power of sound literary
judgment and enjoyment," through " bigotry in the
choice of books."   It seems, at the first sight, to be
an ungenerous caution to a young writer; but it is a
very necessary one.   Beware of your favorites in any
thing, — your favorite author, your favorite preacher,
your favorite instructor, the head of your sect, the
originator of your school in philosophy, the leading
expounder of your type of theology, the representative
man in your *beau ideal* of culture.   Stand off, and
measure them all.   Wait a while : let your judgment
of them take years in the forming.   Receive trustfully
and gratefully whatever they give you which satisfies
the varied cravings of your nature, and helps your
culture to an even balance, but hold in suspense for
a time any influence from them which surfeits some
tastes, and leaves others to starve.

There must come, in the lives of us all, a period at
which we revise our early enthusiasms, and smile sadly
at some of them.   A blessing to us are those authors
and those men, whom, after that ripening period, we
find that we have not *outlived*.   The blessing will be
proportionate to their number and to the range of
culture which they represent.

LECTURE XIV.

BREADTH OF RANGE IN PASTORAL STUDY, CONTINUED. — THE STUDY OF LIVING SPEAKERS.

BEFORE we leave the topic of breadth of range in our studies, an *excursus* deserves a brief consideration, upon the fact that the clergy are under peculiar temptations to narrow discipline. Not all is true which is often affirmed of the literary bigotry of the ministry. Yet the fact of the peril is a reality.

The intellectual intensity of the clerical profession is one source of the peril. It demands intense concentration of mind. Like other men of sense, the clergy must be about their business. They must work at it in dead earnest. Reading, therefore, is at the best but an appendage to professional duty. A very large portion of a pastor's waking hours must be given to mental production, not to accumulation, not to the culture which books give. The temptation follows inevitably to be content with a contracted range of reading; if not with professional reading alone, with a range of other reading which has no freshening variety.

Again: intensity of *moral* excitement in the ministry enhances the peril. Professional duty in the ministry draws deep and exhaustively upon the moral sensibilities. It absorbs vitality, as white-heat does oxygen. A pastor, therefore, is often in danger of having no spirit left in him for literature which does not contribute directly and palpably to professional service. No other profession equals the ministry in respect to this moral pressure from above and around, crowding it down and inward upon its peculiarities. No other enlists such forces of conscience in behalf of its peculiarities.

Further : unenlightened convictions of conscience in the ministry sometimes enhance the peril of a contracted culture. Impulse of conscience must often be balanced by good sense, before it will permit a clergyman to engage happily in any very broad range of reading. Conscientious prejudices against learning constitute one of the perpetual burdens of the church. The clerical right to culture has been purchased at an immense cost of conflict with unenlightened consciences. I have known a clergyman who had passed through a collegiate and professional training of seven years, who, at the end of it, thought it not right for a minister to read Shakspeare. When the Rev. Edwards A. Park, D.D., occupied this rhetorical chair, he formed among the students a Shakspeare Club, for the elaborate discussion of the style, the philosophy, the plots, and the theology of Shakspeare. It encountered so much opposition from timid consciences, in the seminary and out of it, that he thought it necessary to deliver a lecture on the "propriety of studying Shakspeare, and the special usefulness of the study to ministers."

It is to be conceded that the danger apprehended by some fervent pastors, of a spiritual chill from intellectual enthusiasm, is not wholly imaginary. Periods have occurred in which some sections of the church have suffered thus. Such was the case with the Church

of Scotland in that portion of the eighteenth century
in which the characteristic representatives of her pulpit
were such men as Dr. Blair and Dr. Robertson. They
were eminent in the literature of Scotland, but of arctic
temperament in her pulpit. Such periods are singu-
larly alike everywhere. A lenient morality supplants
fervid piety; doctrinal Christianity is held esoterically
as a thing to be believed, but not preached; truisms
and commonplaces make up the staple of sermons; the
clergy give themselves to other avocations than that of
apostolic preaching; and the great bulk of the people
slumber in religious torpor. The awakened mind of
Scotland gave to such a ministry a name which is fitting
to it in all times, by calling it "Moderate." Every
ministry of every age needs protection against the
danger of a "moderate" pulpit. We must admit the
danger, and be fore-armed against it.

But this need not prevent our recognition of the
opposite peril. Our profession appeals so powerfully
to the religious part of our nature, that often a young
minister is obliged to instruct and to discipline his conscience, and to crowd it to a liberal action, before he
can peacefully pursue lines of study which are essential
to his intellectual growth, and therefore to his professional success. Probably we have all felt a momentary
thrill of sympathy with the rule of a certain evangelist, to read no book but the Bible. Yet one sequence
of that rule was, that his range of materials for the
pulpit was so limited, that he was obliged to ask the
reporters not to report his sermons. A pastor should
not cherish a conscience which must be coddled at such
a sacrifice of his intellectual breadth. The laws of God
require it as little as the canons of good taste. A
good conscience is always good sense.

In these several modes, through the mental intensity of clerical duties, through the intensity of moral excitement attending them, and through false convictions of conscience, the clergy are exposed to peculiar temptations to a contracted culture. Therefore we should not read professional literature alone. Even in professional literature we should not confine ourselves to school or sect. One cause of awkwardness and monotony in sermons is often that their authors read little but sermons and kindred theological writings. For the full vigor of the pulpit we need a cross of sermons with other forms of literature. Then, diversity of school and of sect is vital. The Church of England has furnished a very different order of preachers from those of Scotland. The Methodist and the Presbyterian types of preaching are almost antipodes. The Congregational Church of New England has a type of its own. You might search the continent of Europe over, and not find, in all its history of all its sects, a preacher like Dr. Emmons, or another like Dr. Bushnell.

We must be generous, then, in our appreciation of diversities. No other bigotry is so degrading as bigotry in culture. It underlies opinions, and insures bigotry there. Be our reading much or little, we should read always in the spirit of respect for varieties, even opposites, in literary character. I can not more fitly close this review of the necessity of variety in our reading than by quoting the opinion of Dr. Thomas Arnold of Rugby. He thought more profoundly upon the whole theory and practice of education than any other man of our times.

In a letter on the studies of a clergyman, he expresses himself as follows; viz., "I would entreat every man with whom I had any influence, that, if he reads at all, he should read widely and comprehensively; that he should not read exclusively what is called divinity. Learning of this sort, when not mixed with that comprehensive study which alone deserves the name, is, I am satisfied, an actual mischief to a man's mind. It impairs his simple common sense. It makes him narrow-minded, and fills him with absurdities. If a man values power of seeing truth, and judging soundly, let him not read exclusively those who are called divines. With regard to the fathers, in all cases preserve the proportions of your reading. Read, along with the fathers, the writings of men of other times and of different powers of mind. Keep your view of men and things extensive. He who reads deeply in one class of writers only, gets views which are sure to be perverted, and which are not only narrow, but false. If I have a confident opinion on any one point connected with the improvement of the human mind, it is on this."

(8) The principles already named should be qualified by another, which is that a scholarly ideal of study includes the study of unwritten literature. The habit which is practicable to a pastor in this respect is not the appropriation of a great amount of time to the purpose, but the cultivation of professional vigilance in improving such opportunities as fall in his way. Do not waste them by making entertainments of them. Make them tributary to your stock of oratorical knowledge. A great oration, a masterly constitutional argument, a powerful forensic plea, a finished sermon, uttered by the living voice, belong, as much as our libraries do, to the literature of the age. A preacher's

culture must suffer, if he ignores them. Generally, a young man's first awakening to the dignity of a scholarly life is the result of his listening to an oral address. My own first conceptions, which have never been essentially changed, of excellence in English style, I owe to my hearing, at the age of sixteen years, an oration by Edward Everett, at a Commencement of Amherst College. Our debt to such literary models we often undervalue, because they are not a book. We do not see them on our library-shelves. Several things concerning them deserve attention.

This unwritten literature is of great magnitude and variety. Very little, comparatively, of the bulk of cultivated thought, finds its way to the press. The most voluminous and the weightiest part of it is speech, not writing. I say deliberately the weightiest literature of the world is spoken, not written. That, and that only, is literature, which is power in thought as expressed in language. Thought moving other minds at the will of him who utters it, — this is literature. The weightiest volume of it is not in our libraries. Our schools have little direct concern with it. True, it is a paradox to denominate it literature; but the paradox is not deceptive, and no other word expresses it as well.

Earnest conversation is full of this unwritten literature. The table-talk of many other men besides Luther and Coleridge and Johnson is as worthy as theirs of a place on our bookshelves. Emerson says, "Better things are said, more incisive, more wit and insight are dropped in talk and forgotten by the speaker, than gets into books. The problem of both the talker and the orator are the same."

Dr. Johnson became a scholarly authority in England by his conversation more than by his writings. His sway of English literature proceeded from the club-house rather than from the printing-house. Hence that sway is in our day becoming a myth. We do not find good reason for it in his writings. Walter Scott talked more poetry, and Edmund Burke more eloquence, than they ever wrote. Men used to part with Dr. Arnold at midnight, mourning over the loss to the press of the materials of literature which they had heard from his lips in the few hours before. The "Autocrat of the Breakfast-Table" grew out of the request of the friends of Dr. Oliver Wendell Holmes that he would print some of his conversations. There is a humble pastor in Essex County, Massachusetts, who has been repeatedly petitioned by his clerical brethren to save for them in permanent form the seeds of prolific thought which he has scattered at random among them in meetings of ministerial associations. The Rev. Henry Ward Beecher is said to have talked more and sounder theology than he knows how to preach.

Home-life in many cultivated families abounds with unwritten literature. It is often full of healthy criticism of books, of art, of music, of material nature, and full of more than golden links of suggestion which bind these to life and to eternity. A record of the select hours in many cultivated households, through any period of five years' continuance, would form a volume of literature as vital as any in the world.

Specially in crises of history, it does not require knowledge of libraries to create the materials of libraries. In critical periods, like those of the rise of Christianity, the Crusades, the Reformation, the civil

wars in England, the English Commonwealth, the
American Revolution, the overthrow of American
slavery, men and women who have nothing that the
world calls literary culture *live* literature in thousands
of humble homes. They talk literature, though it may
be ungrammatically. Families by thousands, during
the war of the Rebellion, lived books like that of the
"Schönberg-Cotta Family."

In a similar manner, the colloquial instructions of
schools, the interviews of pastors with their parishioners, the emotive utterances of meetings for religious
conference, contain the richest germs of literature.
They contain, often, the latest and the wisest and the
most hearty developments of that which makes power in
books. Say what we may of the dullness of prayer-
meetings, churches are sometimes sensible of an intellectual as well as a spiritual quickening in them, which
they do not get from an equal amount of discourse
from the pulpit. Some pastors are nearer to the very
magazine of literary power: they draw more heat
straight from central fires in their plain talks on a
sabbath evening than in the sermons of the day. The
people know nothing of either as literature; but they
feel the difference none the less. The difference is just
that which they feel between the reading of a bright
book and the reading of a dull one. A pastor in the
city of Boston has been heard to say, "If I must
choose one to the exclusion of the other, between the
pulpit and the dais of the conference-room, give me the
conference-room. On the latter, I and my audiences
are ten feet nearer to each other in more senses than
one."

I once inquired of an alumnus of this seminary, what

lived in his memory as having been the most powerful mental stimulus to him in the curriculum of the seminary. He answered without hesitation, " The Wednesday evening conference." He specified particularly the conferences conducted by one professor. Not all the rest of the instructions he received here had laid him under so deep an obligation as the plain, extemporaneous talks of that one man. In a vast variety of these homely forms are found unwritten volumes. I am not insensible of the ease with which this view may be burlesqued. It may seem to be ludicrously disproved in the very next prayer-meeting you attend. I concede drawbacks, but claim that a residuum remains which is worthy of our libraries. Put into type the very thoughts which fly like shuttles back and forth among living minds in their homeliest intercourse about almost any thing in which they are in dead earnest, and you have in the result books which would live by the side of venerable names in folios.

It deserves note, therefore, that a literary man makes a fundamental mistake, who neglects to observe literature in these homely, unwritten forms. No matter how aspiring he may be in his aims, he can not afford to ignore these low grounds of literary expression. No author can afford to lose the discipline of conversation with illiterate men. It supplies a stimulus, and in some respects a model, which he can obtain nowhere else. Sir Walter Scott expressed his opinion on the subject extravagantly; but he was right in the principle for which he contended, that men are original thinkers and talkers on that which is the business of their lives. The professors of Edinburgh, dining out, were recreating: the merchants of Edinburgh, in their counting-rooms, were working to the extreme of their mental tension. This made the difference to Sir Walter between dullness and earnestness. No man is dull who is really in earnest about any thing, be it but the twist of a pin's head.

Why does literary seclusion, if long unbroken, induce unhealthiness of mind? Why does literary monasticism always fail in its aims? Why was "Brook Farm" a failure? Poets, philosophers, scholars, seers, went there, expecting to pass their evenings in "high converse" of kindred souls. But I have been told, as coming from one of them after he had outlived the dream, that they sometimes went out at sunset, in the desperation of their mental vacuity, and leaned over the pig-sty, thrusting sticks at the swine for occupation. This is a caricature, doubtless; yet it is quite in the order of nature that its equivalent should have occurred. Literary culture revolts from such seclusion as heartily and inevitably as religion does from the monastery and the convent. It is not good for man to be alone.

Specially is it true that a public speaker can not afford to be ignorant of speech as practiced by those who hear him. A preacher can not afford to part with a knowledge of speech as it exists in the homes of his people. If you become men of power in the pulpit, — I mean if you become spiritual chiefs, and not merely conventional figure-heads to your churches, — you will owe your power in part to the very men and women and children who feel it from you. The power comes in part from them to you, before it goes back as power from you to them. When our Lord would teach his disciples a great principle in the philosophy of religion, " he set a little child in the midst of them." So do the great principles of truth in many other things come into clearest light by illustration in the most artless and unconscious exemplars. Common things illustrate profound things. Common people are often the most original. Therefore you will discover, that, to move them with your thought, you must know and respect their thought. To reach them with your style, you must master their style. I do not say must *use* their style, but must master it. To reach them at all, you must know what their mental experience is, what they have lived through, and what experiment of life they are trying, when you try your power upon them. Their mental life and your mental life must run in parallels not wide apart from each other. Otherwise your speech can never bridge over the gulf between. Thinking men will hear you incredulously ; good women will sit solitary under your ministry ; and children will look at you from the corners of their eyes.

Yet again : unwritten literature has a representative character. Whenever it succeeds, it represents a mass of unwritten thought which lies below it. The great orator in real life is the spokesman of those who hear him. He utters thoughts which are floating in dimmer conceptions and more homely words in their hearts. He is the interpreter to them of their own souls. Therein lies his power over them. He plays upon an instrument which is tuned by a more cunning hand. Listening to such a man, therefore, gives insight into the thought of the living generation. It is studying literature in the very process of its formation. What would we not give, if we could listen to-day to Edmund Burke on the impeachment of Warren Hastings, or to Robert Hall on the death of the Princess Charlotte, or to

Webster in his reply to Hayne? To study these phenomena in the very process of their evolution would give to our culture what no books contain. It would be like watching the crystallization of the Kohinoor.

But such, in kind, are the processes of the oral literature of our own times. They are forming deposits, some of which will be permanent. The next generations will read them, as we now read Burke and Jeremy Taylor. They will regret that they never heard the living orators and preachers of to-day, as we regret that we never heard those whose names bore a halo in our youth. You have heard men say that it would be a lifelong regret to them that they never heard Webster, Clay, and Calhoun, the great triumvirate of the United-States Senate. Let us prize while we have them the opportunities of hearing the models of living eloquence in our day. They are the chief representatives of that immense collection of literature which real life is creating in unwritten forms.

Moreover, an oral address is a form of literature which can not be completely represented by the press. The old idea, — as old as eloquence itself, — that the living voice is above all other media of communicating thought, is confirmed by all the ages. This superiority to the press is the birthright of the pulpit. The press, with its thundering enginery, can not represent the *man* in an oral address. Yet the man is the soul of the oral address. His physical framework is part of it. Attitude, gesture, tone, eye, lip, the muscular varieties of countenance, all that goes to make up what the ancients called the *vivida vultus*, and that secret magnetic emanation from the whole person, the origin of which we can not locate in any one member or feature,

— these are all symbols of a speaker's thought as truly as his words are.

In the old Greek pantomime not a word was uttered; yet it sometimes aroused an audience to such excitement, that, on certain subjects, it was forbidden by law. King Ferdinand of Naples, after the revolutionary movements of 1822, addressed the lazzaroni from the balcony of the palace, in the midst of tumultuous shouting, and used no language but that of signs, and yet made himself entirely intelligible. " He reproached, threatened, admonished, forgave, and finally dismissed the rabble as thoroughly persuaded and edified by the gesticulations of the royal Punch, as an American crowd would have been by the eloquence of Webster." Much more may vocalized thought in the oral address surpass written thought in a book. As a type of literature the oral production must have peculiarities which the press can not preserve to us.

This is illustrated in the standing fact of historic eloquence, that, as recorded, it commonly disappoints us. The great orators of the past seldom or never in the reading equal our expectations. Who feels that the orations of Demosthenes equal the reputation of the first orator of Greece? His name could never have held the place it has in modern criticism, were it not for the momentum given to his fame by Athenian opinion. Our best judgments of the orators of the past are the historic judgments : they are the opinions of them which criticism has inherited. If we had picked up the works of Cicero in a nameless scroll on the coast of Siam, it is doubtful whether we should have discovered for ourselves their superlative excellence. So of the Earl of Chatham : his speeches do not explain to us why the House of Commons should have quailed before his utterance of the word "sugar." All that remains of Patrick Henry leaves a shadow of mystery over his reputed power with the House of Burgesses of the Old Dominion.

Among preachers none disappoint us more than the most illustrious of them. We can not discover Whitefield and Robert Hall in their published sermons. We have to accept the traditions of their unintelligible success. Of any one of Whitefield's sermons it is literally true, that, though we have every word of it in print, we have but a fragment. The major part of the symbols of his thought are not in his words. The man is not there. The soul of the orator is not there. The spiritual witness to the union of his soul with the souls of his hearers is not there. These were intangible and evanescent. The audience felt them, but no invention of science could transmit them. One can scarcely read a sermon of Whitefield's, with a remembrance of the effects it wrought, without a feeling akin to that which one has in looking upon a body which is awaiting its resurrection. A living oratory, therefore, should be regarded as a type of literature which can be thoroughly known in no other form.

Once more: a study of printed literature alone may give us false conceptions of what oral eloquence is. Some excellences of printed thought are not adapted to oral speech. You have heard it said of a sermon, "That will read better than it sounds." It is a severe criticism. An oral address ought not to read better than it sounds: if it does so, it is an essay, not a speech. On one occasion, when a speech in the House of Commons was highly praised in the hearing of Mr.

Fox, he inquired, " Does it read well? " — " Yes, grandly," was the answer. " Then," said Mr. Fox, " it was not a good speech." The principle is a subtle one, but the facts of parliamentary eloquence confirm it. The converse of the principle is equally true, — that a production which does *not* read well may for that reason have been a good speech.

From this principle it follows that a man who studies only printed literature may obtain a false theory of oral eloquence. This peril is no fiction. It is working evil in the living ministry. Scores of ministers are preaching after the model of the essay. They are literally " talking like a book." They are not orators. They will not be such, till they form an ideal of eloquence which involves the act of imagining an audience, and constructing thought for expression to the ear.

Here let a brief *excursus* be indulged upon the question, often asked, " What is it in oral speech which distinguishes it from the essay? " I can not answer this very perspicuously by definitions; but perhaps it can be answered by a contrast of examples. The following is an extract from a recent essay on the " End of God in Creation : " —

" What was the final cause of creation? The transition from the unconditioned to the conditioned is incomprehensible by the human faculties. What that transition is, and how it could take place, and how it became an actualized occurrence, it is confessed on all hands are absolutely incomprehensible enigmas. We can not reasonably imagine, then, that, if we are thus ignorant of the nature and the mode of this stupendous fact, we can nevertheless comprehend its primitive ground, can explore its ultimate reasons, can divine its final motive. Nor can we think to unveil the Infinite Soul at that moment, when, according to our conceptions, the eternal uniformity was interrupted, and a new mode of being, absolutely unintelligible to us, was first introduced. We can not think to grasp all the views which were present to that Soul, extending from the unbeginning past to the unending future, and to fathom all its purposes, and to analyze all its motives. If anywhere, we must here repel every thing like dogmatic interpretation of the phenomena, and admit whatever is put forth only as conjectural in its nature, or at all events partial, and belonging far more to the surface than to the interior of the subject."

This is essay. Listening to it, one can not fail to see that it needs to be read in order to be appreciated. To a hearer it is dull; to some hearers, obscure. Yet are not some sermons constructed on this model? Are they not inevitably delivered with intonations and a cadence which almost compel the sense of humdrum in the listener?

Take, now, the same theme, and the same leading thoughts, and the same succession of thoughts, but expressed in the following style: —

"Why did God create the universe? Creation is incomprehensible to man. What is creation? How was it possible? How did it ever come to be? I can not answer. Can you? Every man of common sense confesses his ignorance here. But if we are ignorant of what creation is, and how it is, can we imagine that we understand why it is? Shall we think to unveil the mind of God in the stupendous act? That moment when God said, 'Let there be light,' was a moment of which we can know nothing but that 'there was light.' Shall we think to see all that God saw? Can we look through the past without beginning, and the future without end, and fathom all his purposes and all his motives? Can we by searching find out God? If we must repel assertion anywhere, we must do so here. Whatever we may think, it is but little more than guess-work. At the best, it can be but knowing in part. The most we can know must be on the surface. It can not penetrate to the heart of the matter."

Is not this speech, as distinct from essay? Is not the difference obvious? Is it not vital to oral style? Some critics would underrate it. They would pronounce it superficial, because it has not the ponderous structure, and the swelling cadence, of the original. They would call it popular, as distinct from scholarly, because it can be appreciated in the hearing.

Whatever may be true of such criticism, my point is, that oral speech to any class of hearers requires certain peculiarities which do not belong to the essay, and are not largely illustrated in printed forms of thought. Therefore, by studying those forms alone, a preacher may obtain false ideas of oral eloquence. The natural fruit of such a training is, that a preacher should read essays from the pulpit all his life without knowing it. The mystery of his ministry to him may be, that he can interest his people so much more effectively out of the pulpit than in it. But the mystery is no mystery. It is simply, that, out of the pulpit, he *speaks*, and in it he *essays*. This is the reason why preachers are so often requested to repeat or to publish their extemporaneous sermons, while their written sermons, of vastly more solid worth, lie unhonored in their desks. This is the secret reason why the conference-room sometimes sustains the pulpit which stands in ponderous dignity above it. It is because in the one the preacher talks, and in the other he soliloquizes. In the one he is eloquent therefore; in the other — what shall I call it?

LECTURE XV.[1]

THE STUDY OF THE SCRIPTURES AS LITERARY CLASSICS.

(9) ONE remaining principle, by which other principles of selection in our study of books should be qualified, is that we should study the Scriptures as literary models. It furnishes a cheering solution, in part, to the problem of the practicability of scholarly culture to a pastor, that a very vital portion of that culture may be derived from the one volume which is central to his professional labors. No other profession finds in its most necessary and vital work such a stimulus to intellectual depth and breadth as that which the pulpit finds in the study of the Scriptures. Good cheer is this to an overburdened pastor.

Allusion was made to some of the biblical writers, in speaking of the choice of authors who have been controlling powers in history. I have purposely reserved the consideration of the study of the Bible as a whole, because its study as a collection of literary productions may be advocated by reasons peculiar to itself.

Let me ask you to note first — without comment,

[1] Portions of the lectures on the Study of the Scriptures have been already published in a sermon preached before the government of Massachusetts.

for the point is so obvious — the distinction between
the study of the Bible as a religious revelation and the
study of it as a literary classic.

This suggests immediately the singular neglect of
the Bible by modern literary taste. It is one of the
subtle collateral evidences of human depravity, that
the republic of letters has so generally ignored the
Scriptures as a literary production. Such is the habit
of the scholarly thought of our times, that, when the
idea of a model of such thought is first suggested to
us, it is in connection wholly with uninspired names.
If a stranger at a university were to ask one, on the
spur of the moment, to give the names of ten models
of the first class in the history of the press, the reply
would doubtless be entirely oblivious of the writers of
the Bible.

As purely literary labor, and for scholarly purposes
alone, where is criticism of the Bible ever taught,
outside of theological schools? By the common consent of scholars, commentaries on the Scriptures are
relegated to the curriculum of professional study.
Even there they are often regarded as provincial, not
to say unscholarly. Would the literary study of the
Bible, think you, be welcomed at Harvard College with
the same respectful enthusiasm with which a course of
lectures on Shakspeare, by an expert in Shakspearean
literature, would be received? Could a biblical club for
the literary criticism of the Pentateuch be sustained at
Yale College as vigorously as the Chaucer Club was
sustained at Andover a few years ago? This is one of
the developments of what I have elsewhere denominated the cant of literature. The secret and unconscious antipathy of the human mind to the moral aim

of the Scriptures betrays itself in that vanity of scholarship which affects to despise or ignore their literary
claims.

Or put the case in another way. One can easily
imagine what a stir in the learned world would be
created, if certain portions of the Bible were recent
antiquarian discoveries, claiming no inspired authority.
Suppose that the first chapter of Genesis had been
exhumed, during the last insurrection in India, from
the ruins of an old temple of Vishnu. Conceive that
the Fifty-first Psalm had been just deciphered from a
hieroglyph in the Pyramids. Picture to yourself the
latest importation of a slab from Nineveh as containing the first known inscription of one of the closing
chapters of the Book of Job. Imagine that the Sermon
on the Mount had just come to light from a lost and
recovered book of Seneca, or had been found among the
meditations of Aurelius Antoninus. What an ecstasy
would rouse the dignity of the scholastic world! What
an inundation we should have of literary astonishment!
What exultant monographs from Westminster Reviews.
What eager quotations from the revered authors, as the
peers of Confucius and Plato! Our universities would
resound for a decade with eulogiums upon the resurrection of a noble antiquity.

But because the Scriptures are the word of God,
because they claim authority in morals, because they
press close upon the conscience, the literary mind of
the race has silently turned away from them as models
of literary culture, and has expended itself on gods and
goddesses of its own creation.

Our current systems of education are founded in part
on this perversion of scholarly taste. They assume that

the study of the Bible is not a necessity to a liberal education. It ranks with the study of anatomy or of the law of mortmain. So far as I know, the only exceptions to this view are found in the German gymnasia, where the Old and New Testaments are, or were a few years ago, criticised and taught by the side of Xenophon and Virgil. The study of the Bible in our American colleges — what shall I say of it? Do I wrong it in saying that it is an expedient of collegiate police? Is it not sometimes required mainly because the authorities do not know what else to do with Monday morning? Such at least was the usage in my time.

The fact is a singular one, that in the German schools, where the inspiration of the Bible is often discarded, and where Ezekiel and St. Paul are criticised precisely as criticism deals with Aristophanes and Juvenal, the literature of the Bible is restored to respectable appreciation. It is recognized as a model of scholarly culture. The moment the weight of inspiration is taken off, and a scholar can approach the Scriptures with no response of conscience to them as a religious authority, then respect returns for them as literary classics.

It is worthy of notice, that in this country a positive retrograde has taken place on this subject in the collegiate curriculum. During the first century of the existence of Harvard College, the Greek New Testament was the only Greek text-book put into the hands of its students. The time was, when Hebrew was taught there as an undergraduate study. The professors could some of them converse in Hebrew. How much do the undergraduates of the venerable university know of Hebrew now? How often do its learned faculty regale themselves in Hebrew colloquy?

To appreciate the Bible ourselves, then, as a literary classic, we need to emancipate ourselves from the current opinion of educated men on the subject. We have probably grown into that opinion unconsciously. Uneducated Christians, in their indiscriminate reverence for the Scriptures, may be nearer the truth than we are in our scholarly judgment. We may have a process of self-discipline, more severe than we anticipate, to go through in restoring the Bible to its true place in our literary estimate. It will not do to approach it with prepossessions against it as a literary model.

But, approaching it in an appreciative, scholarly spirit, we find incitement to the literary study of it in the fact that the Bible contains the oldest literature in the world. Interest in antiquity for its own sake is legitimate. That interest is a normal fruit of education, as well as a natural instinct of the human mind. Every mind has roots in the past. A thing is presumptively true, if it is old; and an old truth men *will* revere. We all have historic feelers, which reach out for something to lay hold of, and to steady our faith, amidst the rush of events. He is not a bold man who can tear himself loose from the underground of former ages. It would be an irreparable loss to the educating forces of Christendom, if the faith of the Christian world *could* be destroyed in the descent of the existing races of men from one pair ; so ennobling, and so stimulating to culture, is this instinct of reverence for a long-lived unity. The human instinct of reverence for the old story of a paradise, with its halo of the golden beginning of things, is quickening to high culture.

Much of the disciplinary power of the Greek literature comes to us through our intuitive reverence for the long-lived. So long as Macpherson's imposture was undiscovered, and his works were received as the veritable productions of Ossian, they exerted a perceptible influence upon the men of letters in England through the magnifying power of their reverence for ancient genius. The literary firmament was ablaze with enthusiasm for the great Northern poet. It was like the northern-lights, as transient, indeed, but, while it lasted, as enchanting. Had the poems of Ossian been other than an imposture, it is by no means certain that they would not have perpetuated their first renown till this day, so sensitive is the vision of literary taste to any gleam of genius from a bygone age.

With all the abuses to which this susceptibility of our nature is liable, it is in our nature, and for wise purposes. Within its normal limits, and kept in balance by the spirit of inquiry, its operation is healthful. No grand elevation of society, and no finished culture of the individual, is ever attained without its aid. We have, then, a very obvious ground of literary interest in the Scriptures, which is altogether independent of their inspiration and of their moral uses, in the fact that they contain the earliest known thoughts of our race in literary forms. To give definiteness to this fact, let several specifications be observed in illustration of it.

It is, for instance, a fact, the significance of which infidelity appreciates if we do not, that the only authentic *history* of the world before the deluge is found in the sacred books of Christianity. The world of the future never can know any thing of the ante-diluvians except from the Jewish historian. It would be worth centuries of toil to the socialism of Europe, if it could blot out this one fact in the relations of

the world to the Pentateuch.   The late Professor B. B.
Edwards thought it probable that we have also in the
books of Moses, what no other literature can show, a
fragment of poetry which was actually composed in
the antediluvian infancy of the race.   Does it not help
us to some conception of the venerableness of these
volumes to recall, that, by the commonly received chronology, they were written eleven hundred years before
Herodotus, whom the world has consented to honor as
the father of history?

The Hebrew jurisprudence is by the same chronology
seven hundred years older than that of Lycurgus, and
two thousand years older than that of Justinian.   You
have heard that Thomas Jefferson was indebted, for his
conception of our American government, to the polity of
an obscure church in Virginia.   But republicanism was
foreshadowed in the Hebrew commonwealth nearly
three thousand years before the settlement of James-
town.   The principle of the New-England town-meet-
ing, in which De Tocqueville found the corner-stone of
our free institutions, was originated by Jethro, the venerable father-in-law of Moses.

The lyric poetry of the Hebrews was in its golden
age nearly a thousand years before the birth of Horace.
Deborah sang a model of a triumphal song full five
hundred years before Sappho was born.   The author of
Ecclesiastes discussed the problem of evil five hundred
years before Socrates in the Dialogues of Plato.   The
Epithalamium of the Canticles is nearly a thousand
years older than Ovid's "Art of Love."   The Book of
Esther was a venerable fragment of biography, more
strange than fiction, at least twelve hundred years old,
at the dawn of the romantic literature of Europe.   The

Proverbs of Solomon are by eight hundred years more ancient than the Treatises of Seneca.

Dr. Johnson once read a manuscript copy of a pastoral story to a group of friends in London. They begged of him to inform them where he obtained it, and who was the writer. Imagine their amazement, if he had told them that it was an ancient treasure, written, in a language now dead, nine hundred years before the Georgics of Virgil, seven hundred years before the Idyls of Theocritus, and twenty-five hundred years before the discovery of America, and that it had been remarkably preserved among the archives of the Hebrews; for it was no other than the Book of Ruth.

Jeremiah is as properly pronounced the founder of the elegiac school of poetry as Mimnermus, to whom its origin is commonly ascribed; for they were, probably, for a short time, contemporaries, the Hebrew prophet being by half a century the senior.

The entire bulk of the prophetic literature of the Hebrews; a literature extraordinary; one which has laws of its own, to which there is and can be no parallel in any uninspired workings of the human mind — this mysterious, often unfathomable compendium of the world's future, which the wisdom of twenty centuries has not exhausted, was, the whole of it, anterior to the Augustan age of Rome. Even the writers of the New Testament are all of them of more venerable antiquity than Tacitus and Plutarch, and Pliny the Younger.

What shall be said of the Book of Job? Biblical scholars only conjecture its age; but the argument for its great antiquity appears to me, though not by any means conclusive, at least as strong as that for its later origin. If the first hypothesis be true, this is the oldest volume now existing, at least eight hundred years older than Homer. It was already an ancient poem when Cecrops is conjectured to have founded Athens. When Britain was invaded by the Romans, it was more time-worn than the name of Julius Cæsar to-day is to us. Natural philosophers now turn to its allusions as the only recorded evidence we have of the state of the arts and sciences from three to four thousand years ago. A modern commentator on the book has collated from it hints of the then existing state of knowledge respecting astronomy, geography, cosmology, meteorology, mining, precious stones, coining, writing, engraving, medicine, music, hunting, husbandry, modes of travel, the military art, and zoölogy. Any work, surely, which should be so fortunate as to be of uninspired authority, and should give to the world the obscurest authentic hints of the state of these sciences and arts forty centuries back, would be hailed as a treasure worthy of a nation's purchase. In the study of such a volume we may legitimately feel the same enthusiasm which Napoleon, in the campaign of Egypt, sought to arouse in his soldiers, when he exclaimed to them, " Forty centuries look down upon you."

Whatever is becoming to a scholarly spirit, then, in a love of ancient literature, for the sake of the stimulating and ennobling effect of its antiquity, we have reason to cherish for the Scriptures, considered merely as literary classics.

We find another inducement to the literary study of the Scriptures, in the fact that they sustain a regenerative connection with Oriental civilization. Two things comprise the points essential to this aspect of the subject.

One is, that the Oriental mind is giving no signs of having finished its work in history. What is the law of Providence respecting nations and races which have finished their work as powers in the world's destiny? It is a law of doom. Such nations and races die. Christianity, which is the flower and fruitage of Providence, has always been prophetic in its instincts. It has never bound itself to the soil anywhere. The law of its being is, that it shall pass away from superannuated to youthful races, from decadent to germinant nations, from expiring to nascent languages, from senile to virile literatures. Then those races, nations, languages, and literatures which represent its abandoned conquests die, if they have in them no recuperative power to fit them for future use. Under this law of divine operation the entire Oriental stock of mind, if it has no Christian future, ought now to be evincing signs of dissolution. But this is by no means true of it. The nations which represent it are not, as a whole, dying out. They are not visibly approximating their end. More than one of the Asiatic races seem to be as full-blooded, and as virile in their physical make, and as likely to endure for thirty generations, as they did a thousand years ago. They seem to be waiting in grand reserve, as the beds of anthracite have waited with latent fires, for future use. That ancient development of man which began on the plains of Shinar bids fair to live by the side of its Occidental rival, even if it does not outlive this by reason of its calmer flow of life.

If it does thus live, all analogy would lead us to believe that there is something in it which deserves to live. There is something in it which Providence has a use for in the future. It has energy; it has resources; it has faculty; it has manly tastes and proclivities; it has something or other, which, under divine regeneration, will be a cause of growth, if infused into the life-blood of the Western races. The circle of Occidental development may be enlarged by it. The channel in which our civilization is moving may be thus widened and deepened.

The other fact bearing upon the topic before us is, that, if new systems of thought *are* to grow up among the Asiatics, with any function of control in the world, they must be the creations of the Bible. Nothing else represents the Oriental mind in any form which can ever rouse it to its utmost of capacity. Nothing else, therefore, can ever make it a power in the future civilization. None but a visionary can look for a rejuvenescence of Asia in coming ages from any internal forces now acting there independently of the Scriptures. The history of the East contains nothing which can ever be to the world, for instance, what the revived literatures of Greece and Rome were to the middle ages of Europe. Explorers find nothing there out of which great libraries can grow. They find nothing that calls for or promises to the future great universities, or new systems of philosophy, or advanced scientific researches. The East is the land of pyramids and sphinxes. Whatever that immense territory has to contribute to the civilization of the future must come from the germination of biblical thought. It must be the working of biblical inspiration in the spiritual renewal of Oriental character, which nothing but the religion of the Scriptures can produce.

Why should it be deemed visionary to look for this

as one of the results of the infusion of European mind
now going on in Western and Central Asia? Already
the germs of Christian universities and libraries exist
there which may one day allure literary travel from
the West, as those of England and Germany do to-day.
Inspired prophecy aside, it is no more visionary to
predict the re-creation of Oriental mind in forms of
new literatures superior to any the world has yet
known, through the plastic influence of the Scriptures,
than it was to anticipate the birth of the three great
literatures of Europe as the fruit of the modern revival
of the literatures of Greece and Rome. The minds of
nations move in just such immense waves of revolution. Reasoning *à priori*, they seem impossible: so
do geologic cataclysms to a race which lives in quiet
over slumbering volcanoes. But, reasoning *à posteriori*,
they are only the natural effect of a great force gen-
erating great forces. They seem as gravitation does
to a race which has no conception of what it would
be to exist without it. The diurnal revolutions of the
earth are not more normal or more sure.

The Asiatic races have, indeed, a fairer intellectual
prospect than Europe had at the time of the revival
of letters; and this for the reason that they are to
receive their higher culture in Christian instead of
Pagan forms. Conceive what a difference would have
been created in the destinies of Europe, what centuries
of conflict with barbarism would to human view have
been saved, if the Greek and Roman literatures could
have come into the possession of the modern European
mind freighted with Christian instead of Pagan thought,
and if, thus Christianized, they could have been wrought
into European culture!

Yet this, to a very large extent, appears likely to be the process of intellectual awakening to which the immense forces of Asiatic mind are to be subjected. Asiatic literatures of the future are to be the direct product of centuries of Christian culture in other lands. They are to have no Paganism to exorcise, as European civilization had, from the very models which are to inspire them. In Asia, Paganism is to represent in the future, not only dead institutions, oppressive governments, degrading traditions, and popular wretchedness, but a puerile literature as well. It can never there, as it did in Europe, go into solution with Christianity through the force of a Pagan culture so beautiful and so lofty as to command the reverence of all scholarly minds.

With this view of the future of the Oriental world, it is certainly a remarkable feature of the divine plan that Revelation should be for ever stereotyped, as it is so largely, in an Oriental mold. It looks, does it not, as if the Oriental type of the race were yet to be a power in the world through the Scriptures, as the only vital nexus between its future and its past.

Napoleon used to say that the only theater fit for great exploits was the East. Europe, he said, was contracted: it was provincial. The great races were beyond the Mediterranean. They were in the ancient seats of empire, because the numbers were there. There may be more of truth in this than he meant to utter. The grandest intellectual and moral conquests of the world may yet follow the track of Alexander.

From this train of suggestion, the inference is obvious, that the time can not be distant when enterprising

scholarship will not be content to omit the Hebrew and
Christian Scriptures from its resources of culture. A
mind which is imbued with biblical learning has a home
in the future of literature, and among the majorities of
cultivated races, which no mind can have without it.

LECTURE XVI.

THE DEBT OF LIVING LITERATURES TO THE BIBLE.—
INTRINSIC SUPERIORITY OF BIBLICAL MODELS.

IF the relation of the Scriptures to the future of Oriental civilization should seem to be a distant motive to biblical culture, let us observe one which is more immediate in its influence, in the fact that the Bible is, to a large extent, incorporated into all the living literatures of the world; not into all of them in equal degrees, but into all sufficiently to be felt as a power. When we speak of the literary sway of European and American mind, we speak of the conquests of the Scriptures. The elemental ideas of the Bible lie at the foundation of the whole of it. Christianity has wrought such revolutions of opinion, it has thrown into the world so much original thought, it has organized so many institutions, customs, unwritten laws of life, it has leavened society with such a potent antiseptic to the putrescent elements of depravity, and it has, therefore, created so much of the best material of humanity, that now the noblest scholarship can not exist but as a debtor to the Christian Scriptures.

The debt of literature to the Bible is like that of vegetation to light. No other volume has contributed so much to the great organic forms of thought. No other is fusing itself so widely into the standards of

libraries. Homer and Plato and Aristotle were long
since absorbed in it as intellectual powers. This volume has never yet numbered among its religious
believers a fourth part of the human race, yet it has
swayed a greater amount of mind than any other volume the world has known. It has the singular faculty
of attracting to itself the thinkers of the world, either
as friends or as foes, always, everywhere. The works
of comment upon it of themselves form a literature of
which any nation might be proud. It is more voluminous than all that remains to us of the Greek and
Roman literatures combined. An English antiquarian,
who has had the curiosity to number the existing commentaries upon the Scriptures, or upon portions of
them, found them to exceed sixty thousand. Where is
another empire of mind to be found like this?

Here is a power, which, say what we may of its
results, has set the Christian world to thinking, and
has kept it thinking for nearly two thousand years.
The unpublished literature of the Christian pulpit surpasses in volume all the literatures of all nations. "If
the sermons preached in our land during a single year
were all printed," says a living scholar, "they would
fill a hundred and twenty millions of octavo pages."
The Bible is read to-day by a larger number of educated minds than any other book. The late revision of
the New Testament in our own language is not yet one
year old; yet its circulation amounts to two millions
and a half of copies. This sale, unprecedented in the
history of any other volume, indicates an immense
reserve of interest in the book, which, till now, has had
no such means of expressing itself. The mind of the
English-speaking races must have been saturated with

biblical thought, and to a great extent with biblical faith, for a long time, to account for such a phenomenon. Multitudes are poring over the book, and are feeling its elevating influence, who never think of it otherwise than as an authority for their religious faith.

Our own language owes, in part, the very structure it has received to our English Bible. No Englishman or American knows well his mother-tongue till he has learned it in the vocabulary and the idioms of King James's translation. The language first crystallized around this translation as the German language did in less degree around Luther's Bible. In English form the Bible stands at the head of the streams of English conquests and of English and American colonization and commerce. It must control, to a great extent, the institutions which are to spring up on the banks of those streams the world over.

It is interesting to observe how the influence of the Bible trickles down into crevices in all other literature, and shows itself, at length, in golden veins, and precious gems of thought, which are the admiration of all observers. The late Professor B. B. Edwards, in illustration of this fact, notices the following details; viz., "An essay has been written to prove how much Shakspeare is indebted to the Scriptures. The Red Cross Knight in the 'Faerie Queene' of Spenser is the Christian of the last chapter of the Epistle to the Ephesians. The 'Messiah' of Pope is only a paraphrase of some passages in Isaiah. The highest strains of Cowper in the 'Task' are an expansion of a chapter of the same prophet. The 'Thanatopsis' of Bryant is indebted to a passage from the Book of Job. Lord Byron's celebrated poem on 'Darkness' was founded on a passage in Jeremiah."

Wordsworth's criticism of Milton, that, "however imbued the surface might be with classical literature, he was a Hebrew in soul," is true of very much that is most inspiring and most durable in our modern poetry. Wordsworth's "Ode on Immortality" could never have been written but for the creative effect upon the poet's imagination of such Scriptures as the fifteenth chapter of the First Epistle to the Corinthians and the eighth chapter of the Epistle to the Romans. Pantheism has a cool way of appropriating a great deal of Christian poetry. Thus it claims Wordsworth. But the most autobiographic passages in "The Excursion," descriptive of the communion of his soul with nature, could never have been conceived but by a mind which was permeated by the inspiration of the One Hundred and Forty-eighth Psalm.

> "In such access of mind, in such high hour
> Of visitation from the living GOD,"

is the language in which he himself describes that communion.

Shakspeare's conception of woman is another illustration to the same effect. De Quincey claims it as an absolute original by no other genius than Shakspeare. But in the last analysis Shakspeare's ideal is only the Christian ideal, which suffuses with refinement our modern life. We owe it ultimately, not to poetry, nor to the drama, but to the biblical fact of the atonement. Nothing else has made the conception possible of a Desdemona or an Ophelia growing out of a sex degraded in all other than Christian literatures.

The hymnology of all modern languages has been absolutely created by the Hebrew psalmody. The

ancient classics have not, so far as I know, contributed
a stanza to it. Not a line of it lives, through two
generations, in which the genius of the Psalms of
David does not overpower and appropriate all other
resources of culture. The old English and Scottish
ballads never exerted on the national mind a tithe of
the influence of the Hebrew psalm. The commonwealth of England owed its existence, in part, to the
psalm-singing of Cromwell's armies. On the continent
of Europe, also, the whole bulk of the despotism of
the middle ages went down before the rude imitations
of the Hebrew psalmody by Clement Marot and Hans
Sachs. The battle-song of Gustavus Adolphus was
originally published with this title, "A Heart-cheering
Song of Comfort on the Watchword of the Evangelical
Army in the Battle of Leipsic, Sept. 7, 1631. God
with Us."

The Bible has also formed the best standards of deliberative eloquence in modern times. The Earl of
Chatham was sensible of his own indebtedness to it.
Patrick Henry and James Otis were often likened in
their lifetime to the Hebrew prophets. Lord Brougham
and Daniel Webster both acknowledged their obligations to the same models. Webster was for years the
biblical concordance of the United-States Senate. His
ablest opponents, in preparing their speeches, used to
resort to him to furnish them with scriptural passages
and metaphors to point their weapons against him.
Such was his command of the same resources, that
he could afford to give them liberally, and without
upbraiding.

To all departments of modern literature the Scriptures have been what they have been to modern art.

It has been said that the single Christian conception
of a virgin and her child has done more for the elevation of art than all the exhumed models of Greece and
Rome.   It is a well-known fact that nothing in art
itself succeeded in crushing out the moral abomina-
tions which many of those models expressed until the
Christian religion flooded the whole realm of beauty
with more intense ideas; so that, to the purest taste,
the Greek Venus has become imbecile by the side of
the Christian Madonna. So are the literary models
of the Scriptures working, as germs of power in modern
literature, beyond the depth of Greek and Roman
thought in its choicest and most durable forms.

I will name but one other form in which the obligations of modern literature to the Scriptures is illustrated : it is that of the unconscious debt of infidelity
to biblical resources.   The infidel literature of our
times owes nearly all the vitality it has to its pilferings
of Christian nutriment.   It lives by its unconscious
suction from Christian fountains. " The Cotter's Sat-
urday Night " is not more palpably indebted to the
Scriptures than are some of the finest passages in
Shelley's " Queen Mab."   The " Paradise Lost " and
the " Pilgrim's Progress " are not more really the out-
growth of the old Hebrew soul than are some of the
sublimest conceptions of Lord Byron's " Cain."   No
man could have written " Cain " or " Queen Mab "
whose genius had not been developed by a Christian
civilization, and whose infidelity had not been fired by
collision with the Epistle to the Romans. The power
to *be* so blasphemous grew out of Christian knowledge ;
and the power to express the blasphemy with such
lurid grandeur sprang from the culture which Christianity had created.

The atheism of Great Britain, which is working so disastrously among the artisan classes of the kingdom, owes its chief resources of power over the popular mind to the fact that it holds on to so much of scriptural thought. Its capital ideas are biblical ideas. Strip it of these, and it would have no chance of a hearing in the workshops of Birmingham. What else than Christianity ever gave to the human conscience *spring* enough to enable it to conceive of such a thing as a practical religion without a God? Yet this is English atheism to-day. It is not vice; it is not conscious blasphemy; it is not moral nihilism: it is an aim at morality, moral culture, moral principle, moral progress, even moral worship, after its kind, — all which it audaciously proposes to support without a God for the center of the moral instincts. When did the human soul ever before get force enough of moral instincts to conceive of such a project as that?

Similar to the lesson taught by the atheism of Great Britain is that taught by the most powerful phases of infidelity in this country. It would be entertaining, if it were not too painfully solemn, to observe the depth to which Christian thought has penetrated, and the extent to which Christian colorings of speech have suffused the culture exhibited by the most brilliant of the infidel lecturers and writers among us. Mark it anywhere, — on the platform, in the newspapers, in magazines, in books: the materials of thought which these men are wielding, to the saddest hurt of an unthinking faith, are at bottom Christian products. No other class of literary men are so profoundly indebted to the Scriptures, yet so profoundly oblivious of the debt.

Open one of their books, turn to its most captivating pages, sift its style, weigh its thought; and what do you find of good sterling worth? Wherever you find clear ideas held in honest Saxon grip, you find them vitalized by something or other which they owe to Christianity. Here it is a truth as old as Moses; there it is the power to conceive of the opposite of a truth: again it is an antithesis of half-truths; farther on it is a dislocated quotation, or a warped and twisted allusion: now it is a fungus overgrowing a germ of truth which gives it its power to grow; then it is a Pantheistic turn to language which Pantheism never originated, but which, in its original, Christian souls love. Even down to the indefinable ingenuities of style, you find at work the alert and sinewy fingers of a Christian culture. The very sentences which express or imply semi-Paganism in theology, but the structure of which makes them play in the very heavens of beauty like the coruscations of the northern-lights, are, as specimens of style, the product of our Oriental yet Saxon Bible. Are Confucius, Zoroaster, Socrates, at the root of the thoughts and the forms which you feel in such pages? No: it is Moses; it is Isaiah; it is David; it is St. John; it is Christ. Take away the elements of culture which these have contributed to such literature, and no man would care what heroes or philosophers might claim the residuum.

The most striking illustration, in my judgment, which has exhibited the truth of the fact before us in our own country, is that given by the Rev. Theodore Parker. For twenty years the most vital infidelity in this land was personified in him. He brought to the solitary altar at which he ministered in Boston a generous scholarship, a mercurial genius, a versatile command of thought, and a fascinating style. Taking him all in all, his was a more earnest character than that of any other man who has gained any thing like equal eminence in the ranks of active hostility to what he called "the popular theology of New England." The purity of his life was almost ascetic. For one, I am compelled to concede the power of the man in his lifetime, whatever may be true of it now. I do not think that any candid man among us who knows the classes of mind which were reached, and the momentum given to them, for twenty years, from that Twenty-eighth Congregational pulpit, will feel, that, as a friend of truth, he can afford to ignore that power, or to underrate it.

But it was not the power of his infidelity: it was the power of his unconscious obligations to truth. His vital and vitalizing ideas were Christian ideas. He owed them to the Book which he disowned. He drank them in from all the living literatures which he mastered. He maligned religion as we conceive of it. He ridiculed Scriptures which to us are sacred. He denounced as barbaric the ground-work of our hope of heaven. He scoffed at our ideal of a Redeemer. He uttered words which from our lips would be blasphemy. Yet the interior forces which bore up as on an oceanic ground-swell this mass of error were forces every one of which sprung from that ocean of inspired thought whose great deeps were broken up in the civilization around him.

What were some of those forces? In what ideas did they find their origin? They were such as these: the fatherhood of God, the unity of the human brotherhood before God, the dignity of manhood, the intensity of life as the prelude to immortality, and, more than all else, the application of these ideas to social and national reforms. These were the forces which he wielded. Without them the world would not have heard of him. Yet these are, every one of them, biblical forces. He owed them to the Christian Scriptures; and he owed the susceptibility to them in the popular mind on which he worked so disastrously to that interpretation of the Scriptures which has expressed itself in our New-England theology. Thus it is with every development of infidelity which has force enough to make it respectable. It feeds on Christianity itself, and grows lusty *therefore*.

To the views thus far advanced respecting the literary claims of the Bible should be added the fact that the Bible contains within itself models of thought and expression which are intrinsically superior to other literature. What do we mean when we speak of the literary pre-eminence of the Scriptures? This involves two inquiries.

The first is, What is the bearing of inspiration on literary merit? I answer, It is not such that pre-eminence in literary *forms* follows from inspiration as a thing of course. Inspiration does not save from literary defects even. It does not necessitate uniform excellence in taste, the most perfect conciseness, force, purity, precision, beauty, of style. It does not even protect against false syntax. The Scriptures are open to criticism in these respects, like any other book. It is in the substance and the spirit of the volume chiefly, that its supremacy appears. Literary defects arise necessarily from the freedom of the inspired mind.

In the laws of inspiration God has exercised the same care for human freedom that is displayed in all other divine adjustments. So jealous is the divine mind of the integrity of that inclosure within which a human mind is itself a *creator*, that, even in the anomaly of inspiration, the human mind is not automatic. In the process of constructing a revelation the inspired mind is left to act out itself. A human coloring suffuses the material of the inspired production, because a free, self-acting will is concerned in it. Hence come literary defects.

The central fact in this matter is, that, in the inspired record, God has secured the best literary forms possible to the instruments he chose to work with. He has inspired St. Paul to write as well as, under the conditions of his work, St. Paul could write. He has inspired David and Isaiah to speak as well as, under the conditions existing, they could speak. In neither case has he taken from the man his identity. It is no irreverence, therefore, it is only a recognition of the divine plan of procedure, to say that the Bible makes no claim to immaculate excellence in classic forms.

Again: a pretended revelation, of scholastic origin, would have been very apt to claim absolute perfection. Mahomet did this for the Koran: Jewish bibliolatry did this for the Pentateuch. It is an incidental sign of the divine origin of the Scriptures, that they never do this for themselves. The Scriptures, therefore, come to us in forms of very unequal literary merit. They resemble in this the works of uninspired genius. Genius elsewhere never claims perfection. It never thinks of its own work as literature. It throws itself into its creations with self-abandonment. In its noblest works it is unconscious of its nobility. The very intensity of its conceptions creates defects when crowded into human language. So it is with inspiration acting through the agency of a human mind: if the Scriptures did not exhibit these diversities, the strongest possible philosophical argument would be established that they are not the work of the men who profess to be their authors.

The second of the two inquiries suggested is, What are the things in which the Bible does exhibit the superiority claimed for it? You will readily recall them. I name them only to give definiteness to them as excellences in literature, and not as moral virtues alone, involved vaguely in the gift of inspiration, and therefore outside of our scholarly regard.

The fidelity of the Bible to the loftiest ideals which the human mind can form of *truth* and *purity* is a literary excellence. It is a requisition of good taste, as well as of the moral instincts. That the Scriptures utter no falsehood, minister to no vice, truckle to no conventional corruption, do not ignore the moral affinities of the intellect, never confound moral rectitude with beauty, but, in a word, subordinate intellectual to moral integrity, — these are exponents of literary dignity which the cultured taste of the world must sooner or later learn to esteem as it does not now. They would give to any other literature a dignity which would command the admiration of all scholarly minds.

The *intensity* of the biblical style of thought is a literary excellence. Contrast this with the immense amount of frivolous and aimless thought in all other literature. Inspiration never trifles, never dallies with truth, never sports with "the eternities," never perpetrates a pun, never fawns upon great men, never flatters woman, never deals in comedy, never created such a character as that of Shakspeare's "Falstaff," or the universal clown of the modern stage. As a collection of literary productions, the Scriptures look inward to a great central tragedy. An intellectual intensity, therefore, broods over them, which is altogether unique. Those portions of Shakspeare's dramas which exhibit the same quality are those on which, mainly, his fame rests. In him we do not restrict it as a quality of form only: it is the very substance of all that we admire in a great tragic poem. The same is true of it as a quality of biblical thought.

The *originality* of biblical thought is a literary excellence. This we can not appreciate till we throw our minds back of the Scriptures themselves, back of the whole intellectual training for which we are indebted to them, and think of the mass of novel truth which the Bible has given to the world, and the mass of preextant truth which it has freshened and vitalized. Contrast it with the paucity of ideas in Homer, and are you not sensible of the magnitude of the one and the littleness of the other? If the Greek mind had had a volume containing such a mass of ideas before unknown and inconceivable, temples would have been built for its teaching as the gift of immortal gods.

As the fruit of its originality, in part, the aptness of the Bible to *germinate in uninspired literature* is a literary virtue. Regarded as a fertilizing power to other products of the human mind, no other volume can be compared with it. It is marvelously reproductive of kindred thought. The germs of epic poems, of systems

of philosophy, of political constitutions, and of the
eloquence which sways nations in crises of history, are
the common thoughts of the inspired authors.   The
seeds of such culture as that which effloresces in a
Milton, a Bacon, a Chatham, a Burke, are here ideas
thrown out by men speaking, as if on the spur of the
moment, in friendly letters, in talks, to unlettered
minds and to children.

The sympathy of the Scriptures with *human liberty*
is an excellence, which, in equal degree, would redu-
plicate to the echo the fame of any other literature in
the world.   History is largely made up of struggles
for freedom.   Free thought, free speech, a free press,
free soil, free men, free government, are the objects for
and against which the great conflicts of the race have
been waged.   Much of the scholarly thought of the
world has been committed to the service of autocratic
and aristocratic privilege.   Authors have been, to a
considerable extent, the retainers of noblemen.   Sometimes they have been, like Horace, the slaves of feudal
superiors.   Against the main drift of national literatures the liberty of man has often been compelled to
contend for its existence.   Some of the living standards in our libraries to-day are the product of a muzzled press.

Not a trace of sympathy with such a condition of
things is found in the literature of the Bible.   The
bent of its genius is all on the side of those institutions for which free men have fought, and women have
suffered.   The Bible is pre-eminently the manual of
liberty.   Those words which have been the watchwords
of sanguinary revolutions for the deliverance of nations
from oppression express the favorite ideas of biblical

jurisprudence and song and prophecy. That rulers
exist for the people; that the poor are in law the
peers of the rich, and the ignorant, of the wise; that
mankind are one brotherhood, with equal claims upon
the fatherhood of God and the fraternity of each other,
— are the familiar and central thoughts of biblical
poets, historians, lawgivers, prophets, and apostles.
The whole strain of the volume is one long protest
against the oppressor, and one perpetual song of cheer
to the slave. No other literature is in this respect so
uncompromising and so self-consistent. It is an incen-
diary volume to slaveholders everywhere. Popes place
it at the head of the list of books anathematized.

Yet, on the other hand, the Bible is equally the
manual of *temperate and bloodless reform.* It gives no
place to the malign emotions in warfare against oppression. Fanatics expurgate and denounce it no less
bitterly than tyrants. It tolerates wrong, and incul-
cates long-suffering, rather than to invite convulsive
revolutions. It trusts to time, and the omnipotence of
truth, for the emancipation of mankind. It subordi-
nates civil to spiritual liberty, — a thing which fanatical
reform has never done, and for the want of which it
has always failed. If the spirit of biblical literature
had held sway in history, there would never have been
a servile war, never would a race or a nation have
been emancipated by the sword. Yet the cause of
human liberty would have been centuries in advance
of its condition to-day. The equipoise of opposing
truths, and the consequent smoothness and stillness of
beneficent revolutions, are characteristic of biblical
thought as opposed to the eternal war-song of all other
literature. The ultimate culture of the world will

transpose the passive and the active virtues in its literary judgments.

The *symmetry* of the biblical system of truth is a literary excellence. With no system in form, it is everywhere suggestive of system in fact. The biblical scholar degrades his own work who discerns in the Bible no implications of a self-consistent structure of theology. It is in this respect what every man's real life is, — a plan of God. Every thing in it fits every other thing. What other literature not founded upon it has such balancing of opposite truths, such adjustments of the relations of truth, such diversity in unity, such unity in diversity, such a grand march of progress in the evolution of truth? In one sense the Bible is a fragment, made up of fragments; but it is fragmentary as the segment of a circle is fragmentary.

The number and diversity of *literary styles* in the Scriptures deserve mention. Although immaculate form is not one of their claims, yet incidentally to their loftiness of thought, and purity of character, excellence of form often appears as if by spontaneous creation. The style of some portions of the Epistles, art has never tried to improve. Who has ever thought to improve the form of the Beatitudes or the Lord's Prayer? What reformer or censor of public morals has ever attempted to improve the style of some of the Hebrew prophets? The narrative style of the evangelists, the lyric poetry of the Psalms, the epic grandeur of the Book of Job — what adventurous critic has ever assumed to equal these? They are as nearly perfect as human language permits. Poetic, didactic, philosophic, narrative, illustrative, allegorical, epistolary, dramatic, oratorical, prophetic, styles are all illustrated in the Bible by specimens of the first order of merit.

As the sequence of some of the foregoing qualities, a certain power in the literature of the Bible to *project itself into the future* is worthy of remark. The materials of extant literatures may in one view be classified as literatures of the past and literatures of the future. Some standards of our libraries are only monuments. We admire them, but we never use them. Practically the world has done with them. To high culture the study of them has become a recreation only. They are receding from the earnest life of the world more and more distantly with every generation.

The Bible, as a literary power, is no such monumental structure. Though the oldest, it is still the freshest, literature extant. Covering all the past, it reaches over a longer and grander future. A favorite idea of critics is that of the immortality of literature. The Bible is the only volume which is sure of that. The future belongs to it as to nothing else which the world now reveres in libraries. Its own prophecies are a fair symbol of the prospective vision which illumines it, and assures to it an undying youth.

Such are some of the salient points definitive of our conceptions of the Bible as a literary classic. The majority of them occur to our thought first and most positively as moral excellences only; but good taste approves them as well. The affinities between our intellectual and our moral nature are such, that to ignore either involves deterioration of the other. An eminent English critic says that Lord Byron, in the lack of a keen conscience, suffered the lack of the first quality necessary to a true poet. A more subtle illustration of the same kind of affinity is seen in the power of a lofty morality to elevate the very vocabulary of a language, and the opposite power of degraded morals to degrade a language also.   On the same principle, certain qualities in the Bible which first strike us as moral qualities only, we claim as literary virtues as well.   They augment immensely the power of the volume as an educating force in the discipline of a scholarly mind.   I do not dwell upon them at greater length, because they are familiar; and to expand them might easily degenerate into unmeaning eulogy.

LECTURE XVII.

THE PROFESSIONAL VALUE OF BIBLICAL MODELS TO A PREACHER.

THE claims of biblical study upon a pastor would be but incompletely treated, if no mention were made of its direct professional service. No other single principle of success in the work of the pulpit surpasses this, of its dependence on the models of the Bible as guides to both the theory and practice of preaching.

Every careful student of theology discovers the distinction between truth as it appears in uninspired forms of statement, and the same truth as it appears in the biblical forms. It is not chiefly the forms which attract us in the Scriptures: it is the truth itself, qualified and assisted by the relations in which it is uttered, by its antecedents and consequents in the biblical collocation of materials, by the objects for which it is spoken, by the illustrative elements by which it is pictured, by the frequency with which it is repeated, by the atmosphere which is thrown around it by the religious feeling of the writer, and by the moral authority which it derives from the reader's faith in its inspiration. These often change, by refraction, the perspective in which the truth is seen. It is a vast variety of such things which makes truth appear truthful in the biblical conception and statement of it. It

256

puts on a different look when taken out of the locality in which inspiration has adjusted it to its inspired purpose. In a word, truth in the Scriptures seems to have been *lived*, not said only. A soul breathes in it which speaks as never man spake. The same qualities in the biblical representations of truth which give to an unlettered reader a spiritual quickening give to a preacher a kind of culture which is a powerful auxiliary to his intellectual preparation for professional service. No man needs that culture more.

For the sake of definiteness of conception on this topic, let us follow it in an *excursus* from the main subject upon the contrast between the ultimate impression of certain truths in the biblical teaching, and that of the same truths in the forms of science and in a certain class of sermons.

Our systems of theology do an invaluable service to a preacher. No man can preach the Bible truthfully, who does not preach it with fidelity to a system of truth which pervades it. If we preach it in methods which are reckless of an underlying system, we are sure to derive from it extremes of truth which are not truthful. The best biblical preaching, therefore, is the best theological preaching. The contemptuous treatment of dogmatic theology, sometimes heard from men of pettifogging scholarship, does not deserve refutation. Still our theological systems, as represented in the great historic creeds, are all of them polemic in their origin. They have a belligerent look; they are skeletons in coats of mail. They have been formed in times when some one truth, or class of truths, was believed to be in peril: they have, therefore, an outlook in some directions more eager and defiant than in others. The

majority of them are compromises, in which contending
parties placed each its own construction upon ambigu-
ous language. Therefore, to a later age, they often bear
the look of contradiction.

This is specially noticeable in the drift of our most
scholarly confessions upon doctrines which involve the
freedom of the human will. On this subject, truth has
been of slow and toilsome growth. She has crept and
limped up the great highway of human opinion. "With
a great sum" have we "obtained this freedom." Pagan
theology everywhere has been saturated to the point of
stupor with fatalism. The early Christian thought was
drugged with the same poison. The *clear* enunciation
of the liberty of the human will, and of the theological
corollaries from it, has been, in the main, the product
of the Christian thinking of the last two hundred years.
We owe it largely to the political and civil history of
the Netherlands.

Many of the historic creeds of Christendom, therefore, are wofully disproportioned on this class of doctrines. In some of them, these doctrines are set over
against their related truths in language which gives to
both classes the look of contradictions. They are
stated on the principle of the Duke of Wellington, that
" the way to solve contradictions is to affirm both sides
stoutly." But more frequently these correlated truths
are so stated as to depress the fact of human freedom.
Divine sovereignty is emphasized; human responsibility
is mumbled. The doctrine of decrees is thundered;
that of man's ability is whispered. In all that renders
God august and terrible the sound is the blast of a
trumpet; in all that should quicken man's consciousness of moral dignity and duty the voice is but the
echo of an echo.

As monuments of historic theology, the great creeds of the church are all the more valuable for being just what they are. They mark the struggling faith of believers from theologic infancy upward. We study them with much of the same interest with which one would study the Pinakothek and Glyptothek of Munich, in which is represented the complete history of painting and sculpture. It is no strange thing that they are often illogical, and very far from self-consistent. This is inevitable in the structure of any document which must express the convictions of many independent minds. Macaulay says that "some of the most useful political instruments in the world are among the most illogical compositions ever penned." The same is true of some religious creeds. It grows out of the nature of compromise, in which, from the necessities of the case, the creeds of historic importance have been framed. Compromise of great and sincere beliefs borders hard on contradiction. All honor, then, to these monumental structures of our faith. They have done for the church all that they were ever meant to do.

But who of us have not been sensible of a more powerful *educating* force emanating from the same truths, as they are expressed for a moral purpose, in their biblical forms? It seems as if the human mind, in direct converse with the thought of the Infinite Mind, can not obtain its most formative conceptions of truth, except through the medium of moral sensibilities and a moral aim. Hence it is that we experience such a supreme educating power in the writings of the Hebrew seers, and of the apostles, and in the discourses of our Lord.

Are we not sensible often that a doctrine of our faith in even a masterly theologic treatise is a different thing from the same doctrine in the Bible? It makes a different impression. It may be stated with such refined analysis and with such exactest choice of speech, and set in the frame of a system so symmetrical, that you feel unable to add to it or subtract from it as a theologic formula; yet, in the whole treatise built upon it, it has a different ring from that given by the apostles with the same instrument. It leaves a different resonance in the ear. It starts a different quivering of the sensibilities.

Sermons are sometimes constructed after the model of scientific theological treatises, and therefore exhibit the same contrast with biblical teachings. Have you not listened to discourses on eternal punishment, to the theory of which you could not urge valid objection, but which produced a totally different impression from that of the blended sternness and benignity of the teachings of our Lord? Where do the Scriptures authorize such a final impression of the doctrine as that of President Edwards's sermon on the text, "Their feet shall slide in due time"? Who ever derived from the Bible such merciless conceptions on the subject, couched in such relentless forms of statement, as are found in some of the sermons of Mr. Spurgeon?

Have you not heard discourses on the sovereignty of God, and responsibility of man, not a paragraph of which you would erase as in itself untrue, which yet left an impression unlike that of the ninth chapter of the Epistle to the Romans, interlined with the eighteenth chapter of Ezekiel? Who ever received from the Bible the idea which is embossed on so many brazen sermons, that God's sovereignty is sheer will, almighty will asserting its almightiness? and, on the other hand, that human freedom is an omnipotence of will which God is impotent to control? Where in the Scriptures is the thought ever uttered or painted, even in the wildness of Oriental hyperbole, which was declared by one of our American preachers, that, "in the repentance of a sinner, man is the giant, and God is but an infant"?

Have you never listened to preaching on the doctrine of the atonement, to which you could not object that any single statement was untrue, but which still you felt to be, in its ultimate impression, out of sympathy with the Epistle to the Hebrews? Who ever received from the scriptural imagery of Christ's relation to the Father in the work of atonement, that conception of the Father's vengeance which Dr. Watts has versified in a stanza, which, if it had been sung of the Greek Nemesis, would have surpassed any equal number of lines in Homer? —

> "Rich were the drops of Jesus' blood
> Which calmed his frowning face,
> Which sprinkled o'er the burning throne,
> And turned the wrath to grace."

Our inherited type of preaching on the doctrine of sin is unscriptural in this respect, that it starts with the idea of the mercilessness of a holy God. It assumes that forgiveness is not the original and spontaneous action of the Divine Mind. Such is the nature of sin, that the primary notion must be, in a holy mind, that it can not be forgiven. This is the idea which is wrought into the most profound discussions of Pagan theology. It is the very life of the Greek idea of fate. It was the finality of the theology of Socrates. The same conception pervades much of the later literature

of the world.   Turn to one of its latest and most original productions, — Hawthorne's " Marble Faun."   You
find this notion of the implacableness of innocence
towards the guilty in his appalling picture of the relations of Hilda and Miriam.   Hilda the pure, and
Miriam the fallen — an impassable gulf yawns between
them, which eternity can never bridge over.   The fallen
one stands doomed to an " infinite, shivering solitude,"
in which she can not come " close enough " even " to
human beings to be warmed by them."   " Standing on
the utmost verge of that dark chasm, she might stretch
out her hand, and never clasp a hand of theirs.   She
might strive to call out, ' Help, friends, help ! ' but, as
with dreamers when they shout, her voice would perish
inaudibly in the remoteness that seemed such a little
way."

This notion has often congealed the heart of the
pulpit.   Therefore, in preaching even on the doctrine
of the atonement, we have failed to represent the spon-
taneousness of the love of God as the Scriptures do.
We have fettered it with limitations.   We have qualified it by elections.   We have obscured it by figures of
bargain and sale.   We have counted the elect as if
there were danger that too many souls should be ran-
somed by the price paid.   The inevitable impression on
the common mind has been, that the love of God in
redemption acts under repression, and with divided or
wavering purpose.   All this is just what the Scriptures
do *not* teach in their expression of the love of God in
the atoning work.   There all is free and whole-souled.
The way to the heart of God is wide open.   There is
no conflict in the mind of Godhead.   No antagonism
of nature or of purpose separates God from Christ.

God gives his Son; Christ gives himself: the purpose
of redeeming love is original with both. God, above
all other beings in the universe, is a sinner's friend;
the whole Godhead is a sinner's friend. A preacher
comes into a different atmosphere from that of the
religion of nature, as soon as his mind takes in the
unbroken strain of the responses which the Scriptures
make to the inquiry "What must I do to be saved?"

So of any doctrine which has been hotly contested
in the schools. How few discussions of such a doctrine
are there, which a Christian heart, when in the most
filial communion with God, and reverent fellowship with
Christ, feels to be honestly and artlessly truthful to the
Scriptures as a whole, breathing the same spirit, and
leaving the same impression, without abatement and
without hyperbole!

You will recognize, therefore, the pertinence of the
injunction, that a preacher needs to imbibe the spirit of
the biblical models as an addition to, yet distinct from,
that of the theologic models. I say, "an addition to"
these, not in abrogation of them; because theologic
science must do, and has magnificently done, a work *for*
the pulpit which can not be brought *into* the pulpit.
We must study philosophic truth in its exactness for
the purpose of concinnity of faith, and then we must
come back and drink in the spirit of the same truth in
its inspired artlessness of form for the purposes of
preaching.

Some striking information to the point here is found
in an account, published a few years ago, of the religious state of Sweden. It appears that it was a feature
in the organic law of Sweden, that the schools should
teach all the youth of the kingdom the Lutheran Cate-

chism: as the Swedish pastors termed it, the schools
should "teach religion" to the children. Accordingly,
every Swedish child of suitable age was "taught religion" by catechetical drill supervised by the pastor
of his parish. Probably there was not then, if there
is now, another country on the globe where this duty
was so scrupulously attended to as there. But, at the
time referred to, the complaint was universal among
the clergy and the thoughtful laity of Sweden, that the
vitality of the old faith was dying out. In hundreds
of parishes the youth droned through the Catechism as
a necessity to their civil standing in after-life; but the
ancient faith no longer breathed in the ancient form.

Side by side with this admirably compacted system
of catechetical routine, there sprang up an obscure sect
of "Lascari," as they were termed; that is, "readers,"
as I understand the title. They resembled in spirit
the Methodists of England. They derived their name
from the fact that their religious teachers, with no
ecclesiastical *status* recognized by either Church or
State, were simply readers of the Bible. They erected
plain meeting-houses, like barns, to evade the laws of
the realm against the unlicensed erection of churches.
The people forsook the old temples of their fathers, and
flocked in thousands to the cheerless barns of the
Lascari, to hear the Bible read. The clergy stood
upon their dignity. They scolded the people from
their pulpits. The entire respectability of the kingdom
frowned upon the innovation. But still the people
thronged the meetings of the "Readers." Again they
repeated the old story of Christian reform, — that, as
Dr. Chalmers said, Christianity is *not* a power of
respectability only, but a power of regeneration.

Awakened men and women from far and near came together to hear the voice which had raised them as from the dead. Some of them journeyed from ten to sixty miles for the purpose. Many gave evidence of spiritual conversion. The traveler who published the account in this country expressed the opinion that the hope of Protestantism in Sweden was no longer in the old church of Gustavus Adolphus: it was in the despised Lascari.

The providence of God teaches a significant lesson to the pulpit by such a social phenomenon as this. It is, that to the popular heart there is no other preaching like that which is baptized in the fountains of inspired thought and feeling. The pulpit which is built upon the soundest platform of systematic divinity, and that *only*, goes down before the living man who invites men to listen to the words of God. It is true no man can build up in the popular faith the best ideal of Christian truth, who has not mastered systematic theology in its most scholarly forms; but it is equally true that no man can build that ideal who has studied truth in those forms alone.

This view is confirmed by an acknowledgment which Orestes A. Brownson has made respecting the *catena* of Roman-Catholic theologians. He says, "The fathers studied and expounded the Scriptures, and they were the strong men, the great men, the heroes of their times. The mediæval doctors studied, systematized, and epitomized the fathers; and they, though still great, fell below those who were formed by the study of the Scriptures themselves. The theologians followed, and gave compendiums of the doctors, and fell still lower. Modern professors content themselves with giving compendiums of the compendiums given by the theologians, and have fallen as low as possible without falling into nothing, and disappearing in the inane."

This would be a libel, if affirmed of the brilliant succession of Protestant scholars who have represented the progressive theological thought of the last three centuries. It is specially untrue of those of our own country. But of the Romish schools it expresses, from one who may be accepted as an authority, the tendency to a deterioration of culture which will be always found where theological science has been divorced from a study of the Scriptures.

This tendency is sometimes witnessed in the pulpit, when dogmatic theology is allowed to monopolize its ministrations. Then logic tyrannizes over rhetoric. Theological system overbears homiletic variety and the adaptations of suasive speech. In confirmation of this, it deserves to be noted that the most cumbrous and least profitable kind of *serial* preaching, unless it be executed by a man of rare power in popularizing abstract thought, is that in which a series of sermons is founded upon the church creed. That was a deserved rebuke which a pastor in Boston once received, when, in the midst of such a series on the Catechism, a delegation from his sabbath school waited upon him to inform him that a religious awakening was in progress in the Bible classes, and that they needed other instruction than that which he was giving them; not other truths, but in other and more versatile forms.

This fact suggests another, that no other proportions of truth tally so well with the purest type of revivals of religion as the proportions found in the Scriptures. I can not but regard some kind of severance of truth from the biblical ways of putting it as one reason of the pathological affections which have brought revivals into discredit among thinking men. I refer to the whole class of phenomena which medical science would classify under the titles of hysteria and catalepsy. An epidemic of them at the West, many years ago, received the popular name of "the jerks." Something resembling St. Vitus's dance attacked perfectly able-bodied men under the tempestuous preaching of the time. Athletic men from the backwoods of Kentucky, who sought the Presbyterian camp-meetings with angry challenge of "the jerks," were thrown to the ground before the sermon was half finished, and wallowed there till they were borne out into the air, swearing that "the devil was in it." Probably in some sense he was. But no such phenomena are recorded as attending apostolic preaching, except those which are expressly ascribed to miraculous gifts. Biblical truth in biblical proportions tends always to a certain equipoise of effects. The whole man is reached by it. It produces a quickening of so many and such varied sensibilities, that each balances another. Opposites limit and regulate each other. Paroxysmal excitement is impossible. " *Peace* I leave with you" is the message which symbolizes the spiritual economy in the working of biblical truth in its biblical adjustments.

To the views thus far presented, I would add, if the time would permit, a more extended notice of one other topic which I will now name, with only a synopsis of the train of thought which it suggests. It is that the study of the Bible as a literary classic has a tendency to blend scholarship with Christian sensibility in such proportions as to render each a help to the other in the

growth of character.   The prominent thoughts on this
topic are the following ; viz., the difficulty which Christian scholars often experience in harmonizing in their
own. character accomplished scholarship and religious
faith ; the fact that the ministry contains men of religious ardor but imperfectly regulated by scholarly discipline; the opposite fact, that it contains also men of
superior scholarship, who sympathize but feebly with
the popular developments of religious fervor; the fact
that historically these two elements of character are
actively combined in the most vigorous periods in the
life of the church, and signally so in the most useful
men; the fact that disaster always follows any marked
and prolonged disproportion between them in the administration of the pulpit; the fact that no other clerical
study is so healthfully regulative in this respect as
that of the literary models of the Scriptures; and the
fact that a biblical discipline of piety thus blended
with scholarly culture will work its own way to the
most essential principles of art in public speech.

LECTURE XVIII.

3d, Having thus far, in our discussion of a pastor's literary studies, considered the objects of the study and the selection of authors, we now proceed to observe the methods of literary study by a pastor.

It is necessary here, at the expense of repetition, to recall and re-apply the two preliminaries which were named at the outset of our discussion of the selection of authors; viz., that the principles bearing upon the subject must in practice qualify each other, any one of them by itself constituting an impracticable basis of culture; and that, even with this qualification, the principles collectively constitute at the best only a theoretic ideal of study.

These preliminaries are even more significantly true of methods of study than of the selection of authors. No one principle can have a monopoly. All combined give us only an ideal : the realization of it is a matter of degrees. A nearer approach to it is practicable in some cases than in others; but in all cases it is of value to have it as an ideal. It is worth much to know what *is* scholarly reading. If it is but partially practicable to a man, it is worth something to him to

know *that;* to be able, therefore, to adjust his plans
to that. It is worth much to save time and force
from useless struggles, and specially to save himself
from the narrowness of underrating a high ideal, because *he* has tried it, and found it impracticable. I
repeat, therefore, that these preliminaries are more
necessary as qualifications of the principles we are
now about to consider than of those named respecting
the selection of authors.

1. Bearing them in mind, let us observe, that the
ideal of scholarly reading is critical reading. Here,
again, the distinction between reading and study is
elemental. It lies at the foundation of the whole
business. In mere reading the mind is passive: in
study the mind works. In reading we drift: in study
we row.

If Professor Stuart in his prime had been asked how
many hours in a day he studied, he would have said,
"Three and a half." But he spent at his study-table
ten, often twelve, hours. Such was the difference in
his estimate between study and reading. A young
man wrote to me not long ago that he was studying
fourteen hours a day. From my knowledge of his
temperament and habits, and from the fact that he
adds that he is "growing fat upon it," I doubt whether
he is studying two hours in a day. A man does not
grow fat upon fourteen hours of study in a day.

Critical reading establishes acquaintance with an
author. It discloses also the very process of his literary work. Every author's work is a panorama of
his mental processes to one who has the critical insight
by which to discover them. They are more easily discovered in some than in others. Some writers are

secretive: they do not let themselves loose in their speech. But these are inferiors in literary power. The great minds liberate themselves; they move on winged utterances; they throw the whole force of their own being into their creations. Then, like other works of creation, the thing created bears the image of the creator. It is impossible, for instance, to read with scholarly care the sonnets of Shakspeare, or Byron's "Cain," without discovering somewhat of the personal life and character of the author. Even a heedless reader can not escape the discovery of the hidden character of the author's mind in reading Hawthorne's "Marble Faun" or "The Scarlet Letter." They present a still picture of the man which is more suggestive than an autobiography.

That is unscholarly reading for a professional man, reading for his own culture as a public speaker, which does not disclose somewhat of the process of authorship. Not the man only, but his work, needs to be made visible. To achieve this requires study, as distinct from reading. The majority of educated men read a vast deal more than they study. The old adage, "Commend me to the man of one book," was founded upon the invaluable worth of critical reading. We do a permanent evil to our own minds, if we read a valuable book as we skim the newspapers. It is impossible to appreciate an athletic literature without some degree of the strain of a mental athlete in the study of it. Specially is this true of that mastery of the process of authorship which a public speaker needs to acquire by his reading.

To illustrate this critical method in reading for professional discipline, we should observe such things as

the following. Respecting the materials of thought,
Are they true? are they relevant? are they original?
are they intense? are they the obvious outflow of a
full mind? are they suggestive of reserved force? do
they mark a candid thinker, a sympathetic thinker,
a mind which puts itself *en rapport* with the reader?
Respecting the style of the work, such points as these
need attention: Is the style clear, concise, forcible, picturesque? Are the sentences involved? Does a Latin,
or a German, or a Saxon model prevail in their structure? Do laconic sentences abound? interrogatives?
antitheses? parentheses? rhythmic clauses? clauses in
apposition? quotations? epithets? long words? short
words? obsolete words? archaic words? euphonious
words? synonyms? monosyllabic words? Is the vocabulary affluent, or stinted? Is the style as a whole
that of oratory, or of the essay? Is it as a whole natural to the subject and the discussion? Is it as a whole
peculiar to the author, or imitative of other authors?
Does it indicate in the author the habit of weighing
well the forces of language? Does it contain fragments void of thought? Robert Hall's well-known
criticism of his own production, which a friend was
reading to him for the purpose, illustrates critical study
of style: "'Pierce' is the word: I never could have
meant to say 'penetrate' in that connection."

It is sometimes said that this critical reading is a
pettifogging process, — the mind is contracted by it.
Not so, if the volume in hand is one of great and
enduring power. A great mind works as the great
powers of nature do in producing a multitude of di-
minutive creations. We can not neglect these, and
yet know that mind thoroughly in its best moods of

authorship. Lord Bacon says, " He that can not contract the sight of his mind, as well as disperse and dilate it, wanteth a great quality." Reading in this manner, one acquires not only a knowledge of an author's mental character and habits of thinking, but somewhat of the very process of production in the case in hand. Even a little of such acute reading will create a new perceptive power in all other reading. The knowledge gained will approach the accuracy and intricacy of self-knowledge.

Are there not some authors with whom already you have formed this kind of personal intimacy? If you should happen upon an anonymous extract from them which you had never seen before, you could pronounce confidently upon their origin. You know it by a word, a tone of thought, an idiomatic sentence or illustration, as you recognize a friend in the distance by his gait, or the swing of his arm. The authorship of the " Waverley Novels " was detected by readers of the " Scottish Ballads " and " The Lay of the Last Minstrel," long before Walter Scott acknowledged the authorship. This critical reading which makes it impossible for an author to secrete himself from readers is the basis of all mastery of books.

2. Scholarly reading is reading in the spirit of philosophical inquiry.

There is a difference between literary curiosity and literary inquiry. Curiosity contents itself with facts: inquiry seeks for the principles which underlie the facts. Curiosity asks " What? " inquiry asks " Why? " Why is one discussion masterly, and another feeble? Why does one volume suggest material for two? Why is one order of thought superior to another? Why does one page require a second reading? Why does one structure of discourse excel another? Why is one style of illustration more vivid than another? Why is one construction, one length, one emphasis, of a sentence, more effective than another? Why is one word better than another? Why say "pierce," and not "penetrate"?

Some anomalies in literature force upon a critic the philosophical inquiry. Let us note an illustration of this. Has it never occurred to you what a singular violation of congruity occurs in the first stanza of one of the dearest hymns of the church, perhaps the hymn which above all others has won the affection of Christian hearts? On what principle can criticism justify such lines as these? —

> " There is a fountain filled with blood
>   Drawn from Immanuel's veins,
> And sinners plunged beneath that flood
>   Lose all their guilty stains."

Do we ever fill a fountain? Is there no jar upon æsthetic feeling in the anatomical specification of veins? Would any thing but the necessities of rhyme induce a poet to prefer that image to the "heart"? Is the picture, when finished, an attractive or an impressive one to the imagination? Is there any congruity in an interchange of the images of "flood" and "fountain"?

These æsthetic difficulties have been submitted to several of the most accomplished Christian critics of the country. They were unanimous in condemning the incongruities on æsthetic grounds, yet as unanimous in saying that no art can improve the stanza on moral grounds. James Montgomery was so sensitive to these imaginative defects of the hymn, that he once published it revised by his own hand, with this stanza adjusted to the demands of taste. But who has ever sung the revised edition? In what collections of psalmody has it ever found a place? It has fallen still-born. Christian worship clings to Cowper's original. Christian hearts will love it in all its æsthetic deformity; and more, Christian feeling denies the deformity, let criticism say what it will.

There is a reason for such an apparent anomaly as this. Genuine taste and Christian sensibility never conflict in reality. The following explanation has been suggested by a living scholar whose æsthetic taste and religious sensibility both entitle him to a hearing. He says substantially that the whole conception of the atoning work of our Lord is so august and so mysterious, that the mind does not demand in a lyric expression of it the sharpness of congruity which it would demand in the expression of a less solemn or a less obscure thought. The whole idea of the atonement is an anomaly. Æsthetic anomalies are in keeping with it. It overawes æsthetic feeling in its common forms. It exalts the moral sensibility in the place of that feeling. An Oriental confusion of metaphor, arising out of luxuriance of imagery, is therefore invited by the strange abnormal character of the thing expressed. The poetic mind declines to trace such a thing in imagery exact and finished, like that in which it would paint a rainbow, or fringe a cloud. In such a mind the Christian feeling which loves the stanza as it is, is more truthful than the æsthetic feeling which would condemn it. Whether or not this is a satisfactory explanation of this example, the example itself illus-

trates the working of philosophical criticism, and the
necessity of it in the explanation of anomalies.

Again : philosophical inquiry gives dignity to criticism. By means of it criticism constantly makes incur-
sions into mental science. The rhetorical force of one
word may be attributable to a fundamental principle
in philosophy. The words " power," " cause," " ought,"
are unanswerable arguments for certain philosophical
truths. The existence of those words is a philosophical fact. The true philosophy of mind can not be
evolved without them. Yet the proper use of them is
one of the things with which rhetorical criticism concerns itself. This is but one of a multitude of ways
in which criticism and mental science work into each
other's domains.

Moreover, philosophical criticism often reverses our
first judgment of authors. A search for the reason of
an opinion will often lead a candid mind to give up the
opinion. So our judgments of authors are often hereditary judgments. In our maturer culture we can not
defend them ; and we discover this by asking why we
attribute to such authors the qualities we revere. Our
first impressions of authors are also often our juvenile
impressions. We find that our literary manhood does
not support them ; and we either discover this, or are
confirmed in it, by raising the philosophical inquiry,
Why? The glare of a false literature is often thus
found out, when a more indolent criticism would be
dazzled for a lifetime.

3. The most useful reading is done by a scholarly
division of labor. By this I mean, that critical attention
should be directed to one thing at a time. We can not
wisely bring to critical reading the habits we form in

accumulative reading. Deep boring must be done in spots. The surface we cover with our reading should be dotted over with points at which we sink a shaft of critical inquiry. An inspection of your present habits of reading will probably disclose to you that they have thus far been almost wholly acquisitive and discursive in their character. You have read for information and entertainment, not for critical culture.

Acquisitive reading for critical purposes is wearisome, because it is unproductive of results. No man will long continue it. Did you ever attempt to drag a tree through a narrow gateway, with the branches headed to the front; and did you not discover a very convenient principle of mechanics when the bright thought occurred to you to turn it end for end? The single trunk obeyed you, and drew after it the supple branches which were so refractory before. Like such a juvenile error are attempts to carry a great diversity of critical processes along side by side in our reading. The diversity bewilders. The objects of our critical attention straggle out on this side and on that. Our thought seizes one and another at random, and drops each to attend to a third, till, by dint of tug and heat, we advance by inches to the discovery that we are losing all pleasure, and gaining no discipline but such as is the common lot of saints. At last, bruised and irritated, we give it up in despair. Reverse the process, fix attention on one thing at a time, and you advance with ease and with the consciousness of progress.

For the sake of definiteness in our conception of this method, let several applications of it be noticed. Thus division of labor may be applied to the study of diversities in kind of literature. For example, the essays of our language form a department by themselves. Study them as such. Get a clear idea of the English essay, — what it is, what is its relation to other departments of our literature, when it originated, who are its chief masters, what are their peculiarities, and what is the control of the essay over modern opinion. Do not burden your study of the essay by trying to carry abreast with it in your reading English poetry, history, biography, philosophy. Let each of these monopolize your time in turn. One week, or its equivalent, devoted to a study of the essay alone, will give you a very valuable knowledge, even to some extent a critical knowledge of it, which will assist you in the studies of a lifetime.

Division of labor may be applied to criticism of single authors, if they deserve it. Study an author by installments. Study first the sentiment, then the construction, then the illustrative materials, then the style, and, finally, his place in the fraternity of authors and in the history of his times. The severest labor of such reading is near the beginning. One advances in it with accelerated speed. You are constantly taking side-glances, also, at other things which you can not help noticing, as you see things out of the corners of your eyes. This relieves the monotony of your work, without burdening your attention with unmanageable varieties.

This analytic method of study may be applied to the several parts of a discourse or of a poem. It is the method usually adopted in lectures on the structure and composition of a sermon. We study texts by themselves; introductions are considered alone; propositions, divisions, conclusions — each receives dis-

cussion in its place. The same division of labor may
be applied to other species of composition, — to orations, to works of fiction, to histories. This principle
of division of labor is the one on which we pursue all
other intelligent courses of study: we study theology
by topics; we read history by periods, by royal reigns
and dynasties; medical science is studied by classification of diseases: why should not the criticism of
literature be facilitated by the same principle? This
method in the study of books tends to secure profound
knowledge at the vital points of literary history. We
can not otherwise discover the vital points; for we
shall not otherwise study any one thing long enough
to discover its relations to other literature. But, with
a few things thus thoroughly mastered, we shall know
that our culture is well anchored. We can trust ourselves: gales of false taste will not drag us from safe
moorings. What we know, we know; and we know
that we know it. If our judgments differ from those
of others, we can afford to wait for the decisions of
time.

By this method, ultimately, even the extent of our
literary knowledge will be most effectually enlarged.
The chief objection to this painstaking study is that
the work is slow. But in truth it is the best method
for acquisitive study in the end. Dr. Johnson, in his
"Lives of the Poets," says that the reason why the
ancients surpassed the moderns in literary acquisitions
is, that they had a more truthful conception of the
limitations of human powers, and confined themselves
to one thing. The measure of our knowledge is not
so much that of what we gain as of what we hold
and use. In war, military policy is not to conquer a

strategic point till force enough is at command to hold
it. So, in literary pursuits, conscious mastery at a few
points will soon extend itself to others. The points
of conquest will soon begin to communicate with each
other. There are certain signals in a man's consciousness of knowledge by which mastery in one thing helps
mastery in another. An interchange of tribute is carried on, by which knowledge assists all other knowledge. We are not conscious of that, except through
profound and thorough scholarship: nothing less than
that deserves the name of culture.

LECTURE XIX.

**METHODS OF STUDY, CONTINUED. — LITERARY COMPARI-
SONS. — CULTURE OF WEAK TASTES. — COLLATERAL
READING.**

4. CONTINUING the discussion of the scholarly ideal
of reading, I remark that it involves studious comparison of authors with each other.

Literary comparisons are often involuntary. One
can not read, even cursorily, two such authors as Adam
Smith and John Ruskin, or two such as Jeremy Taylor
and Robert South, without unconsciously instituting
comparisons between them. We obtain a more definite
conception of each by contrast with the other. From
time immemorial the two great orators of antiquity
have lived in literary criticism chiefly by means of
such comparison. We know Cicero and Demosthenes
to-day mainly in the fact that each was what the other
was not. The literary mind of to-day would never
have known Plato *as* it does but for the existence of
Aristotle.

This law of comparison rules even our judgment of
national literatures. We have a conception of the
Greek literature which we never could have had, if
the Roman literature had not been superinduced upon
it. The Greek idea of beauty is more vivid in our
thoughts than it could have been but for the Roman

idea of law. The German and the English and the French literatures are thus illuminating each other in modern critical judgment. Is the allegory of the three artists, illustrative of the differences in the three national minds, too well known to deserve rehearsal? The legend reads that three painters — an Englishman, a Frenchman, and a German — were commissioned to paint a picture of a lion. The Frenchman started the next day for Africa, and there drew his picture of a lion from the life. The Englishman went to the British Museum, and painted his picture from the authorities he found in the library of natural science. The German shut himself up in his own library, and evolved a lion from the depths of his own consciousness. The caricature will live a long time as a representative of the three literatures and the national minds which they express.

Comparisons connect different departments of literature. We see the structure of Edmund Burke's mind the more clearly for our knowing his early passion for the poetry of Milton. The eloquence of Massillon is the more intelligible to us when we learn his predilection for the poetry of Homer. The dramatic power of Whitefield we understand when we are told of his youthful studies of Shakspeare. Criticism would be deprived of one of its most powerful auxiliaries, if it were dissevered from this study of resemblances and contrasts by comparison of authors.

The value of this expedient is seen, also, in the fact that comparisons have associated certain names in literature with certain names in art, in current literary opinion. Criticism often expresses its most profound judgment of an author by saying, that, if he had not

been an author, he would have been equally eminent
in painting or in sculpture. Canova's remark respecting Pitt and Fox was founded on the law of mental
resemblances.   To the Athenian mind, Pericles and
Phidias were of the same stock of mental character;
though it is not known that the one ever handled a
chisel, or the other ever spoke in public. "Paradise
Lost" has suggested to more than one reader the fres-
coes of Michael Angelo. Disraeli observes that Milton,
Michael Angelo, and Handel are parallels to each other
in their respective arts.   Each represents the same
epoch in the history of his art.   Dante's "Inferno"
and the painting of "The Last Judgment" have a
deeper ground of reciprocal suggestion than similarity
of theme.   One of the keenest of modern critics has
characterized the poetry of Shelley by likening it to
the coloring of Titian.   The relics we have of the
speeches of several great generals to their armies confirm the criticism which their military exploits alone
have suggested, that they might have been great orators.   Many lovers of eloquence have regretted that
Cæsar and Napoleon were not restricted by force of
circumstances to the senates of nations, rather than to
their battlefields.   Mr. Everett, characterizing Daniel
Webster, compares him to the Prince of Condé, on the
eve of the battle of Rocroi, and to Alexander before
the battle of Arbela.   These are not fanciful suggestions: they are founded on real similitudes of genius.
They illustrate the value of literary comparisons as
auxiliaries to critical knowledge of authors.

The most delicate qualities of authors are scarcely
discoverable without the aid of comparisons. Delicate
distinctions of color you can not discern, except by

placing them side by side. So it is in the study of
books. Wholesale criticisms of authors, either in praise
or censure, are almost sure to be false, because they
overlook the refinements of criticism. They would be
corrected often by more patient comparisons. Criticism
is often like color-blindness, by reason of its inability
to see the lights and shadows of literary character.

This was the defect in Jeffrey's criticism of Wordsworth. One must have accustomed one's taste to enjoy
serene and lunar models of beauty before one can come
to a poet like Wordsworth with an appreciative spirit.
This can not be gained without a considerable range
of comparative criticism.

Comparison of authors assists us to a true estimate
of the relative value of different qualities in literature.
Not all the qualities of good writing are equally valuable. Mr. Webster owed much of his success in oratory
to the justness of his estimate of strength as superior
to beauty in argumentative debate. Men of the first
order in senatorial discussion often choose abruptness
of speech, so that their power shall not be inwreathed,
and therefore entangled and impeded, by appendages
of beauty. Edmund Burke failed in public speech,
because of his failure to appreciate the qualities of oral
as compared with those of written address. Burke's
speeches are essays. His friend Sheridan was a more
powerful debater in his day; yet Lord Brougham says
that he played to the galleries, and indulged in claptrap. If Burke had brought the solidity of his genius
to a fair expression by those qualities which Sheridan
exaggerated, he would have been to the English Parliament what Demosthenes was to the Greek republics.
Yet such balancing of opposite virtues in composition

is not gained otherwise than by critical and candid comparison of authors distinguished for each.

5. As far as possible, our reading should be made tributary to the correction of our own known deficiencies in literary production.

Variety in selection of authors is not sufficient to insure symmetry of culture. Our existing tastes may tyrannize over our reading so far as to defeat the object of that variety. Let your mind swing loose in the act of reading, and you will inevitably be swayed by your tastes in appropriating what you read. You will appropriate only those elements which are kindred to your present tastes. An imaginative mind will coin fancy out of metaphysical definitions, if it reads passively. A prosaic mind will fashion a creed out of poetic imagery, if it exercises no control of itself in reading. It requires often self-denial to restrain our ruling tastes, and to seek, by dint of patient criticism, for those things which we most need, but do not want. Few scholars achieve this self-conquest whose literary enthusiasm is not largely pervaded by religious principle.

Observe an illustration of the need of the principle before us to remedy one of the most common defects of preachers; viz., the want of illustrative power. There is a class of preachers who are men of good sense, who have read extensively, who are well-informed as men of the world, whose discourses are clear, consecutive, well-aimed, and enforced by an earnest spirit. Yet they do not preach breathing sermons. They can not make truth vivid; they can not freshen stale truths. They are not live men in the pulpit: therefore their preaching is humdrum. Pious hearers who carry in their own souls a coal from a burning altar will call it "good preaching;" but they are not really moved by that preaching any more than the wicked and the indifferent are, who call it stupid. They are self-moved.

Such a preacher has no right to quiet his conscience by the self-assurance that he has done his duty because he has preached the truth. He has not preached the truth truthfully; he has not preached it scripturally. In the Scriptures truth is alive. It is all aglow with vitality made to appear vital by the dramatic resources and the quickened sensibilities of the writer. Our friend the preacher has a new process of culture to go through. The imaginative element in him needs to be aroused, and his reading needs to be so directed as to achieve this. He needs to study the great poets, the dramatic masters, the picturesque historians, biographers, essayists, of our language, and the most dramatic orators and preachers. By such a process of self-discipline the most prosaic mind may acquire somewhat of the genius of an orator. Every man has that genius in his nature: every man will show it, if his house takes fire. The elements of eloquence, of dramatic power, of painting, of whatever is vivid in conception, and forcible in utterance, are in the germ in every human soul. They need development in every preacher to make the pulpit a throne of power.

This principle is sometimes needful to remedy a defect the opposite to that just named; viz., an inability to preach logical, direct, and severe discourses. This, though a less frequent defect, is by no means uncommon. It often results from a neglect to cultivate dormant tastes. I can best develop this by an instance which came under my own observation. A young man began his ministry with me who possessed some of the

choicest elements of character which it has ever been
my lot to witness in one of his years. He was passion-
ately attached to the ministry as his life's work. The
only lamentation he uttered on his death-bed was that
his disease would cost him his profession.

The chief defect of his character was a beauty developed into a deformity. He was by nature a poet, and
by culture he had made himself nothing more. All
truth to his mind assumed imaginative forms, and expressed itself in rhythm. The sternest truths of religion
dissolved into images of beauty. Law, predestination,
sin, retribution, put on a roseate hue. On themes
kindred to his overgrown tastes he could preach, to a
solitary and dreaming hearer here and there, with the
voice of a charmer. But the majority of his hearers
were not moved even to a cold admiration of sermons
into which he poured his whole soul. His materials,
his methods of division, his style, his indirect, imaginative, shrinking appeals, were too ethereal for this homespun and corrupt world. To the masses his was an
unknown tongue.

Some subjects he could not discuss at all: it was not
in him. Retribution, depravity, decrees, he would
never have preached upon definitely to the end of time.
He probably never made a direct appeal to a hearer's
conscience. For robust talk in the pulpit he seemed
to have no heart. Yet, strange as it may seem, he had
by no means an effeminate nature. In defense of an
unpopular opinion he was lion-hearted. In times of
persecution he would have been sure to be in the
minority and a martyr. He could never have been
Luther, but he would have been Melanchthon: Luther
would have loved and leaned upon him. His few

friends revered him for his purity of character. Men
who experienced none of the difficulty which he had
in obtaining a pulpit felt self-reproached when they
communed with him.

The thing which he needed to make him a preacher
was more hardihood. He should have forced it. He
ought to have studied Edwards on the Will. He should
have read Dr. South, and the prose of Milton, and
Cromwell's speeches. He ought to have taken as his
models John Knox and Richard Baxter and President
Finney. He should have gone upon the wharves, and
talked to sailors. His brethren in the ministry felt
relieved, for his sake, when God removed him: we
thought, in reverent remembrance of him, of that feature in the felicity of the redeemed which seems in the
Scriptures to represent them as instructors of angels.
He appeared to be better fitted to that service than to
any demanded in a world like this.

By the views here expressed, it is not meant that
natural tastes are to be suppressed. Symmetry is not
worth the loss of vitality. A motionless equilibrium
of tastes is more fatal than a vivacious distortion of
them. No fault is greater than a tame faultlessness.
But there is a practicable regulation of one-sided proclivities, which is not the extinction or the enslavement
of them. Within reasonable limits let the natural
tastes have their way, but develop the dormant tastes:
that is the point, and it is practicable. Defects can be
so far corrected, that, while you will always do some
things better than others, you can still do the others
well. No man of common sense in the pulpit needs
to be dumb on some subjects, and imbecile to some
hearers, for the want of the tastes requisite to " become

all things to all men." Still less need any man who is called of God to the ministry be such a deformed man that he *must* make a one-sided preacher. Put your culture into the weak points of your intellect, as you put your principle into the weak points of your character. You are in no danger in either case of landing upon a dead level.

6. A scholarly ideal of reading includes a study of the biographies of authors and the history of their times. A book is part of an author's life. In itself it is incomplete; by itself it may be false: we need to see it as a part of the man. It is, therefore, a good general rule not to read an anonymous book. Now and then an exception occurs, like "Ecce Homo;" but exceptions are rare. Still more significantly is an author a fixture of his age. He is set in the age like a stone in an arch. It is never true literally that men write for future times. They write for their own times: they are made by their own times. The avenue to immortality for any man's influence lies through the life-blood of a living generation. Matthew Arnold means just this when he says, that, "for the creation of a master-work of literature, two powers must concur, — the power of the *moment* and the power of the man: the man is not enough without the moment." The law of nature is inexorable in this conjunction of the man with the time. Even the literature of inspiration is not free from its working. The Bible is intensely a local book: it is historic in its structure. To be understood, and still more to be felt as a power, it must be studied in its historic surroundings. Isolate it from those surroundings, and you have one of the most unintelligible of volumes.

So it is with uninspired authorship: it can not shoot

over its own age. Every author is the growth of his
own times: the roots of his thinking are there. If we
would know him well, we must see him there in his
natural birthplace, in the very homestead of his literary
being. We must first see him as his contemporaries
saw him; then we are prepared to see him with eyes
which they had not.

One or two illustrations of this principle will indicate
the importance of it in the history of the pulpit. In
the age of the Reformation and that next succeeding,
few preachers, so far as I know, preserved strictly what,
in modern homiletics, would be regarded as unity of
discourse. Often the whole system of grace was presented in one sermon. A preacher would have subjected his evangelical spirit to suspicion, if he often
discoursed without introducing the doctrine of justification by faith. It was then that the old homiletic rule
was originated, that a man should never preach without
saying so much of the gospel, that if a hearer should
never hear, and had never heard, another sermon, he
should not be ignorant of the way of salvation.

Modern homiletic science has abrogated that rule.
The taste of modern congregations would soon weary
of the sameness of the preaching which that rule would
create. But how does such preaching appear when seen
in the times which created it? Set it, like a picture,
in the frame of its age, and it seems the most becoming, because the most necessary, style of preaching.
The people were emerging from Romanism. The doctrines of grace were a novelty. Preaching itself had
become a rare accomplishment. Elementary views of
doctrines, and those often reiterated, were demanded by
the intellectual knowledge and the religious culture of

the times. It was more than pardonable, therefore, if
Luther and his contemporaries repeated and reiterated
the doctrine of justification by faith, and preached it by
remote connection with other themes, and dragged it
without connections into their conclusions. The emergencies of the times demanded this homiletic lawless-
ness, and the rude taste of the people did not condemn
it. To have forced upon the pulpit of that age, with
Athenian severity of taste, the homiletic canons of later
times, would have been neither good preaching nor
good sense. The people of the age were not Athenians.

Take an illustration from the English pulpit of the
seventeenth century. A certain preacher in the reign
of the first king James selected for a text the words:
"There are spots in your feasts of charity." He an-
nounced his subject thus, "*Maculæ in Epulis.*" He
proceeded to divide his discourse as follows: 1. "*Mensa
Sybaritica;*" 2. "*Mensa Centaurica;*" 3. "*Mensa Thy-
estea.*" Then, by way of contrast, he considered, 1.
"*Convivium spirituale;*" 2. "*Convivium sacramentale;*"
3. "*Convivium cœleste;*" which last division is ampli-
fied as being "*επουρανιοσ-ευωχια,*" which is still more magnificently developed by the subdivisions of "*visio
divinarum,*" "*societas angelorum,*" and "*consortium sanc-
torum.*"

True, he translated this gibberish. But our modern
criticism, in its impatience, says that he must have been
a fool. Perhaps not. Turn to Bishop Latimer, whose
power in the pulpit was such that his enemies did not
know what to do about it, except to burn the man to
ashes. Yet we find him guilty of the same pedantry.
The text of his famous "Sermon of the Card," he
announces in Latin, "Quis es?" Turn to Jeremy

Taylor,—no fool surely,—and you find, that in sermons which he artlessly tells us were preached to "the family and domestics of his patron, with a few cottagers of the neighborhood," there occurs a profusion of classical allusion, which seems like the echo of an Oxford lecture-room. Quotations from Plautus and Homer occur in a singular medley with others from Cicero and Seneca.

As sensible men, we must condemn all this; and we marvel that he had not the good sense to condemn it also. But we do him great injustice, if we judge him by the tastes of this age. One of the most curious inlets to the character of the English pulpit of those times is located just here. Not only is it true that this pedantry accorded with the scholastic taste of that age, but the popular taste refused to respect preaching which was not sprinkled with it. I open almost at random the sermons of a contemporary of Jeremy Taylor, and I find the text quoted in Latin, two Greek quotations on one page, and four Latin extracts on another. Reverence for the classic languages had descended to the seventeenth century from a century earlier, when there was no literature to speak of in the vernacular tongues of Europe. Erasmus risked his life in a mob, because he would not talk Italian. He abandoned a benefice offered to him in England, because he would not stoop to learn the English language. He often refused to converse in German, though he knew the language expertly. He thought the Reformation degraded by Luther's preaching and writing in German. This was the general taste of the scholars of his age. Erasmus was the most liberal of them all. They looked upon the classic tongues as the only tongues in which a scholarly literature could ever exist.

The common people, therefore, did their best to ape the folly of their betters. Through that whole period, down to a time long after Jeremy Taylor, this was the inherited taste of the people. They could not read or understand Latin and Greek; but they could hear it, and their ears were elongated by that. The relics of that taste remained to our own day. So lately as in the last decade of the eighteenth century, Clarkson published a pamphlet in England against the slave-trade, which he thought it politic to publish in Latin, lest he should not attract the attention of the learned men of Europe. It is within the remembrance of men now living that German scholars began generally to think it respectable to write commentaries in German.

In the time of Jeremy Taylor this taste for pedantry was, in one aspect of it, a virtue in the people, whatever it was in the scholars of the age. In the people it was, in part, the natural expression of their respect for learning. They objected to the learned Edward Pocock, professor of Arabic at Oxford, that he was "a plain, honest man, but no Latiner." Even modest George Herbert, when he began to preach, thought it necessary to awe the people by preaching to them a prodigiously learned sermon, in which he showed them that he was equal to the best as a "Latiner;" but in his pious simplicity he informed them that he should not generally preach to them so learnedly as that, but henceforth he should try to save their souls.

These illustrations show the practical necessity of the principle before us to a sound judgment of literature. To know an author well, we must know the man; and, to know the man well, we must know the times of which, by an irrevocable law of nature, he was the representative and the child.

Collateral reading will often disclose to us the secret of otherwise inexplicable effects of literature in the age when it was written. Contemporary influence is often the mystery of the next age. Our American pulpit already contains remarkable illustrations of this. President Edwards's sermons, as we read them, do not explain to us the astonishing effects of some of them. His elocution had almost no concern with them, except to moderate their fiery pungency. No audience of to-day could be plunged into an incontrollable fit of weeping by the sermon on the text, "Their feet shall slide in due time." An eye-witness testifies that Mr. Spurgeon's audiences listen to sermons from him which resemble that one from President Edwards, not only without a tear, but with signs of the most stolid indifference. To explain the experience of the church at Enfield, we must take note of the idiosyncrasies of that age as they are pictured in the history of the " Great Awakening."

LECTURE XX.

7. A PRINCIPLE fundamental to a preacher's study of literature is that it should be accompanied with habitual practice in composition.

If rightly conducted, a pastor's compulsory habits of production are rather a help than a hinderance to the scholarly character of his reading. Criticism and production re-act favorably upon each other. Nothing else is so powerful a tonic to the mind as composing: in certain conditions of the cerebral system it is a direct tonic to the brain, if conducted on the principle of alternation. Composition is creation. It is athletic exercise. The weakest minds are the most active absorbents, with the least capacity of production. The working of a healthy mind in study is like respiration: inhalation and exhalation are reciprocal. Without such reciprocity, a very large portion of our reading must be useless. It passes through the mind, but does not remain there. The power of retention needs the stimulus of production.

What knowledge is that which is most indelibly fixed in your memory, — that which you have learned only, or that which you have taught? What accumulations are most perfectly at your command, — those which are stored by the dead-lift of memory, or those which you have used by reproduction? The discovery is often disheartening, but it is healthful, that one is making a mere valve of one's mind, opening it for a stream of reading to run through, and shutting it upon nothing.

Again: study, without mental production, creates in the mind itself inferior habits of thinking. We think very differently in the two cases, of thinking for the purpose of expression, and thinking passively. We think more clearly and less discursively when we think for the purpose of communication; we analyze more accurately; we individualize more sharply; we picture thought more vividly; we are more apt to think in words.

Test this view by your own experience. Why is it that reverie has such a debilitating effect upon your mental energy? Why is it that nothing else so surely unfits you for a morning's work in composing as to begin it with a waking dream? And why is it that nothing else breaks up the dream so sternly as the act of thinking with the pen? Some of the most accomplished writers have formed the habit of taking the pen in hand as the most efficient aid to quick, consecutive, clear, profound, and vivid thinking. Robert Southey says, "It is the very nose in the face of my intellect that I never enter into any regular train of thought unless the pen be in hand."

Professor Stuart, who was one of the most fluent composers of his time, once told me, that, when he was a young man, he was often compelled to quit his sermon, and walk in his garden, in sheer vacuity of thought, not knowing what to say next. "But now," said he, "my mental working is all instantaneous and

incessant. Results flash upon me. I draft a plan of
a sermon as rapidly as I can move a pen. I could keep
a dozen pens in motion, if I had as many right hands."
He attributed that state of mental productiveness to
his lifelong habit of associating study with composing.

Mental production, when reduced to a habit, pro-
motes originality of thinking. In a perfectly healthy
mind the act of composing is a stimulus to invention.
The mental state in composing is an elevated state;
the mind then has a masterly sweep of vision. Sir
Walter Scott says, "My imagination is never so full
of a new work as when I approach the end of one in
hand." Clergymen often say that they are never so
ready for their week's work in sermonizing as on Sunday evening. Dr. Thomas Brown, the celebrated professor of mental science at Edinburgh, was so confident,
from his experience, of the power of composing to
stimulate his invention, that he at last trusted to it
for the suggestion of his most original thoughts. His
lectures were written chiefly in the evening before
their delivery. Many of his most brilliant trains of
reasoning never came to him in his calmer hours.
They were originated by the extemporaneous tug of
composition, and he lost them if he did not use them
then. President Edwards somewhere laments the loss
of a thought which came to him while composing a
sermon, but which he did not pause to note down, and
which he mourns over as so much mental treasure lost
for ever.

This is the secret of the most brilliant extemporaneous eloquence. When Henry Ward Beecher's "Life-
Thoughts" were first presented to him in manuscript,
he said he was not ashamed of them : he would

" father them, if he had ever had them." But many of
them he did not recognize. They had come to him in
moments of extemporaneous exhilaration, and had gone
from him. All such phenomena of literary experience
illustrate the secret and unconscious spur which composing gives to invention.

Further : study without composition destroys the
natural proportion of executive power to critical taste.
True, in a scholarly mind critical taste will always be
in advance of executive power. Every studious man
knows better than he can do. Still there is a certain
proportion between these two things, which can not be
impaired with impunity to executive genius. Destroy
that proportion, and you create a morbid taste respecting every thing which you do yourself. Thus fettered,
a man becomes a fastidious and discouraged critic of his
own productions. The excellences of authors do not
inspire, they only intimidate him. His own failure is
always a foregone conclusion. They affect him as the
first study of Alexander's campaigns affected Cæsar.
His sensibility becomes diseased; and his own efforts
of executive skill cease to be elastic, because they cease
to be hopeful. There is in all intellectual experience a
principle corresponding to that moral principle which
gives efficacy to prayer. The mind must have faith in
order to achieve any thing.

With such disproportion between taste and executive
power comes the temptation, almost irresistibly, to
relapse into the habits of an amateur, and abandon
original composition altogether. A similar weakness has
infected other departments of labor. It was such an
excess of critical taste which led Leonardo Da Vinci
and Washington Allston to leave so many unfinished

paintings. It is notorious that the majority of American artists who go to the galleries of Italy become only copyists : they cease to attempt original production. Said one of the most eminent portrait-painters in this country, after a year's residence in Florence, "I can paint no more. These fellows are painters; not I." Even of Michael Angelo it is said that he worked in a frenzy while the fever of his first conceptions was at its height, but that, when a work was finished, he relapsed into a chill, and his work disgusted him. His ideals and his works were thus in incessant conflict in his mind.

I suspect that the secret of the unwieldy style of Dr. Chalmers is discovered in the fact, which he confesses, that the difference between his ideal and his execution "produced a constant strain." His style is just that, — the straining of a mind in painful labor. It is not the bounding of a mind at ease, drinking in the exhilaration of its work. He never writes as if he loved to write. Robert Southey speaks of his own good fortune in not discovering certain faults in his own work too soon. He says, "I might have been spoiled, like a good horse, by being broken in too early." Tasso came near refusing to publish his "Jerusalem Delivered," because of the painful sense he had of its failure to equal his own critical standard. Dr. Arnold speaks of a certain subject on which he must write; and he says, "I groan beforehand when I think how certainly I shall fail to do it justice." Such a state of mind is debilitating, like a south wind. No man can do his best on a theme which he approaches, "groaning beforehand." When such debility becomes chronic, a man is in peril of a permanent prostration of

the executive forces, so that composition shall never be
to him other than a drudgery and a sorrow. The evil is
never outgrown by neglect of composition; and culture
by other means than composition only aggravates it.

Let us now observe some of the methods by which
the study of books may be associated with practice in
composition most successfully. Of these, certain methods of imitation of authors deserve mention. These are
of long standing, and of high repute among rhetorical
writers. One is that of translation from a standard
author to one's own language. The method is to take
a page from Macaulay, for example, and by a few read-
ings familiarize your mind with the materials, and then
reproduce them in your own words. Another of these
ancient methods is that of translation from one standard author to another. The idea is to take a passage,
as before, and, instead of reproducing it in your own
language, to reproduce it in a style imitative of another
distinguished author. Transfer thus a page from Milton into a page from Hume. A third of these ancient
methods is that of originating your own materials, but,
in the expression of them, imitating one or more
authors of good repute.

These methods agree in the principle of imitation.
They have been practiced from time immemorial by
masters of composition. In ancient times, when the
literature of the world was less abundant than now, it
would have been deemed folly to dispense with such
elaborate methods of self-discipline in the education of
a public speaker. You will recall the example of
Demosthenes in the study of Thucydides, and of Cicero
in the study of several Greek authors. On the revival
of the ancient literatures in the middle ages, this imita-

tive study of the Greek and Latin classics was carried
to an almost fabulous extent.

In our own times, Daniel Webster, Rufus Choate,
Edward Everett, and John C. Calhoun all submitted
to this kind of drill. They owed to it, in part, their
marvelous command of English style. Webster acquired such skill in imitation, that his reproduction of
John Adams in one of his orations has been supposed
by many well-informed critics to be a quotation. Indeed, some fragments of it were quotations from the
letters of Mr. Adams to his wife; but they were not
so extensive or important as to affect Mr. Webster's
title to the authorship of the passage in question. Edmund Burke's imitation of Lord Bolingbroke, in his
" Vindication of Natural Society," Bolingbroke's edit-
ors thought it necessary to disown by a card to the
public.

It will not do to ignore, still less to sneer at, these
methods, which are supported by such names and such
success. Yet I do not recommend them to preachers,
and this for the reason that they are impracticable to
preachers. They presuppose leisure. But the early
years of a pastor give no such leisure as that which
commonly attends the early years of a young man in
any other profession. I have never known these
methods of discipline to be adopted by a young pastor.
I doubt whether a preacher has ever given them a fair
trial. I pass them, therefore, to notice a more practicable method.

It is the habit of preparing the mind for daily composing by the daily reading of a favorite author. In
the suggestion of this method I have specially in view
the necessary habits of preachers. Preachers must

be prolific writers : they can not depend on favorable moods for composing. They have before them, not a life of literary leisure, but a life of professional toil, the chief burden of which is mental production. Said one of the most eminent pastors of Massachusetts in a recent lecture to candidates for the ministry, " I have been twenty years in the pastoral office; and in all that time I have done but one thing, — to get ready for next Sunday." So the work appears to successful preachers. They can not afford to spend much time as if in a Friends' meeting, waiting for impulses of speech. They must live in a *state* of mental production ; and, for this, daily composing is the most natural and the most successful expedient. It has been adopted by the most prolific authors and the most laborious preachers. Luther's rule was " *nulla dies sine linea.*"

Assuming, then, daily composing as the usual habit of a preacher, the plan here recommended is to commence each day with an hour or more of studious reading, and then to pass, without interval, from that reading to the work of composing. The advantages of this method are numerous. One is, that it is practicable, and is therefore more likely to be adopted than the more laborious methods which imply ample leisure. Another is, that it is an agreeable method, and therefore easily becomes habitual. A third is, that it can be made to fall in with other objects of study. It can be made both critical and accumulative in its character. In the act of quickening the mind for its own productive labor, you can multiply your resources of thought.

A fourth and the chief advantage is the direct stimulus which the mind may thus obtain for its own work. A wise selection of authors may render this stimulus almost invariable. Do not the majority of young writers spend an hour before composing in the mental toil of uplifting the mind to the level of its work, and concentrating its attention? That hour given to a suggestive author will commonly achieve the object much more easily, with less wear of the nervous system, and with less of spasmodic action in the work of composing.

Let it be added, in leaving this topic, that the method in question is supported by the practice of many eminent authors. Voltaire used to read Massillon as a stimulus to production. Bossuet read Homer for the same purpose. Gray read Spenser's "Faeric Queene" as the preliminary to the use of his pen. The favorites of Milton were Homer and Euripides. Fénelon resorted to the ancient classics promiscuously. Pope read Dryden as his habitual aid to composing. Corneille read Tacitus and Livy. Clarendon did the same. Sir William Jones, on his passage to India, planned five different volumes, and assigned to each the author he resolved to read as a guide and an awakener to his own mind for its work. Buffon made the same use of the works of Sir Isaac Newton. With great variety of tastes, successful authors have generally agreed in availing themselves of this natural and facile method of educating their minds to the work of original creation.

8. One principle remains to be noticed, by which other principles should be affected in our methods of study, which relates to the spirit of criticism. It is that in our studies a generous appreciation of the genius of others should be balanced by a just estimate of our own.

Two opposite errors are suggested here, against which we need to be fore-armed. The first is that of censorious and illiberal criticism. Gibbon classifies bad critics in three divisions,— those who see nothing but beauties, those who see nothing but faults, and those who see nothing at all. If you see nothing but faults in a great writer, you are in no mood to receive scholarly culture from him. De Quincey says that a surly reader is inevitably a bad critic. A sarcastic spirit in study is its own punishment. The truth is not in such a spirit. That spirit is receptive only of what is mean and degrading. "One can never know how small a small man can look till he has seen him trying to look down upon a great one."

Dr. Arnold says of historians, "If a historian be an unbeliever in all heroism, if he be a man who brings every thing down to the level of a common mediocrity, depend upon it, the truth is not found in him." The seat of the scoffer is not the seat of wisdon. The late Professor Reed of Philadelphia illustrates the spirit with which a young man, or any man, should read the great lights of literary history. In a letter to a friend he says, "I have just finished a lecture on Hamlet. My reverent admiration for the myriad-minded man has deepened by this study of his dramas: in the lowest deep a lower deep. John Milton is before me in awful grandeur for Monday next." Carlyle says that "great souls are always reverent to that which is over them: only small, mean souls are otherwise." Prescott the historian, by years of genial study, acquired such an affectionate reverence for the great minds in the history of literature, that he requested, that, when he came to die, his remains might be arrayed for the grave, and left for a while alone in his library, in the midst of the volumes in which he had found the scholarly companionship of his life. By that loving fiction he would pay his last tribute to the friends who had cheered him in his blindness. Such is the spirit of a genuine scholar.

But an error opposite to that of illiberal and sarcastic reading is that of self-depreciation in the contrast with illustrious men. I have already spoken of this as the result of a want of exercise of one's own powers. Sometimes the cause of it lies deeper than that: it is innate. A young writer does not trust his own pen, because he does not trust himself in any thing. The very thought of literary greatness oppresses him: therefore he does not let himself loose in composing. He is an ascetic, practicing upon himself a severity of criticism under which no abilities can expand freely.

Walter Scott, speaking of Campbell the poet, said, "What a pity it is that Campbell does not give full sweep to his genius! He has wings that would bear him to the skies. He does now and then spread them grandly; but he folds them up again, and resumes his perch, as if afraid to launch away. The fact is, he is a bugbear to himself." Often is it true that discerning critics see in a young man powers which success has not yet brought out into the light of his own consciousness.

These two elements — reverence for greatness in others, and respect for one's own powers — are correlative parts of one virtue: neither is healthy without the other. I have observed so many instances of the latter of these two evils, that I venture to give you in a brief *excursus* two or three suggestions for its correction. You will anticipate me in the thought that

liberty in original production is not to be gained by a
permanent sacrifice of your own ideals. Cling to your
best ideal of any thing. Fail with it, if need be, rather
than sacrifice it to success. " Be true to the dreams
of your youth."

A second thought is, that, in a state of mental dejec-
tion through self-depreciation, you should write with
temporary recklessness. The chief thing needed in such
a state of servitude is to *write*. Do something: create
something. The servitude must be broken through at
all costs. Try your own abilities: give them a chance
to prove themselves. Create, somehow, a little independent history of effort to stand upon. Till you can
obtain that, you have no " πov $\sigma\tau\omega$ " for the fulcrum of
your self-respect. If you can not obtain it under law,
seize it without law. *Be* an outlaw in the world of
letters. Violate the rules; defy principles; get loose
from shackles; clear your mind of the gear of the
critics; write defiantly. Give the rein to your powers
of utterance : let them career with you where they will.
Criticise their wild work in your after-thoughts, but
try them again. Apply the curb as they will bear it,
but put the coursers to their speed.

By such a passionate practice you may develop the
germs of your natural forces in composing, be they
what they may. You will discover them; not much,
probably, to speak of, and less to boast of, but something worth having and trusting. One Being has
thought them worth an act of creation. You will
know that you have them. The training of them will
come in due time. Robert Southey says, " Write rapidly; correct at leisure." Of one of his own poems he
says, " ' Madoc ' would be a better poem if written in

six months than if six years were given to it." If he
had said six weeks, instead of six months, he would
have been nearer the truth.

A third suggestion is, that, in a state of mental
despondency, you should write with dogged resolution.
Dr. Johnson says that any man can write who will keep
doggedly at it. Never yield the point that you can
write, and write well. Be indebted to obstinacy, if
need be. Pluck is a splendid virtue. Not only strike
when the iron is hot, but make it hot by striking.
Mind, like iron, is full of latent heat. It is more
malleable in some cases than in others; but in all it is
susceptible of white-heat. Therefore make it an invariable rule not to give up a subject of a sermon on
which you have begun to write. A vast amount of
waste of clerical effort is caused by succumbing to discouraged effort. The wasted introductions of sermons
are "an exceeding great multitude." When indicative
of a habit, they signify mental debility. Finish, therefore, every thing you undertake, for the sake of the
mental discipline of success. Make something of the
refractory theme and the barren text. The process will
not intoxicate you by its results. You will often floun-
der through the sermon, not much wiser at the end
than at the beginning, and hardly knowing how you
got through. You will be sometimes reminded of
Aaron's luckless attempt at statuary. You need not
dance around it; perhaps you will dash it in pieces;
but go through the process of making of it a likeness
to some living thing in the heavens, or in the earth, or
under the earth. You will be the stronger in will-
power over difficult themes, if in nothing else.

Take encouragement from the example of Sir William Hamilton: —

"There is scarcely a case on record where there existed a greater antagonism between an author and his pen than in the case of Sir William Hamilton. In reading his pure and limpid language, it is hard to realize that he was not a ready writer. But even while occupying the chair of logic and metaphysics in the University of Edinburgh, and every day delivering from it those lectures on metaphysical science which have made him famous throughout the world, he could never take his pen at any time, and write a certain required amount. Indeed, he always took up his pen with extreme reluctance. Owing to this aversion to composition, he was often compelled to sit up all night in order to prepare the lecture which was to be the wonder and admiration of every person who heard it the next day. This lecture he wrote roughly and rapidly, and it was copied and corrected by his wife in the next room. Sometimes it was not finished by nine o'clock in the morning, and the weary wife had fallen asleep, only to be wakeful and ready, however, when he appeared with fresh copy."

One other suggestion is, that you should trust the predisposition of the world to receive favorably the work of a young man. You have nothing to fear from the world's criticism, unless you invite it by self-conceit. The severity of criticism falls on middle-aged and old men. A young man, and specially if he is a clergyman, has every facility he can reasonably ask for for a successful beginning of his life's work. Wait ten years, and you will yourself marvel at the patience of your first parish. The "dead line" of "fifty years" is a long way off. If you live to reach it, you may have achieved a success which will make you indifferent to it. If you have not, it will not be owing to any want of generosity in the verdict of your contemporaries upon you as a youthful preacher.

LECTURE XXI.

THE PRACTICABILITY OF LITERARY STUDY TO A PASTOR. — PRELIMINARY SUGGESTIONS.

4th, I HAVE thus far endeavored to give you some ideal of the true study of literature in respect to its objects, the selection of authors, and the methods of the study.

The peril attending any such endeavor is, that it will only awaken in you a sense of the impracticability of the study to one who is immersed in the cares of a pastor's life. That is a profitless kind of advice which only impresses upon its recipients a sense of its uselessness to them. I wish to make the hints I have given you a real help to you, if possible. Therefore, before leaving this subject, I propose to add some suggestions upon *the practicability of literary study to a pastor.*

1. Let me ask you to observe several preliminary suggestions respecting a plan of scholarly reading.

(1) It is frankly conceded, as has been already remarked in the preface to this volume, that any scholarly plan of study must, to the majority of pastors, be, to a greater or less extent, an *ideal* one. The practicability of it is a matter of degrees, exceedingly variable at different times, as well as to different persons. The ideal element must enter largely into any plan that shall be largely useful. If there are any to whom it

can be only an ideal, it is not therefore useless, even to them. The *negative* value of a lofty ideal of scholarly life is not to be despised. It may act as a censor of a preacher's sermons, keeping alive a taste which will exclude unscholarly methods and material which he knows to be such, but which he will not avoid, except through a silent respect for his dumb library. The very sight of a library of a thousand volumes well chosen is a stimulus to a pastor who for months may not be able to read a volume. Says Bishop Hall on "The Sight of a Great Library," "Neither can I cast my eye casually on any of these silent masters but I must learn somewhat."

But the large majority of educated pastors *can* read something, if they will. Evidences abound that they *do* read very considerably. The charge can not be sustained against our American clergy, certainly not against the clergy of New England, that they cease to be scholars when they become pastors. Look at the reports of "ministers' meetings," and clerical "associations," and at the pastoral contributions to the weekly and quarterly press. The subjects there discussed show that our pastors are men of books as well as men of affairs. In the meridian of their labors, and at the head of large and exacting parishes, they do not turn the key upon their libraries. They are vigilant observers of the current of scientific and theological thought around them. The only question is, whether their reading is regulated by the wisest economy in choice and methods. One does not beat the air, then, who endeavors to give to youthful preachers a high and enduring ideal of a scholarly life. They are entering into a fraternity of scholars who find time and mental force for *some* ideal.

If further evidence is needed on this point, look to the pulpits of other lands and times.[1] Calvin was as laborious in the pulpit as out of it. He often preached, for weeks together, every day in the week; yet there are his immense folios to speak for him as a scholar. Bochart ministered daily while building his " Phaleg " and " Hierozoicon." Owen was incessant in preaching while his exposition of the " Hebrews " was in progress. Lightfoot was faithful to his pastoral duty while he was amassing his wealth of Talmudic learning. Lardner and Pye Smith and Hartley Horne had pastoral charges in London. Bloomfield was a vicar. Trench, Alford, and Ellicott were among the working clergy when they planned their learned works, and published a part of them. Stier was a pastor: so was Ebrard. Henry, Scott, Doddridge, Adam Clarke, were laborious and able ministers. Kingsley was a hard-working pastor: so, at one time, was Stanley. These men illustrate, by their union of pastoral duties with a scholarly life, that where there is a will there is a way.

But much is gained, if the presence of a scholarly ideal in the furniture of a pastor's mind achieves no more than to arrest the habit of reading at hap-hazard. This is the bane of the existing habit, probably, of the large majority of educated men. The time we spend in reading print of some kind is more considerable than the majority of us suppose. I once inquired of a hard-worked metropolitan pastor how much time daily, on the average, he spent in reading of all sorts, aside from that directly necessary to his preparation for the pulpit. He replied, " Not an hour." Then, correcting his hasty count, he said, " Two hours." Again reflecting, said

[1] See North British Review for 1860.

he, "I read the magazines. Yes: three hours and a half would cover it all." Well, a great deal can be done in three hours and a half a day. A distinguished commentator wrote five volumes of commentary in less than three years, working but three hours and a half a day. The Rev. Albert Barnes wrote sixteen volumes in less than an equal number of years, devoting to them only the hours before breakfast.

But the precious three hours and a half dwindle to a very small fragment, if one hour is given to the newspaper, and another to the magazine. They are largely wasted time, through the habit of reading without plan. More than time is wasted by it. Mental force is wasted, and mental debility is invited in the place of it. It is worth a great deal to a man's whole character as a man of culture, if that waste is forbidden by a scholarly ideal of what good reading is. Be it so that scholarly reading would restrict a pastor to few, some to very few, volumes in a year; better that than the wasteful and debilitating effect of reading at random. Be it that a pastor can read but ten, five, three volumes in a year: those few, well chosen and well read, may make all the difference between a scholar and a boor in his mental tastes and professional habits. A good ideal of scholarly reading is not useless, if it can regulate wisely an imperfect culture.

One good book is a great power in the making of a youthful mind. Is there not somewhere one *man* to whom you expect to be grateful for ever for his formative power over the development of your mind? What is one *book* but the mental being of one man? Why may not your obligations to the book be as incalculable as to the man? Reverently read the one book, then,

if you can do no more. Better this than none at all.
Better this by far than the slipshod mode of life which
befits only indolent minds, and invites an oblivion of
libraries. Oblivion of libraries is akin to softening of
the brain.

To bring to a definite point this vexed question, is
it too much to claim that every educated pastor not
disabled by disease can perpetuate in active life the
amount, if not the kind, of literary culture *which his
collegiate curriculum once created in him?* Is it not a
decline from *that* level which commonly creates the
"dead line of fifty"? And is that decline ever a necessity. "*Incredulus odi.*" In proof I could name to
you an eminent pastor, for forty years in the city of
New York, whose habit through all that time, with rare
and brief suspensions, was to read daily at least ten
lines in some Greek or Latin classic. That simple expedient drew after it, and *made* practicable to him, other
expedients of culture which kept his mind rich and
full and strong till the day of his death. At seventy
years he had found no "dead line."

(2) The study of books need not be made impracticable by the study of men, which has been so earnestly
recommended. The latter study does not require re-
tirement and mental concentration. It is discursive.
One may pursue it in the streets. Pastoral duty gives
large opportunity for it. It requires chiefly the mental
habit of professional vigilance. Let a pastor live in a
state of alertness towards all resources of oratorical
knowledge, and he will find them in every thing that
he sees and every thing that he hears. That habit
of literary lookout which led Walter Scott to pause in
the street to make note of a new word, and which led

Stothard to travel with a pencil tied to his finger, with which he made a drawing of every apple-tree he met with in a journey, illustrates the state of professional watchfulness which a pastor needs in his study of men. Carry thus the image of your pulpit always with you. Never give way to an idle mind. Never vegetate. Hours of physical recreation aside, that is never necessary to a healthy man. Be for ever on the lookout for tribute to your pulpit. You will find it in every thing, everywhere. One preacher was once led to correct an ungainly posture in the pulpit by observing the crooked gait of a lame man in the street. Another was set upon a course of voice-building by noticing the resemblance of his natural tone to the quacking of a duck. Live in such a state of professional outlook, and you may pursue the study of men daily, and yet not take an hour from the time consecrated to your library.

(3) It should be remarked, further, that some plan of scholarly reading must be *made* practicable, if a pastor would save himself from intellectual decline. The chief peril of a pastoral office is that of a *busy* intellectual stagnation for the want of persistence in liberal studies. This was the peril which was so fatal, as Professor Tholuck thought a quarter of a century ago, to the Protestant clergy of Prussia. It can not be said to be unknown in this country. In my judgment, the existence of the "dead line of fifty" is not wholly but chiefly due to it.

It should therefore be a foregone conclusion, when a young man enters the ministry, that some plan of literary study shall be made practicable. Sacrifices must be made to it, — sacrifices of ease, sacrifices of needless recreation, sacrifices of notoriety, and sacrifices of pecuniary interests. If a young man does not value it sufficiently to make such sacrifices to it, it *is* impracticable to him.

(4) The best culture for success in the pastoral office is not consistent with the appropriation of any large proportion of time to the miscellanies of the church.

I refer here to that department of clerical labor which is made up of executive affairs. A certain amount of this is necessary to the fellowship of the churches: therefore every pastor must so far supervise it. It would be dishonorable to shirk it. But, outside of the individual church and its immediate sisterhood, there is an amount of executive duty, which, as many practice it, becomes a profession by itself, to which the pulpit and its tributary studies are subordinated. The management of institutions, the direction of societies, the care of the denominational press, leadership in ecclesiastical assemblies, membership of innumerable committees, of boards of trust, of special commissions, all inflicting an endless amount of correspondence, — these form a distinct department of clerical labor, and create a distinct class of clerical workers. There are men, as you well know, whose chief usefulness is in this line of service. Their pulpits are secondary to it, and their libraries are more distant still from their chief ambition. If one of them were called to account for the neglect of his library, he could only plead, as did the ancient prophet of Judæa, "Thy servant was busy here and there."

It need not be said that this class of clerical workers are performing a very useful and necessary labor, which somebody must do. Those who drift into it are commonly men whose tastes and tact enable them to do it well. They deserve commendation unqualified. But the point I press at present is this, that this department of our profession is not intrinsically congenial with the genius of a preacher and the tastes of a scholar. As a rule, therefore, it must be conducted at a loss of the highest clerical discipline. Eminence in it can not be combined with eminence in the pulpit. Some of its duties can as well be discharged by laymen.

Exceptions to the rule occur, as in the case of Dr. Chalmers, who, both as a preacher and as an executive, was a genius. But such cases are not numerous enough to affect the rule. Every young pastor, therefore, should canvass and decide for himself the question whether his mission of usefulness to the church lies in seeking. or accepting any large amount of this kind of work. The inquiry should be answered early in his professional career. I very well remember the form in which it presented itself to my own mind in my early manhood. I trust to the freedom of the lecture-room in referring to it for the sake of the glimpse it will give you of the opinions on the subject entertained by a considerable class of the older ministry.

The question lay between my immediate entrance upon a pastoral charge, and my taking a fourth year of study. The ecclesiastical body under whose direction I was studying so kindly interested themselves in my plans as to appoint a committee to express to me their judgment that I should accept the pastoral service without delay. The argument of the committee was, that a certain moderate average of power in the pulpit, subordinated to a large inventive faculty in miscellaneous labors, was a more useful ideal of the clerical life than that of a more able pulpit to which learning and studious habits should pay tribute. Letters from several very estimable pastors confirmed that counsel. Said one, "The church needs workers, not students." A judge of the Supreme Court of Massachusetts sent a message to me, saying, "It does not require many books to convert souls." Of them all, but one man dissented from the general drift of opinion. He advised a fourth year of preparatory study. "Lay a broad foundation," said he, "and then build high."

I saw that the problem covered, not merely one year or two, but the whole character of my ministry; in fact, it was whether I should be a preacher, with the tastes and the studious habits which a preacher's life requires, or should make the pulpit an appendage to a life of miscellaneous activities. I chose the pulpit and the study. The fourth year at the seminary was a fraction of a life's plan. I have no inducement to speak of the results of my choice any further than to say that I should repeat it if the same alternative were again before me.

The same question will force itself upon you substantially, though the form may vary. The miscellany and the study will array themselves before you as rivals, and you must choose between them. The board of directors, the board of trustees, the ecclesiastical council, the prudential committee, the managers of this, and the delegation to that, will stand before you as competitors of your pulpit, and you must make your selection. Will you be a committee-man, or will you be a preacher? Will you be a man of affairs, or will you be a scholar? Will you be in demand as the ubiquitous delegate to councils, or the executive leader of your presbytery, or will you be a prince in your pulpit, with the accessories of culture which that implies? Every pastor should decide the question with an enlightened policy, knowing what he gives up, and why. Mediocrity, I admit, can be gained in both departments of service. But ought any young man to *plan for* mediocrity? The world is not suffering for the want of that commodity.

I think I have seen more deplorable waste of ministerial force in needless dissipation of time upon executive miscellanies than in any other form which has come under my notice, which did not involve downright indolence. For one thing, you will soon discover, if you go into this kind of work to any great extent, that it costs a large amount of time for ten men to do the work of one. When did ever a committee of ten men on any thing work fast? William Jay, the celebrated pastor at Bath, once said, that, if Noah's ark had been intrusted to a committee for the building of it, it would still be on the stocks. It is inherently difficult to secure unanimity among an able committee, so that work can go on rapidly. Remember always that your most brisk and efficient work must be solitary work. One hour in your study is worth three in the committee-room. You do this miscellaneous work, if at all, at this enormous cost of time.

In this dissuasion from excessive labor upon the miscellanies of the church, you will understand that I speak of the policy of pastors in old and organized settlements, to which the majority of you will minister. Missionary labor, and work on the frontier, must, of course, come under a different *régime*, because they must meet different necessities. One such frontiersman I could name to you, who is a hero beyond all earthly fame. He might have been the man of whom the preacher said, " One man among a thousand have I found."

The conclusion of the whole matter, then, is this: if in God's providence you are called to the charge of a well-established church in the midst of such churches, and if you are led by God's teaching to believe that the pulpit is the throne of power for you, give yourself to that pulpit. From it you may speak to less than a hundred souls. Remember that Jeremy Taylor did that at Golden Grove. Dr. Chalmers did that at Kilmany. President Edwards did it at Stockbridge. You may have as clear a self-knowledge in this respect as Richard Hooker had when he wrote to his ecclesiastical superior, Archbishop Whitgift, " I am weary of the noise and oppositions of this place. God and nature did not intend me for contentions, but for study and quietness." And he proceeds to pray that he may be removed to "some quiet parsonage, where," he says, " I may see God's blessings spring out of mother-earth." It was this modest but true self-knowledge which put it into his power afterwards to write the " Ecclesiastical Polity," which has brought his name down to our times.

I repeat, therefore, if it is given you to see that the pulpit is your throne, give yourself to it and to the scholarly life which is essential to it. Ally your study with it, and make your home there. Leave executive bishoprics of the church universal to other hands. There are men enough who can do that service, whose tastes develop genially towards it, and whose success shows that they were created for it. It will never suffer for the want of aspirants. When did ever an office of executive duty in the church go begging? If you have been created for the other thing, *do that thing*. Preach; let other men govern. Preach; let other men organize. Preach; let other men raise funds, and look after denominational affairs. Preach; let other men hunt up heresies, and do the theological quiddling. Preach; let other men ferret out scandals, and try clerical delinquents. Preach; let other men solve the problems of perpetual motion of which church history is full. Then make a straight path between your pulpit and your study, on which the grass shall never grow. Build your clerical influence up between those two abutments.

(5) Any plan of clerical study will fail which is not founded upon a stern physical discipline. You must know the laws of health, and must observe them, if you would succeed in a lifelong plan of literary effort. High culture, like high attainments in piety, depends largely on a subordination of the body to the mind. The body needs a gentle training to the endurance of brain-work. By patient training we can educate the body to endure double the amount of intellectual labor which is generally possible to it at the age of twenty-five years. I need hardly say that no great intellectual success can be attained by a man whose body is in subjection to *any* appetite.

(6) Any plan has little probability of success which is not assisted by certain moral virtues. You can not work well with your brains and your heart in conscious conflict with each other. Especially your intellectual aspirations must have the approval of your conscience. If questions of conscience about any thing in your intellectual life are yet unsettled, settle them as the very first duty you have to perform. Agree with thine

adversary quickly. Your chariot will drag more heavily than Pharaoh's in the Red Sea, if your conscience blocks the wheels.

Of the special virtues necessary to a pastor's success in literary pursuits, the chief are, reverence for literary work as religious work, persistence in your own work as that for which God created you, patience with yourself, incessant prayer for success, and trust in divine promises of success. The whole business of ministerial culture needs to be thus baptized in the religious spirit as absolutely as the administration of the Lord's Supper. Do not begin it till you can see the truth of this.

Without such moral auxiliaries as these, you must become an ungodly man in order to succeed. You must gain unity of soul in one direction or the other. One reason for the brilliant success in literature of some intensely irreligious men is that they had rid themselves of all religious scruples. Their whole being was a unit in literary pursuits. Goethe and Byron and Lord Macaulay seem to have been instances of this: hence their marvelous literary acquisitions, and power of execution. One reason for the success of Satan in the dominion of this world is the absolute intellectual singleness of his being. He concentrates power, with no drawbacks caused by conscientious relentings, doubts, scruples. In a moral being, intellectual force pure and simple, unregulated by moral sensibilities, is Satanic force.

(7) No plan will probably succeed which is not in some important features your own. You can not wisely import whole into your culture the literary advice of another mind. Take the advice, but take it for what it is worth *to you*. Scarcely two men can execute well the same plan of a scholarly life. Some men

have more carburet of iron — the stuff that steel is
made of — in their blood than others. Their mental
constitution is affected by it. Each man, therefore,
must, in some respects, frame his own plan. All that
an instructor can do is to give you hints, principles,
facts from the experience of others. The question is
not what is absolutely the superior plan, but what is
the best for you, with your health, with your power
of mental appropriation, with your amount of time for
literary work, in your parish, and at your age.

The yeomen of the Carolinas framed out of their
own experience and common sense a better plan of
civil government than John Locke framed for them
with the most profound philosophy of the age, and a
thousand years of European experiment in government
at his command. So you are in some respects wiser
than the most learned of your teachers concerning
what *you* can do in literary culture. You need also
the discipline of forming your own plan to qualify you
to execute any plan.

(8) No plan will be likely to succeed which is
founded upon a scholastic ideal alone. The scholastic
mind can not be, without amendment, a model for the
professional mind. Yours, from the nature of the case,
must be the professional mind. It must be scholarly,
yet not scholastic. Leibnitz, Gibbon, Descartes, Coleridge, Wordsworth, Southey, were by profession *literati*.
They were nothing else. The experience of such men
needs to be tested by the professional judgment, before
they are applied to men in a profession to which
literary pursuits must be but an appendage. A pastor
should frame a plan adapted to professional necessities,
and then he should respect that plan as profoundly as
if it had the imprint of a score of universities.

(9) You should so arrange your plan of study as to secure as much concentration of effort as is practicable. It is not wise to have more than one or two great lines of study planned and in operation at one time. A day can not be of much value for studious labor, if it is whittled up into shavings of time. Different departments of study must be pursued in succession, time enough being allotted to each to secure the benefit of continuity. The details of such a plan every man must devise for himself; but the principle is invariable, — that the plan be so adjusted as to obtain mental concentration; and for concentration you must have time for continuity of impression.

Recent psychological investigations into the conditions of brain-force disclose the fact, that the most effective force of the brain in continuous labor requires *duality* of objects of pursuit. Rest of brain does not require cessation of work, but change of work. Change is more restful than idleness. This indicates that the true economy of power in study is found in having two lines of study between which the mind may interplay.

(10) You should so form your plan of study that it can sustain interruptions. Any plan of study in pastoral life must be interrupted. Times will occur when it must be suspended. Awakenings of the popular conscience may absorb all the mental energy of a pastor in perpetual production. Our profession is one which abounds with emergencies. These must be anticipated. A power of sustained purpose must be cultivated, which can hold study in reserve when study is impracticable, and not be demoralized by the suspension. We must plan for interregnums, so that they shall not result in anarchy.

(11) Your courage in pursuing any plan you may devise should be sustained by the certainty of your mental growth. You will not always be what you are now in point of intellectual strength. Growth is your destiny. Your professional labors will compel growth. They are more productive of mental enlargement than the life of a literary man without a profession. The kind of growth which they will necessitate in you will re-act with a power which will surprise you upon your efficiency as a reader. Your power of mental appro- priation will increase marvelously : hence will come the faculty of rapid reading. Nothing is more sure to disclose itself as a result of years of scholarly reading, and professional composing in alternation, than the gift of rapid mastery in both. As you will write sermons rapidly, so you will appropriate books to your stock of thought rapidly. Some volumes which now would cost you a second reading you will by and by master with one. Some which now require a full and cautious study, by and by you will appropriate by their tables of contents and their prefaces only.

This destiny of growth should be largely trusted by a youthful preacher. Without it, his life would be hopelessly overladen. I well remember, that, when I began my ministry, a good doctor of divinity said to me, "Be content to work hard for ten years, and then you can take it easy." His advice was on a level with his grammar. He should have said, "Be content to work hard for ten years, and then you can begin to work harder; but it will be with more cheering results." No other work of God in creation was so grand as the creation of a *man :* so nothing else in life is so grand a thing as the *growth* of a man.

LECTURE XXII.

A PLAN OF PASTORAL STUDY IN ENGLISH LITERATURE.

2. Passing now from the preliminary suggestions already made, I wish to apply as far as possible the principles advanced in the preceding Lectures to a plan for the study of English literature. My aim here is to give you a method by which *substantially* the majority of pastors can *make* practicable, by dint of self-discipline, a lifelong study of the literature of our language, which shall be sufficiently productive of results to save them from intellectual decline.

(1) Run a line of professional reading through the history of the literature. A line of professional reading should be the backbone of every clergyman's literary life. I have not here in view the bulk of the professional literature, but a historic line of it only. The advantages of this may all be summed up in one, — its naturalness. It is natural for a professional man to make his profession the center of his culture. This is only adjusting your studies, in form and by design, to what they will be, and must be in fact. This is the principle of all wise methods in real life. Necessities must be first cared for. The spinal cord of real life is labor to meet necessities. So it should be with literary pursuits in the midst of professional avocations. A

pastor will obtain his most valuable knowledge of our literature by building it up gradually alongside of the clerical profession.

(2) Pursue collateral lines of reading as they are suggested by professional studies. Any great trunk of literature, like that formed by one of the professions, will be dense with branches running out from either side, into which study will diverge naturally. For instance, you can not familiarize yourself with the English pulpit of the seventeenth century without discovering that you must acquaint yourself also with that most creative period of English history. The Revolution, the Commonwealth, and the Restoration are in the heart of it.

By the law of literary association, collateral lines of reading will branch out in all directions. You will be surprised to find how large a portion of the entire body of the literature is covered by the immediate and obvious lines of collateral study. Let me illustrate this by a single example. At the first view it appears unnatural to associate the pulpit with the stage. How can a pastor's professional reading lead him naturally to the study of Shakspeare? I answer, No two things are more indissolubly connected in English history than the sermon and the drama. There are one or two periods in the history of the English pulpit in which we can not judge well of it without taking into account the taste of the people for theatrical displays. Whitefield and Shakspeare are thus brought hand to hand. The sermons of Bishop Latimer can not be appreciated otherwise.

(3) Portions of our literature which are remotely connected with the pulpit should be read by depart-

ments. Do not read the plays of Ben Jonson to-day, and Izaak Walton to-morrow, and Charles Lamb on Wednesday. Read continuously for a while by departments. English poetry, for instance, forms a department by itself. A few great divisions will classify the whole of it. A very few names should be its *nuclei*. Beginning with Chaucer (who died in A.D. 1400), advance two centuries, and you come to Spenser and Shakspeare, contemporaries. Proceed half a century, and you overtake Milton, and, a quarter of a century later, Dryden, who died precisely three hundred years after Chaucer. A century and a half farther on, you find Wordsworth, who died four hundred and fifty years from Chaucer. English poetry can all be gathered in clusters around these names; and it is of little moment with which of them one begins one's study of that department.

(4) Generally plan to occupy fragments of time with standard literature. In a pastor's life, fragments of time must be utilized, or the loss in the aggregate is immense. Do not be prodigal of Monday mornings: there is no need of it. We should keep at hand in our own libraries, on our study-tables, such authors as the four great poets, such prose-writers as Bacon, Hooker, Milton, Burke, Butler, Macaulay. The habitual intercourse of our minds with a dozen of the leading spirits of our libraries, in the freedom of fragmentary reading, will create innumerable little feeders to our culture, which will keep it full and rich and pure.

(5) Much of the light literature of the language may be naturally reserved for periods of relief from professional labor. English fiction has become a very

vital department of the national thought. Clergymen used to ignore it. That is no longer wise, if it ever was so. We must know it; but we need not give to it our most valuable time. It is wasteful to read Charles Dickens in the midst of a winter's campaign of professional toil. A healthy mind in a healthy body does not need such costly recreation: reserve it for vacations. More than economy of time is thus gained: we gain sympathy of daily pursuits. Seek mental recreation from change of mental labor. Do not unbend to the extreme every day. That is not natural relief to spring from extreme to extreme. A well-trained mind husbands its strength most effectively by passing from a greater to a less degree of mental tension, not to no tension at all. Remember the physiological law of duality. We must dare to be ignorant of light literature till the natural time for it comes in our plan of life.

(6) I pass on now to give you a line of professional reading as illustrated from the history of the English and American pulpit, from which the most that I expect is, that it may be suggestive to you of some more minute plan, or some other, yet, for the purpose, an equivalent plan of your own.

In the following pages I attempt to combine four features; viz., to distinguish the most eminent of Engglish and American preachers, to group these in historic clusters, to assist your memory of our literature as a whole by associating these clerical names with their secular contemporaries, and to arrange these groups in chronological order. I select only representative names, and from the most strongly marked periods in the history of our pulpit. Of course a multitude of eminent names must be omitted.   Of the names which I recite, I will ask you to underscore those which I shall designate as specially deserving of study, either as professional representatives or as literary standards.

The dates I arrange as nearly as possible in the center of the public life of the authors clustered around them, reckoning a quarter of a century on either side of the date specified.   This method is sufficiently accurate.   You will generally find it convenient, in your attempts to fix dates of authors in your memory, to associate the name with some central date of authorship, rather than the date of birth or death ; unless one of these happens to synchronize with the beginning, or middle, or end, of a century, as is the case with Chaucer and Dryden and Wordsworth.

Beginning, then, with the earliest period of the British pulpit, the first date I name is A.D. 1350.   This being long before the Reformation, the pulpit had scarcely an existence in England.   But one name deserves mention in so condensed a catalogue as I am attempting to form. Within a quarter of a century on either side of this date lay the public life of JOHN WICKLIFFE.   Underscore his name as the only representative of the infancy of the English pulpit.   It may assist our mastery of the secular literature of the language to note that Wickliffe was contemporary with Geoffrey Chaucer; the one sustaining to English preaching the same relation that the other did to English poetry.

From this period nothing appears to our purpose for about two hundred years.   Note the date A.D. 1550. Within twenty-five years of this date, before and after, lay the major part of the public life of WILLIAM TYNDALE, Miles Coverdale, JOHN KNOX, HUGH LATIMER,

THOMAS CRANMER, John Fox, and William Cartwright.

The most vital literary activity of the reign of Henry VIII. was concentrated upon the translation of the Bible. Upon that the revival of the pulpit hung suspended. It was a question of life and death to preaching. To very few men are the English and American churches so much indebted through all time as to Tyndale. The "blasphemous beast," as Sir Thomas More called him, gave to the church the chief model of King James's Bible. Underscore the name of Tyndale as the pioneer in the work of translating the Scriptures, that of Knox as the father of the Scottish Reformation, that of Latimer as one of the earliest martyrs to the liberty of the pulpit, and that of Cranmer as the founder of the Anglican Church.

It may assist us, in connecting the religious with the secular literature of this period, to remark the fact that these men were wholly, or in part, contemporary with Sir Philip Sidney, the author of the "Art of Poesy," and Roger Ascham, the father of English educators; and to this and the succeeding period belongs the name of Sir Walter Raleigh.

The next date of importance is A.D. 1600. The half-century of which this is the center covers substantially the public life of a very small group, of which RICHARD HOOKER, Dr. Donne, Bishop HALL, and George Herbert are the chief. Through the whole of the long reign of Elizabeth the pulpit had to struggle for leave to be at all. Brilliant as the age was in other departments, the literature of the pulpit was meager in the extreme. Queen Elizabeth did not take kindly to preachers: she said that two in a diocese were an ample supply. In London many churches were closed for the want of preachers. Says Bishop Sandys, preaching before the Queen, " Many there are who do not hear a sermon in seven years, I might say in seventeen." In Cornwall, Neal says there was not one man capable of preaching a sermon. At one time the University of Oxford had but three preachers, and these were all Puritans.

This state of things was the inheritance which the Church of Rome had bequeathed to the Church of England. The depreciation of preaching in the Church of England which exists to-day had its origin then. Hence, also, arose the extreme poverty of the pulpit at the date before us. Hooker, the darling of the Church of England to this day, is declared, by one of the best-informed critics of English literature, to sustain to English prose somewhat of the same relation that Chaucer sustained to English poetry; he having written the first solid prose-work of logical structure, and clear, forcible style. Bishop Hall was one of the earliest writers of laconic and racy English: he has been called the " English Seneca." The gentle George Herbert, the humble country parson, will live long after his infidel brother, Lord Herbert, is forgotten. This little group of clerical writers were surrounded by Shakspeare, Spenser, Beaumont and Fletcher, Philip Massinger, and Ben Jonson, of dramatic fame; and Lord Bacon was their contemporary.

Passing on a little more than half a century, let us, for the convenience of the synchronizing with the Restoration of the Stuarts, select the date A.D. 1660. This year is in the heart of the most eventful period of English history, and of the golden age of the pulpit as well. Within a quarter of a century of the Restoration, on either side, we find two parallel columns of great names. In the Established Church appear Archbishop LEIGHTON, JEREMY TAYLOR, ISAAC BARROW, Archbishop Tillotson, ROBERT SOUTH, Edward Stillingfleet, and William Sherlock, all of them men of great power in their day, and some of them authors of standards in literature which will live as long as the language lives. Among the nonconformists we number Joseph Calamy, RICHARD BAXTER, John Owen, John Flavel, JOHN BUNYAN, STEPHEN CHARNOCK, and JOHN HOWE. England has not seen since their day an equal number of men of equal rank in her pulpits. Contemporary with these galaxies of clerical genius, it will help our memory of the period as a whole, to recall John Locke, Sir William Temple, Sir Thomas Browne, Abraham Cowley, Samuel Butler, John Dryden, and, *princeps inter pares*, John Milton.

A sad decline appears as we advance another half-century. The revolution of 1688, with the oppressions which preceded it, and the confusion which followed it, and the outbreak of infidelity in the persons of Hobbes, Shaftesbury, and Bolingbroke, greatly depressed the pulpit. Its ablest productions were controversies with infidelity. The close of the seventeenth century was a dark day for the spiritual vitality of both England and Scotland.

Adopting the year A.D. 1700 as the next center, we find before and after it Bishop Lowth, Bishop Atterbury, SAMUEL CLARKE, Bishop Hoadley, RALPH ERSKINE, Bishop BUTLER; and, on this side of the Atlantic, we note the first name which lifts the American pulpit to the level of that of the mother-country, in the person of Cotton Mather.

Contemporary with these, wholly or in part, were the essayists who founded "The Spectator," Addison and Richard Steele; the originators of the English novel, Richardson, Fielding, and Smollett; also Pope, Gay, and Prior, noted as the Jacobite wits of the day; Hobbes, Bolingbroke, and Shaftesbury, the trio of noted freethinkers; and Congreve, Sir Isaac Newton, and Bishop Berkeley. Isaac Watts deserves mention as the first man who redeemed English hymnology from doggerel, although he wrote not a little of it himself.

Advancing another half-century, we reach the date A.D. 1750. This was the age of tame politeness in the Church of England, and the secession of Methodism from it. Within twenty-five years of this date comes the public life of Dr. HUGH BLAIR, Bishop Horsley, Dr. WILLIAM PALEY, and, outside of the Establishment, Philip Doddridge, JOHN WESLEY, GEORGE WHITEFIELD, the senior EDWARDS, Joseph Bellamy, SAMUEL HOPKINS, and Samuel Davies.

These numbered among their contemporaries the club of which Dr. Johnson was the autocrat, including Goldsmith and Edmund Burke; the three great historians of the empire, Hume, Robertson, and Gibbon; William Cowper, who wrought a revolution in English poety; Dr. Reid, the father of the Scotch philosophy; the elder Earl of Chatham, who stood at the head of parliamentary eloquence; and Benjamin Franklin.

Advancing to the beginning of the present century (A.D. 1800), we find not one man in the Church of England who deserves to rank with the following names out of it: Andrew Fuller, ROBERT HALL, JOHN FOSTER, THOMAS CHALMERS, and, in this country, Dr. TIMOTHY DWIGHT, Dr. NATHANIEL EMMONS, Dr.

Jonathan Edwards, Dr. John M. Mason, Dr. Edward
Payson, Dr. Edward Griffin, and Dr. WILLIAM E.
CHANNING.

To this period, for the most part, belong, in secular
literature, Robert Burns and Samuel Rogers; the Lake
Poets, Wordsworth, Coleridge, and Southey; also the
earlier group whose names commonly occur together,
Walter Scott, Lord Byron, Shelley, and Keats; Charles
Lamb, Thomas Moore, Thomas Campbell; and, in the
Scotch philosophy Dugald Stewart, and Dr. Thomas
Brown.   The chief literary revolutions of the time
were Scott's originating of the historical romance, and
Wordsworth's simplifying and humanizing of English
poetry.   The latter movement has affected all the
literature of the language since that day: Charles
Dickens could not have existed but for the advent of
Wordsworth.

Adopting one more date, A.D. 1850, we come into
groups of names, some of which are fragrant in the mem-
ory of the living : William Jay; Dr. EDWARD PUSEY,
the father of the ritualistic re-action in England;
William Archer Butler; Archbishop WHATELY; Dr.
Henry Melville; FREDERICK ROBERTSON; Dr. Thomas
Guthrie; Mr. Spurgeon; and, in this country, ALBERT
BARNES; Dr. Lyman Beecher; Dr. Nathaniel W. Tay-
lor, the father of the so-called "New-Haven Divinity;"
HORACE BUSHNELL; Dr. CHARLES FINNEY, the most
noted revivalist of modern times; Dr. Gregory Bedell;
Dr. Stephen Olin; Dr. FRANCIS WAYLAND; Dr. James
Alexander; and Dr. James H. Thornwell, the most
eminent pulpit orator of the southern half of our
Republic.

Contemporary with these names should be associated

those of Alison, Mackintosh, Hallam, Prescott, and Motley, as historians ; Macaulay, Carlyle, Jeffrey, Sydney Smith, Talfourd, De Quincey, and Washington Irving, as essayists; Cooper, Thackeray, Dickens, and Hawthorne, as novelists ; Tennyson, Bryant, Longfellow, and Whittier, as poets; and Sir William Hamilton as a metaphysician.

This catalogue of clerical names, you will understand, I give you as only a representative one, with which it is desirable to be acquainted as far as possible. Of these, I have distinguished about thirty names of men whose writings and memoirs would give you a very fair knowledge of the entire history of the pulpit in our language, so far as that is extant in libraries. These thirty names a pastor at the meridian of his labors *can* make himself acquainted with, even if he will give to them only fragments of time. It is a kind of study which does not necessarily demand the severest, long-continued, and unbroken application. A man of affairs can make it a supplement to his professional life.

I would not be understood to limit our method of beginning the study of English literature to the study of the pulpit. I advise this only as the most natural one to a pastor in active life. It is natural to build the literature around the profession as its center. But some may find an equally suggestive help in an historic line of English philosophers from Lord Bacon downward. A similar line of suggestion might be framed on the history of the English essay. A very superior one might be drawn, making English poetry the historic center from Chaucer to Wordsworth.

The least valuable method, in my judgment, is that

which is, perhaps, the most frequently chosen. It is the basis of many abortive attempts to master the bulk of our literature. I allude to that which arranges the contents of English libraries along the line of political history, and associates the illustrious names with the royal dynasties of England. This method, plausible in theory, will be found cumbrous in the experiment. Better by far is it to follow some historic line drawn within the literature itself, and then make excursions from that laterally into other departments.

It is of less importance than at first appears, what specific line be made central. I have chosen that of the pulpit. But our profession suggests others of perhaps nearly equal value. Theological science is splendidly developed in our language. An historic line drawn in that department would command the professional enthusiasm of many pastors, for the purposes of study, more powerfully than the homiletic line. The history of churchly organization may be more stimulating to another. The liturgic development in the history of English thought may be attractive to some. The line of English commentary on the Bible may be the more awakening to others. The sway of the English Scriptures over our entire literature is very marked. The very structure of our language has been in part modeled by them. It matters little what be chosen as the central line of research, except that it should, in the majority of cases, be within the natural range of the profession, so as to command the zest of professional enthusiasm, and the unity of mental life, which the labors of the profession create. Find such a line of central development in something. Such are the natural affiliations of all great departments of thought, that any one will be found to be suggestive of every other one. There have been no isolated developments of the national mind: therefore there are no isolated representations of it in books. A book which *is* a book is kindred to every other book. Even two such diverse expressions of genius as English poetry and English art are in close sympathy with each other. We have before remarked the natural affiliation of the English pulpit with the English drama. George Whitefield and David Garrick were mutual helpers. Build a nest, therefore, for your thought anywhere in an English library, and the flight from it to the whole circumference will not be unnatural, or on weary wings.

I add in closing, without extended remark, several auxiliary suggestions.

It is not necessary for your purpose to read very largely in any one author, except those of inspired authority.

It is not necessary to read an equal amount in all.

It is not necessary to read in chronological order. A beginning can be made in the middle. One method recommended by some critics is to begin with the present time, and read backward.

The more distant an author is from our own times, as a general rule, inspiration aside, the less important is that author to modern culture. This is the reason why, in the list given in the foregoing pages, the most recent group is the most numerous.

In some instances, the preachers named in this catalogue have not left a large collection of sermons in print. This is true of Whitefield and Tyndale. Our knowledge of their public ministry must be obtained from their memoirs, and the history of their times.

Their influence on the history of the pulpit is too important to permit the omission of their names.

In the reading of sermons, a few specimens thoroughly criticised are more valuable to our culture than volumes read for purposes of literary refreshment.

For mental quickening in the act of composing sermons, one should follow eclectically one's own tastes. If the forty-seventh proposition of Euclid starts your mind upon a track of original invention, study that proposition. Find out by experiment what *will* arouse your thinking power, and make it articulate, and then study that. The range of your mental affinities, as I have before remarked, will surely widen. The floriculturist sets a geranium to sprout in a very small receptacle; but it soon outgrows its birthplace. So an intellectual taste will expand beyond the scope of its germ. Nothing is more sure to grow.

Pursuing literary study by any plan equivalent to the one here recommended, you will not fail of a very encouraging success. Progress will be slow at the first, but it will increase in speed as you advance. Your power of mental appropriation will grow immensely as you approach middle life. It is no cause for discouragement, if its full growth is long delayed. Some of the richest fruits of autumn are the late fruits. So are there minds which are richly endowed by nature, but which develop slowly. Whenever your maturity does appear, be it late or early, you will be able to read rapidly. Many valuable books you will be able to master without a plodding pace through the whole of them. Fragmentary reading of them will suffice. In the maturity of a man's culture, if it has been wisely regulated, and vigorously nurtured, very few books demand of him a reading entire.   That which he brings *to* a book will often be so large a proportion of what he finds *in* it, that he has only to give a glance of recognition to many pages, and pass on.

Even a little of such reading as is here advised, though sadly unsatisfactory to your growing tastes, will still keep alive, as nothing else can, a scholar's vigilance over your sermons, and make them worthy of a scholar's hearing.   One of the most eminent of the Presbyterian pastors of New York, of the generation just now passing away, was once inquired of how he could have made his habits of argument in the pulpit so uniformly exact, without even a momentary slip in his logic; for such was the reputation of his masterly pulpit.   He replied, that he was accustomed to imagine a legal mind, like that of Daniel Webster, among his hearers, and he aimed never to present in his pulpit a train of reasoning to which the great jurist could object.   Every preacher needs such imaginary critics of his sermons. We can find them in the silent friends who throng our libraries.   Make a friend of every good book you own. " There is a friend that sticketh closer than a brother."

INDEX.

Accumulation not the chief object of a scholar's life, 20.

Acquisitive reading compared with philosophical methods, 279.

Adaptation to professional labor, 111.
one object of literary study, 111.
the study of it must form the clergy, 112.

Adaptations, Jesuit theory of them, 111.

Addison, Joseph, state of masses in England in his time, 37.
his charge of affectation upon English literature, 197.

Adolphus, Gustavus, his battle-song, 242.

Affectations in literature, 195.

Affinity, law of, in the choice of clerical labor, 118.

Africa, life of a missionary in, 119.

"Agawam, Simple Cobbler of," quoted, 153.

Ages, dark, the work of the European mind at that time, 124.

Alexander, Dr. James, quoted, 61.

Allegory illustrative of the three great literatures of Europe, 282.

Allston, Washington, his fastidious taste, 298.

Amateur studies, peril of selfishness in them, 153.

American literature, intrinsic merits of it, 178.
its English affinities, 181.
its poetry compared with that of England, 179.

American poetry in action, 179.

American pulpit, the question of its decline, 180.

American theology as judged by German scholars, 190.

American theologians have been eminent preachers, 187.

Amusements, Christian theory of them, 22.

Ancient classics in the American college, 149.
ideal of a liberal education, 83.

Analytic reading, 276.

Angelo, Michael, his mode of professional working, 299.

Anglicizing foreign literatures, 157.

Anglo-Saxon language not spoken out of Great Britain, 163.

Anomalies in literature, 274.

Antiquity of biblical history, 229.
of Hebrew jurisprudence, 230.
of Hebrew poetry, 230.
of Hebrew prophetic literature, 231.
of the Book of Job, 231.
of the Book of Ruth, 231.
reverence of the human mind for it, 228.

Aristotle and Plato one in their final influence, 108.

Arnold, Dr. Thomas, his advice to a young preacher, 210.
affection of him for Aristotle, 104.
his conversational powers, 213.
his opinion of censorious critics, 304.
his opinion of Coleridge's "Literary Remains," 155.
his opinion of making literature a profession, 155.
his opinion of reading inferior authors, 144.
his self-distrust, 299.

Arnold, Matthew, his opinion of authors in relation to their times, 289.

Art, resemblances between it and literature, 283.

Artists, American, in Italy, 299.

Asiatic literatures in comparison with modern, 161.

341

Gibbon, Edward, his classification of critics, 304.
his method of reading, 134.
Goldsmith, Oliver, and the "Literary Club," 200.
Gray, Thomas, his use of Spenser's "Faerie Queene," 303.
Greek drama, resemblances of it to the pulpit, 43.
literature, leading representatives of it, 138.
pantomime, its intelligibility and power, 219.
Griffin, Edward Dorr, his early judgment of himself, 114.
Growth of the power of mental appropriation, 324.
Guizot, François Pierre, his criticism of Shakspeare, 85.
his opinion of affectation in French literature, 197.
his opinion of the French and English drama, 165.
Gymnasia of Germany, criticism of the Scriptures in them, 227.
Hall, Bishop, his thought on the sight of a library, 310.
Hall, Robert, his criticism of his own style, 272.
his servility to Dr. Johnson in his youth, 202.
Hamilton, Sir William, his difficulty in composing, 308.
Harvard College, its early teaching of the sacred languages, 227.
Hawthorne, Nathaniel, his character in his works, 271.
his place in English literature, 138.
theology of the "Marble Faun," 202.
Hebrew jurisprudence, its antiquity, 230.
literature, leading representatives of it, 137.
lyric poetry, its antiquity, 230.
prophetic literature, its antiquity, 231.
psalmody, its influence on English history, 242.
psalmody, its influence on modern hymnology, 241.
Hellenistic Greek literature, its leading representatives, 137.
Hengstenberg, Ernst W., his support of despotic re-action, 56.
Henry, Patrick, his motto respecting studies, 17.
his methods of studying men, 90.

Henry VIII. of England, literature during his reign, 330.
Hercules, the torso, 97.
Herbert, George, his use of Latin quotations, 293.
Holmes, Dr. O. W., his conversational power, 213.
the origin of "The Autocrat of the Breakfast-table," 213.
Homer's "Iliad," admiration of the English aristocracy for it, 38.
Homely literature, 215.
Hooker, Richard, estimate of his relation to English prose, 331.
his judgment of himself and his adaptations, 319.
Humboldt, Alexander, his opinion of William Prescott, 180.
Hymnology, its debt to the Hebrew psalmody, 241.
"Hypochondriac" pastor, an example, 80.
Hysteria in revivals, 267.
Ideal of the studies of a pastor necessary to any plan of study, 309.
the negative value of an ideal plan of study, 310.
Ignorance of the world among the clergy, 26.
Illustrative power, want of it in preaching, 285.
excess of it in preaching, 286.
Imitation of authors in disciplinary composition, 300.
Impracticable plans of study, 315–322.
Incidents, biographical, illustrating rhetorical principles, 3.
Individual character is power in speech, 6.
Infidelity and reform, 54.
in Germany, and re-actions from it, 56.
in the United States, its debt to the Scriptures, 244.
Influence, clerical, the law of it, 119.
Inspiration, its bearing on the literary merit of the Scriptures, 247.
not a protection against literary defects, 247.
Integrity of intellect, 199.
Intellectualism, those who preach it not moved by it, 7.
Intensity of biblical thought, 249.
of moral excitement in the ministry, 207.